# Shotgunned

The long ordeal of a wounded cop
seeking justice

*Paul F. Healy Jr.*

## Dana Owen

*Dana Owen*

*with*

## Ron Gollobin

*and*

## Athena Z. Yerganian

Shotgunned, LLC

# Shotgunned

*Book cover by Anita Brown*
*Book format by Dana Owen & Athena Z. Yerganian*
*www.shotgunned.net*

**First Edition: June 2014**

DISCLAIMER:
The author is a pretty good story-teller. With that in mind, he has tried to tell his story by recreating events, locales and conversations from memory. In some instances, to maintain their anonymity, he has changed the names of individuals and places, and may have changed some identifying characteristics and details such as physical properties, occupations and places of residence. Everything here is true, but he may have occasionally embroidered. Although the author has exhaustively researched many sources to ensure the accuracy and completeness of the information contained in this book, the author assumes no responsibility for errors, inaccuracies, omissions or any other inconsistency herein. Any slights against people, organizations or places are unintentional.

Owen, Dana
    Shotgunned, the long ordeal of a wounded cop seeking justice / Dana Owen
    with Ron Gollobin and Athena Z. Yerganian
    ISBN - 13: 978-0-9905170-0-9
    ISBN - 10: 0990517004
    Library of Congress Control Number: 2014910214

    1. Owen, Dana. 2. Shooting - Massachusetts – Biography. 3. Shooting - Massachusetts – Investigation. 4. Crime - Massachusetts - Boston Area - MDC Police. I. Title. II. True Crime.

First Edition: June 2014
10 9 8 7 6 5 4 3 2 1

Printed in the United States of America

*To my wife Sandy*

*our daughters Heather and Kendra*

*and our six grandchildren*

# Photograph Captions and Credits

Non-listed photos provided by the author from his Memory Book

# Table of Contents

# CHAPTER ONE
## *Monday - June 16, 1975*

*I was bleeding from two gunshot wounds to my head. Lying motionless in the street, I could barely see but I strained to bring the chaos around me into focus. Leaving me to die, the hijackers disappeared into the darkness. I closed my eyes but tried not to slip away. I thought about how my family and I celebrated my little daughter Kendra's birthday, just a few hours earlier. And I thought about how my own Dad died when he was only thirty-two. I couldn't let that happen to my children. Then, I asked myself, "What was so valuable in that truck that someone would actually try to kill a cop?"*

I was the cop, a Metropolitan District Commission (MDC) patrolman. It was June 16, 1975. On my way to work that afternoon, I listened to a song called *Monday, Monday*, sung by The Mamas and the Papas (written by John Phillips), on my car's AM/FM radio and couldn't get the lyrics out of my head.

*"...Monday, Monday, can't trust that day..."*

My 4:00 p.m. to midnight shift started out quietly, as expected for a Monday at the beginning of summer. My partner and I had just finished dinner at the Bickford's Pancake House in Medford. As we walked across the parking lot to our marked police cruiser, I told Bob about the birthday party we had that afternoon for my youngest daughter, who turned four that day. The hit of the party had been the clown, a North Reading cop's wife who dressed up for kids' parties. We got into our cruiser and Bob notified headquarters by two-way radio we were back on the air.

Bob Power had been my partner for almost a year. He was a Vietnam veteran, six years older than I at thirty-three, but I was the senior man, with more time on the job. He was a big man - 6' 2" and 220 pounds to my 5' 10" at 180 pounds. He had a dry sense of humor and I was more serious, but we got along great. Our regular assignment was to patrol the Middlesex Fells Reservation in Medford and Somerville, two adjacent towns just north of Boston.

Just before sunset, with the noises of rush hour almost gone, there was a general broadcast from Headquarters Dispatch, known as Met Control.

"Met Control to all units...A tractor-trailer has just been hijacked by two armed white males at the Congress Street on-ramp to the Central Artery in South Boston...last seen heading north toward Interstate 93...no further description or plate number available at this time."

*Two Boston Edison Utility Company employees working on a manhole in the street witnessed the crime and phoned the information to the Boston Police. They radioed it to my agency, the MDC Police with jurisdiction on the I-93 Expressway (which runs from North to South through the city of Boston).*

I was the driver of our marked patrol car, a beat-up, dark green and white 1972 Ford station wagon, which doubled as an ambulette - a station wagon cruiser equipped with a fold-up stretcher. I enjoyed the control behind the wheel, especially during high speed responses and stolen car chases, my specialty. My partner handled the blue lights and the public address system. In addition, he worked the awkward police radio system, which required him to switch between Channel 1 - to talk with Met Control, and Channel 2 - to hear the other cruisers.

If the hijacked truck was heading North on I-93, we were in a good position to intercept. I set up on the right side of the busy highway in Somerville, at the on-ramp from Mystic Avenue, five miles north of the hijacking scene.

We had been waiting there for only a few minutes when a tractor-trailer (TT) with two white males in the cab passed by us, heading north. It was unusual to see two people in the cab of a TT. The best police work usually stemmed from hunches and I thought we should check out the vehicle. I pulled out and drove up to the rear of the truck, while looking in the rear-view for a 'follow-car,' almost always used in a hijacking. (A follow-car contains other hijackers to back up the hijacked truck and to provide a getaway vehicle.)

> *I read every police bulletin I could. I was aware of another hijacking pursuit, where one of the gang was in the back of the fleeing trailer, armed with a machine gun. He opened up on the pursuing officers.*

With that in mind, I played cat and mouse with the tractor trailer. I drove behind it and then passed it on one side, dropped back and then passed it on the other - always looking into my rear-view mirror for the follow-car.

My partner informed Met Control we were following a vehicle, northbound on I-93 in Medford and gave a complete description.

"The 302 car (our unit call sign) is following a truck, possibly suspected in that hijacking," Bob spoke clearly into the mic.

The response was a calm, "10-4," from the dispatcher.

Bob called in our location, "Approaching Roosevelt Circle."

Another, indifferent, "10-4," came from the dispatcher. It was obvious from his tone he did not believe we were tailing the right truck. The problem was the other cruisers could only hear Met Control's composed 10-4s over Chanel 1 and had no idea what we were involved in.

It was time to find out if we had the right truck - one way or the other.

I said, "Bob, I am going to pull up next to the passenger's side and see what we've got."

I drove up beside the truck, and looked up at the white male in the passenger's seat, who looked down at me. He quickly covered the right side of his face with his hand and turned away. Bingo!!! I knew we had the right truck.

I dropped back behind the truck and turned on the high beams, while Bob activated the PA system and blue lights. Over the roof-mounted loudspeaker Bob said, in an authoritative voice, "In the truck! Pull over to the right and stop!"

After a few more commands over the PA, the truck sped up. Bob switched on the siren, and we saw smoke billow out from the eighteen wheeler's twin exhaust stacks, as the TT barreled northbound up I-93. The smell of the diesel exhaust poured into our unit. The Chase was on!

# CHAPTER TWO
## *The Chase*

How do you stop a tractor trailer with a cruiser? Answer: you don't...you just stay with it. I followed the truck, at what I felt was a safe distance in case we came under fire. I was worried an armed suspect might be waiting to kick open the back door of the trailer and start shooting at us. And I was still scanning for the follow-car. The adrenaline rush was building and hard to control. I started taking deeper breaths to calm myself. I held the steering wheel tighter...

"302...is now in pursuit of a tractor trailer unit...New Hampshire registration number Golf Papa 5692...north bound on I-93 in Medford!" radioed my partner, his voice getting a little louder with each word.

Met Control believed us now. The dispatcher advised us to use caution - the hijackers were armed.

"Use caution? No shit!" I thought.

My job was to drive and my partner's was to keep HQ informed of our location and circumstances. So, I kept quiet.

Met Control's radio squawked, "All units...the 302 car is in pursuit of a hijacked tractor trailer unit...northbound on Interstate 93 in Medford."

"302...requesting back-up units and a road block set up!" Bob yelled into the mic.

"10-4, 302...Met Control to any units in position to assist the 302 car!" The dispatcher's voice had become excited. We were traveling north of the MDC patrol jurisdiction, so any responding units were south and behind us.

Our speed hit 80 mph. I hoped that cruisers from the Massachusetts State Police (MSP), or other cities or towns would intercept or block the road at the intersection of I-93 and I-95, the next major interchange about three miles away but coming up fast. Still driving on I-93 northbound, we approached Spot Pond in Stoneham, and the truck started to slow down. It looked as though it was pulling over into the breakdown lane, under the overpass. As the truck screeched to a stop, the burning smell of overheated asbestos brakes permeated the warm, humid air.

I stopped my cruiser about ten yards behind the truck and a little to its left, our blue lights reflecting off the trailer in the early evening light. The lights lit up the sparse area adjacent to the reservoir - there were no houses for at least a mile. We knew the suspects were armed and at any moment this could become a gunfight.

I heard my partner radio our location.

"302…we have the truck stopped under the overpass of Route 28. Get us some backup!" Bob shouted into the two-way police radio.

"Any unit...we need back up for the 302 car!" The dispatcher almost pleaded. "Units responding? Acknowledge!" In the excitement, we didn't hear any response. Our attention was focused on the truck.

We opened the doors on both sides of our cruiser and, crouching down to the ground, took cover behind them. We drew our .38 caliber service revolvers, knowing something was about to happen. (In 1975, a route car was not equipped with a shotgun.)

Over the PA, Bob issued an order, "You in the truck! Get out with your hands up!"

It was dusk - still warm and hazy. As the day light faded, the sweat started to make my shirt collar wet and time seemed to stand still. In the cab of the tractor trailer, there was no movement from the two men. My partner ran to his right as he maneuvered for cover, and positioned himself against the abutment of the overpass. From that location, he had a better view and a much better angle of the passenger's side of the truck. Still crouched behind my open door, I noticed, out of the corner of my left eye, a brown, four-door sedan, just like an unmarked cruiser. It slowly rolled past me.

Immediately, I knew it was the follow-car I had been looking for. The right rear door of the brown car was open. I saw the shadow of two men in the front seat, but could not see clearly who was seated in the back - only the open door. Slowly, the car drove the length of the truck, pulled over and stopped just in the front and to the left of the truck, straddling the breakdown lane.

Now sweating profusely, I had to stay focused on what was happening beside me and in front of me. I saw a man in a tan trench coat appear from in front of the cab of the TT unit. He never really looked at me, but I saw a revolver in his right hand. He had come from the passenger side of the truck and made a dash to the waiting getaway car.

"Bob, get back here!" I called for my partner to get back in our cruiser. The suspect must have seen Bob in the side view mirror of the truck cab and bailed out before Bob had him in view.

"Police...Freeze!" I yelled.

Pointing my gun at the trench coat, I had him in my gun sight and thought about firing a round at him.

> *I knew the rules of engagement well. He had not pointed the gun at me, but was a fleeing felon which, under the rules, would allow me to shoot. From a distance of about forty yards, a shot was too risky to take, even though I was a decent marksman. If I missed, my bullet could have easily hit an innocent driver or passenger in a vehicle.*

I didn't shoot. The armed suspect ignored my command to freeze and dove into the back seat of the waiting car. With tires screeching, the follow-car, now the getaway, car sped off. The strong smell of burning rubber lingered in the air.

We jumped back into our cruiser. I jerked the gear shift into 'Drive' and floored the accelerator. The quick, forward movement of the cruiser slammed our doors closed for us.

Just then, the driver of the TT unit appeared, standing in the street with his hands up.

As we drove past him, he pointed to the fleeing getaway car, yelling, "I've been hijacked!"

Even if he was really one of the gang, we chose to go after the fleeing robbers in the brown Ford, which was heading into the high-speed lane and accelerating faster. We left him behind and sped off in pursuit - with lights and siren shattering the air.

> *The truck driver waited and watched as cruiser after cruiser, both state and local, flew by him with lights and sirens blaring. He waited, but no one stopped. Then he climbed back into his truck and, per his company instructions, headed on to his original destination, White River Junction, Vermont, which was about one hundred and fifteen miles to the north.*

Even though our 1972 Ford cruiser was beaten up on the outside, it had come back from the shop that day with a brand new 365 horsepower, 429-cubic-inch Police Interceptor engine. The four new 'police pursuit' tires were about to be put to the test.

We quickly gained on their slower Ford and could see a lot of movement by the four robbers inside their car. Maybe they were getting ready to do battle.

The fleeing sedan, hindered by traffic, veered into the left breakdown lane, onto a crushed rock surface. We were right on their tail. As our speed hit 100 mph, it became obvious they could not outrun our cruiser. I was just a few feet off the rear bumper.

With the I-95 interchange about a mile away, I felt I could stay with them and I knew it was only a matter of time before we would hit a police road block. The hijackers must have had the same feeling, because they suddenly veered to the right, crossing all four lanes of traffic. We were still right behind them. I was good at pursuit driving and I was not about to let them get away.

They exited I-93, just before the I-95 exchange, onto the Montvale Avenue ramp, and blew through the stop sign at the bottom, making a hard left turn towards the city of Woburn. With the extra weight of four men in the getaway car, it was a wide, skidding turn. I was able to gain ground on them with a much tighter turn. This was a 'slam-the-gas-pedal-to-the-floor, then marry-the-brake' chase.

As we headed down Montvale Avenue, I had a gut feeling we were about to be fired upon by the desperate hijackers.

I told my partner, "Put a couple of rounds in their rear window, before they open up on us!"

As he leaned out of the passenger window to shoot, a blue station wagon came off the south-bound ramp, between the getaway car and us. I slammed on the brakes to avoid crashing, the new tires skidding on the dampened pavement. I saw a young girl, maybe age six, her face and hands pressed to the rear-side window of the station wagon. She must have heard our siren and had been watching the police chase.

*It is amazing how clearly and logically the human mind works in periods of great stress and fast action. My partner later told me all he saw in his gun sight was this young girl with a look of wonder on her face, just as he was about to pull the trigger. We both had daughters that age and couldn't live with shooting a child.*

Bob saw the face of that young girl and held his fire, just in time.

The chase was approaching the busy intersection of Montvale Avenue and Washington Street. I was familiar with this area and knew we would pass Bickford's Pancake House on our left. Up ahead, I saw the blue lights of a police cruiser, parked in the middle of the intersection with a Woburn police officer standing beside it.

"A road block!" I thought, "It's almost over." But, to my amazement, the cop waved the robbers' car through!

> *I later found out the driver of the getaway car had been flashing his high beams. As our siren wailed from behind, the Ford looked and sounded like an unmarked police car, just as it had first appeared to me. These guys were not going to go easily and they were surely not amateurs.*

The chase continued. Every few minutes my partner notified Met Control of our direction and location, but he had to shut off the siren to be heard clearly over the radio. We had rolled down the hand-cranked windows - MDC policy denied air conditioning in those days - and the siren wail was deafening inside the cruiser.

We took a left onto Washington Street and headed toward the town of Winchester, but we had to cross over railroad tracks near a cemetery - not a good omen. At a high rate of speed, we drove over the tracks, but instead of just rattling the cruiser, we became airborne! We landed, front wheels first, with a hard thump. The jolt lurched us upward and our heads hit the roof liner. The car jerked us every which way as we accelerated after them.

Then, it happened. The muzzles flashed in the darkness and we heard a distinctive *POP! POP! POP!* We were under handgun fire from both rear-side windows of the fleeing vehicle.

Our headlights and rotating blue lights cut through the haze and reflected off the gun smoke from their handguns.

"SHOTS FIRED!" my partner yelled into the mic.

The Dispatcher announced, "Met Control to all units...shots are now being fired in the pursuit!"

I counted twelve rounds, six from each side of the car.

> *A classic police academy drill was to 'count the rounds.' If they had revolvers (a good guess in 1975), they were out of ammo.*

We were passing cars and tearing down a two-lane residential street, as a thick ground fog formed in the humid night. I drove in a zigzag pattern, trying to keep up but from a safe distance, nearly impossible in a flat-out pursuit. Either we stayed close, or we would lose them. We stayed close.

"Brace yourself, Bob. I'm gonna ram them!" I shouted.

But before I could accelerate, the rear window of the getaway car exploded outward, in slow motion. It was a shotgun blast! A fireball of yellow and white belched towards us and the loud roar of a 12-gauge weapon startled me so much I jumped in my seat.

> *Each round of 00-buckshot from a shotgun carries 9 pellets, each the size of a .32 caliber bullet.*

The shotgun roared again! I thought the windshield had been blown out. I got a face full of glass and felt something hard hit the top of my head. The windshield was still intact but, as I drove faster, the wind raced through a bullet hole somewhere in the windshield. Suddenly, our headlights stopped working, blown out by the shotgun blast. The only thing that illuminated the getaway car from our viewpoint was the almost hypnotic rotation of our blue lights. Headlights or not, I did not slow down.

The chase began to seem so surreal. Had I been hit by the blast? Denial kicked in. Somehow, I told myself, a rock had been kicked up from the street during in the chase, not a bullet.

Then, I realized blood was running down my face. And reality kicked in.

I wiped it away, without even looking at my hand, and said simply, "Bob, I'm hit."

My partner looked at me as the blood poured from the wound on the top of my head. The big pellet had entered high on the windshield and deflected down, slamming into the top of my skull - making a six inch long, nasty-looking wound.

Bob asked, "Wanna give it up?"

I responded, **"If it's the last thing I ever do, I'm going to catch these guys!"**

> *I knew if they shot at a police officer, they would shoot at anyone. I committed myself to capturing or killing them. As fast as things were happening, I still had time to think how dangerous these guys were and how they had to be taken off the streets.*

Bob must have radioed Met Control that I was hit, but didn't really remember. I was not about to give up. I would do my duty and we would catch these guys.

Shots came in our direction, again! Either they reloaded or they had extra guns. I fell back behind the brown Ford and drove in an irregular pattern. I ducked down and then popped up in my seat to avoid being hit...again. The gunfire continued, but sporadically.

We had been in pursuit for about fifteen minutes when we found ourselves headed for the center of Winchester, a quiet, affluent and residential town where there **had** to be a road block. The getaway driver recklessly passed five or six cars on Washington Street, a 35 mph speed zone.

If I did not pass that same line of cars, I was going to lose them. They had accelerated away at about 80 mph. I saw their tail lights swerving drunkenly, as the rear of the loaded car fish-tailed on the very edge of control. I was losing sight of them.

"Hold on," I told my partner, as I blindly passed the slower line of cars, with the siren wailing and the blue lights spinning.

As we came over a rise at the intersection of Washington and Swanton Street, just shy of the center of Winchester, the brown Ford was blocked by what looked like a red Mustang at the intersection. I knew in my bones, as we closed in on them at high speed, they were going to open up on us with handguns…and that shotgun.

As I started to duck down, hugging the door to my left, my hunch was validated - flashes from the handguns and a ball of yellow-orange flame came at us, from the sickening blast of that powerful and deadly 12-gauge shotgun. Swerving to avoid the incoming fire, I heard the buck shot slam into the front of our cruiser.

Things started to move in slow motion, and seconds seemed like drawn-out minutes. Another shotgun blast! I was hit…again. As this second bullet slammed into my forehead, it hit like a baseball bat. That 00-buckshot pellet hit me square in the front of my skull, just at the center of the hairline.

> Had I not ducked down, it would have hit me dead center in the chest. Ironically, our bullet proof vests and riot helmets, issued for the civil unrest of the times, were in the back seat of our unit. Back then the vests were simply too heavy and hot to wear in the summer. Once the chase began, we had no time to strap them on.

Immediately, I knew I was out of action, so I had to protect my partner. I wanted to use the car as cover for Bob, so he could shoot back. My right foot stomped the brake pedal to the floor and I spun the steering wheel. The car swung sideways, as it came to a skidding stop, almost onto the sidewalk in front of a White Hen Pantry convenience store. My side of the cruiser faced the robbers.

Gun fire came from close range in front of the store. It sounded like distant thunder of a departing storm, even though it was only a few yards away. My range of vision was down to a few feet and shrinking fast - all sounds were distant and fading, distorted and muffled.

I was sure one of them was going to finish me off. So, I drew my service .38 caliber Smith &Wesson Model 64 revolver, and tried to bail out of the our bullet-riddled patrol car. But my left foot got caught under the brake pedal!

My body started falling ever so slowly toward the street, my gun tumbling from my hand in gradual, rotating motions that seemed to go on forever. The blue lights of our cruiser reflected off the shiny stainless steel service revolver, as it tumbled downward. I counted the rotations of my gun as it floated just out of reach, my hand trying desperately to catch it in mid-air.

Just then, I saw the street coming up quickly and I knew my face was about to smash onto the pavement...hard. I put my hand to the left side of my face and hit the ground with a hollow thud. My revolver hit the street at about the same time, the clanking of metal skittered loudly across the pavement. It rested inches from my right hand, but I couldn't move my arm. I felt my body shutting down as half my body hung out of the cruiser, with my head lying on the ground and my ankle still stuck under the brake pedal.

Lying there on the street, I heard Bob radio, **"Officer down at Swanton and Washington Street!"** Then, I heard the roar of an engine and the squeal of tires as the brown Ford sped off, but I couldn't see it.

My partner raced to me and said, "Hang in there! I have an ambulance on the way."

I whispered from the pavement, "'*Officer down?'*...Bob, you've been watching too many cop shows on TV."

It all seemed too dramatic to me, as I felt like I was drifting pleasantly away to someplace else. But the look of horror and concern on Bob's face told me...maybe it wasn't too dramatic. His face told me I was in bad shape, but then his face faded away too and I only heard his voice far, far away.

"Bob, I don't think I am going to make it," I said matter-of-factly. The darkness started closing in.

His response was angry and impatient. "Don't be stupid! You're going to be fine! Stay with me and fight!"

That was the best thing he could have said to me, because he was right and I had all but given up. Lying on the street, in the gutter, I felt embarrassed. I gathered all my strength and tried to stand up. No use...I was paralyzed and maybe blind.

I was semi-conscious, but felt no pain at all. Blood dribbled out of my head wound and dripped onto the roadway. I was in shock and I knew shock could kill. I struggled to stay awake. My life did not flash before me, but I did think of how my Dad died at age thirty-two, leaving my mother a young widow. *My* wife would not become a widow at age twenty-seven and I would not leave *my* two girls without a Dad. *NO way*!

But death was near and was very seductive. All I had to do was let go, close my eyes and slip into a deep resting state that would carry me to eternity.

I heard a woman screaming in the distance but I couldn't see her. "Oh my God, they killed the poor officer! They **killed** him!"

She just kept screaming over and over again.

My vision was only good for a few inches from my face, almost like in a dream. The wide, bluish-gray brim of a Massachusetts State Trooper's 'Smokey Bear' hat blocked what I assumed were the head lights of the cruisers that had suddenly gathered at the scene.

The Trooper leaned toward me and asked, "What can I do for you, brother?"

I groaned, "Get that screaming woman out of here...and get me to a hospital!"

Then, I recognized the voice of one of the men on my shift. Now, I was sure I was blind because I could not see his face. He asked me if I could describe any of the hijackers - maybe he thought he should get my 'dying declaration.' I did the best I could.

Time stood still as I lay in the street in an ever-growing puddle of my own blood. I found myself on my back, but did not know who had rolled me over. There were no smells, my vision was gone. Even sounds had grown more distant. Everything had faded.

I was loaded onto a stretcher by two MDC officers, who were close friends. I must have been carried to the back of what I knew had to be their station wagon cruiser.

> *I wanted to be taken to Massachusetts General Hospital, known to have the best trauma unit for the treatment of gunshot wounds in New England. Instead, they wisely transported me to Winchester Hospital, only a few blocks away. Later, I was told I would not have survived the twenty-minute drive to MGH.*

For the first time, I felt fear. We sped to the hospital with blue lights flashing and the constant warble of the siren. I felt what injured people I had driven to the hospital must have experienced. Officer Dave Daley rode in back with me and the wooden box containing an oxygen bottle slid and slammed around, when we took the corners on two wheels. He held a 4"x6" inch sterile gauze bandage pad from the cruiser's first aid kit, over my head wounds, trying to slow the bleeding.

Officer Jerry Gately drove as if the hounds of hell were after him - trying to save my life before it slipped away. I knew it was going to be a close race. These were two very capable cops and I was their badly injured brother officer. They pushed the limits to save me.

On the short, harrowing ride to the hospital I told Dave, "Don't let me lose consciousness...Just keep talking to me."

I feared if I lost consciousness, I would die.

Dave said, "Relax. You'll get a medal and be assigned to the MDC pools and rinks, where it's safe."

I laughed and coughed. He knew I hated babysitting a swimming pool, but it didn't sound bad at that moment.

We arrived at Winchester Hospital, a small community healthcare facility in those days. As I was taken out of the police ambulette on a stretcher and loaded onto a hospital gurney, I started to see things again. My vision for close up things was actually coming back! As I looked down, I saw I was still in full uniform, my light blue shirt almost completely dark blue from staining blood.

There were several nurses, doctors and attendants already outside, awaiting my arrival. They had been notified I was coming. They seemed excited and I did not like the look of concern on their faces, as they triaged me. Just then, everything went black.

THE NEXT THING I remembered, I was lying under a very bright light in the emergency room, with several medical staff shooting questions at me and cutting away my uniform shirt.

I heard them talking in the ER, "He will never make it to Beth Israel," (a major Boston hospital, where the best neurosurgeon was on duty). The decision was made to send a cruiser to escort the surgeon to me. The staff did not hide the talk of my condition or how they would proceed. I remembered at some point a small TV set was carried into the Emergency Room by someone, which seemed strange. This was not a place used to high police drama.

My vision became clearer and I was beginning to feel pain, as they started to shave my forehead hair to see the wounds better.

I recalled a nurse saying, "We can't give you anything for pain. You're too critical."

"Great...Can I at least bite a bullet?" I joked.

"Sure, I will have your buddies get you one," she smiled softly.

Listening to every spoken word, I heard the order to get my wife and transport her in an unmarked police car. It would be driven by the Watch Commander, who was en route to the hospital from HQ in Boston.

Officer Daley said to me, "I'll go with the Watch Commander to your house and we will pick up Sandy." He knew my wife and had been to our house before.

I made him swear he would call her first. I had promised her, "If they call, I'm still alive."

I said to Daley, "Don't tell her I've been shot. Say I was in a cruiser accident."

Dave gave me his word he would tell my wife exactly that.

## CHAPTER THREE
### *Sandy's Chapter*
By Sandra Litchfield Owen

*Author's Note: In 2012, thirty-seven years later, we asked my wife to tell us about her feelings on the night I had been shot. She hand wrote what follows, in one sitting.*

It was dusk - well, just after. June 16, a warm summer eve, just four days shy of the longest day of the year - and I was in a hurry for it to become dark so the girls would be asleep.

I was exhausted from the day, but was busily cleaning up the aftermath of our youngest daughter's fourth birthday party. The girls were tired too, but still winding down from the excitement of the day. I had them all bathed, night gowned and in their room, but I could hear them bustling around in there and just knew they were probably kneeling on our oldest daughter's bed, lifting the curtain and peeking through the open window at all the older neighborhood kids who gathered to play in the cul de sac in front of our house until the street light came on. That was the cue in all the households that it was time to come home for the night. I was sure that as soon as that happened, they'd immediately fall asleep.

The party, thankfully, had been outside in the yard on such a beautiful day. We had only invited a few other four year olds, but with the siblings, moms, not to mention the uninvited kids that came anyway because we had hired Jelly Bean the Clown, it turned out to be quite a crowd and more to clean up than I expected. The yard was done, the kids were done and now it was just the rest. Dana had also been there in the afternoon to enjoy the festivities, one of the pluses of being a young cop working evenings; he saw plenty of his kids during the days, which we all loved. He got a kick out of the "clown birthday" and stayed as long as he could before jumping into his uniform and speeding down the highway to the city in time to stand roll call at 4 o'clock.

The street light had come on, all had become quiet both inside and out and the only sound coming through the screen doors and open windows was the soft breeze and a few peepers in the swamp behind our yard. As I neared the end of my "clean up siege" I was in the kitchen alone with my thoughts. I was thinking about Jelly Bean the Clown. She, like me, was a cop's wife and a mom, a little older than I was and had started her own company with another local friend, where they hired themselves out as clowns for kid parties and other events. Pretty innovative I thought, but definitely not my cup of tea.

No, I loved being a nurse. I worked part time night shifts at a hospital down in the same city area where Dana worked on his pm shifts. I loved the unpredictability of it since, as a part timer, I never knew where they would send me: Medical Surgical, Intensive Care Unit, or the Emergency Room. I loved the challenge, the autonomy, the responsibility, my supervisors, doctors and co-workers, not to mention the two nights a week respite from being a suburban mom. It was the perfect balance. It was all good! No, clowning was definitely not for me for sure! I was more exhausted from watching Jelly Bean work the party than I ever was at the end of a night shift, I chuckled to myself. In fact, as I tidied up the last loose end from the day, I was planning my own clean up - a shower and curl up on the couch in front of the TV and try to stay awake, waiting up for Dana as I did almost every night: but I knew tonight that once I hit the couch, I'd never make it till 1 a.m.

The phone rang. It was Dave Daley. Dave worked with Dana and on occasion was his partner for a shift, but as a rule, it was Dave and Jerry Gately and Dana's partner was Bob Power. I knew Dave from husband and wife police functions and we'd been to a couple of parties at his house. Everyone liked Dave and it was easy to feel comfortable with him. But why was he calling me?

"Sandy, Dana wanted me to call you and tell you he was Okay, but that he had a little accident in the cruiser tonight and he'd like it if we came up and brought you down to the hospital. He's in Winchester" --- As exhausted as I was, I immediately went on the alert! I was wide awake now! Dana and I had made a pact when he graduated from the police academy five years before, that he never wanted me to worry when he went to work and if anything ever did happen he didn't want me to go through the trauma of a "home notification" by the department and he would always call first. And we already had done a few dress rehearsals for this evening over the past few years. Dana, being a young enthusiastic and aggressive cop, had already been in a few scrapes that landed him in a hospital: minor cruiser accidents and more frequently over the past couple of summers when he was assigned to a foot beat in Revere Beach at closing time for all the liquor establishments. That was good for a couple of stitches and a phone call from Mass General about twice a summer. But he always called himself. This already sounded different.

And Winchester? Winchester *Hospital*?

First of all, what was he doing in Winchester? Very little of the patrol route was even there. It was all in the surrounding cities and towns. Winchester was an upper middle class town that had its own, very small, community hospital. No one really went there. Oh, they did some minor surgeries there and had a maternity ward, but the place had a reputation for being where the well to do folks went in for "a rest." I didn't know a soul that actually worked there and in nurse circles the joke was that's where we would go to do private duty for some rich client as a retirement job. I guessed they must have had an ER where they probably dealt with bumps and bruises and hangnails so I guessed it couldn't be serious.

"Okay Dave," I said. "Can I talk to him?"

"Well no, he can't come to the phone. That is why he asked me to call you. Do you have someone who can stay with the girls?"

Dave knew Dana and I had no family nearby. They all lived way south of Boston and well over an hour away. And we didn't see them that much anyway. I guessed I could call a neighbor and how soon were they coming?

"Now."

Miriam was one of my neighbors. She lived eight houses up the street, had four kids older than mine, didn't drive (which I could never believe) and was a stay at home mom who did child care in her home before day cares began to spring up and became the trend. From time to time I had bartered with her for child care in exchange for driving her or her kids places. I called her.

She was just wrapping up getting her own kids settled for the night. It was the last week of school and it seemed everyone needed money, special lunch or something before the next morning, but sure, she'd come and sit in my house while I went to the hospital. She'd walk down soon.

*I remember Mom on the phone in the kitchen. She was trembling...not sure if she was on the phone with Miriam or the policeman that called her. I remember coming into the kitchen...I distinctly remember having a feeling in my stomach that something was very wrong and feeling nervous. (I had the same feeling the day the phone rang the morning we were told that Nana Colburn died before anyone even told me.) I'm almost 100% sure that I started to cry and Mom told me "everything was Okay" but I didn't understand and also didn't believe her [Daughter Kendra's Memories].*

Now I was alone with my thoughts and began to digest things. I guessed I had about fifteen minutes till they got to the house. It seemed like an eternity, but in actuality, not even time to freshen up and gather a few things in my purse. Something wasn't right about this, but I just couldn't put my finger on it.

But then I reassured myself; no, it can't be serious. His buddies would never have taken him to Winchester Hospital if it was. In those days, they didn't have modular ambulances and EMTs. All cops were considered capable of first aid and a certain percent of the cruisers were station wagons called ambulettes. Very rough but functional: a collapsible stretcher, ambu bag, oxygen tank and metal first aid box and no real careful way to load a patient in there. No, two cops loading a victim in an ambulette was a lot like how we throw bags of groceries into the back of an SUV today. Rough.

Living at the end of a long winding dead end street abutted by woods and swamp was very quiet. If you heard a car coming down the street, it was probably coming all the way and was a visitor for you. I thought I heard a car and peeked out the window, seeing headlights on the bend of the road in the distance. But the shadow from the street light didn't reflect a station wagon with police lights on the roof, so no; this couldn't be "them."

But it was. When I heard car doors open I saw a dark green sedan parked in front of the house, no police lights on top. In my peripheral vision coming down the street was the shadow of someone walking - must be Miriam, spotting the sedan at the same time I did - The shadowed walker was hastening their step, now cutting across my lawn and coming into plain view under the front porch light. Coming up the walk, I recognized Dave in uniform and a tall, older gentleman in a suit - my mind flashed forward - wait a minute! This wasn't Jerry and this wasn't their ambulette cruiser --- this was not good. Not good at all.

Miriam lay back, letting them come to my door first. The gentleman in the suit stood tall and silent.

Dave did all the talking and with a matter of fact calmness, he said, "Sandy, this is Captain Skopetz."

The older gentleman extended his hand and simply said, "Ma'am."

I shook his hand and was aware of Dave saying something calm and benign, but don't remember what.

Miriam squeezed past them and came in the front door, flashed a nervous smile at me and said, "Don't worry about the girls - we'll be fine."

I nervously said back, "I'll call you when I know what's what."

Grabbing my purse, I slipped out the door and followed Dave and Capt. Skopetz to the unmarked cruiser. No, this was not good at all.

Now they say in peak moments of stress, things flash forward and everything is a blur. But it was just the opposite for me. All my senses increased with heightened acuity and I remember as clearly as if it were today: Capt. Skopetz got in the driver's seat, quietly said something into the mic of the police radio and then turned down the volume. Odd. Dave opened the door to the back seat for me and then got in the back seat with me. No, this definitely was not good. And I remember the distinct dirty and stale smell of the inside of the cruiser - just like what Dana's uniforms smelled like when he came home from a shift.

As we drove up our street, the ride was careful, slow and silent, but as we worked onto the main roads of town the speed picked up, I could see the piercing blue flash of behind-the-grill lights. The watch commander had turned them on while we hastened toward the ramp to I-93. Dave was making calm conversation about "You know Dana" --- "got in a chase" --- "had a little accident with the cruiser" --- It was light enough talk that I actually started to relax again; I made some conversationally appropriate small talk with him. Now we were racing southbound on I-93. As I listened to Dave's small talk, I became aware that the northbound traffic was eerily sparse - granted, rush hour had long since been over, but this just didn't look quite right. No sooner had the thought left my head when, as we came over the rise, all I could see were blue lights - a sea of flashing blue lights that lit up the whole sky and then more cruisers than I had ever seen in my life - and they were parked everywhere, the side of I-93, across the northbound lane, on the median. There was even a helicopter overhead. And they were from everywhere: state, local, MDC, cities and towns and K-9 dogs and cops everywhere. My mind shifted gears and my thoughts immediately froze. I had figured it out and it all made sense. A police chase alright - but the "little accident" had been a fatal. Dana and his partner Bob must have been killed to warrant a bigger-than-TV drama dragnet like this - and this must be why neither Dana, nor his actual partner had called me and why Dave and a watch commander had come to bring me to the hospital --- Winchester Hospital, of all places. Obviously it was the closest place for the pronouncement of a DOA. I turned to Dave and calmly in a soft voice said, "He is dead, isn't he."

"No, Sandy. Honest. I wouldn't lie to you." He nervously looked out the window. But of course he would lie to me if he had been told to and I knew he must be. And he knew that was exactly what I was thinking. We were close to the hospital now and slowed down, as we were off the highway and on Winchester streets. The last two minutes of the ride seemed like an eternity in dead silence.

As we pulled into the back entrance of the hospital there was more bustling going on: a few cruisers, a few cops mostly in jeans and plain clothes, a lot of general bystanders, kind of just milling around like they were waiting for something. I was not as mentally acute as I had been at the beginning of the ride; I was working on stabilizing my mind and preparing myself for what was waiting for me inside. I was promising myself that I would not have a meltdown and become hysterical and was really working hard on getting there in my mind. But all the while the anxiety was mounting in me. It was really a hard balance to juggle.

Capt. Skopetz walked ahead of Dave and me, calmly asking people to step aside as we approached the entrance to the ER. I was very aware of the people staring at me as they complied. I was aware of a priest standing just inside the entrance off to the side. I visually scanned the ER: the usual desk, some chairs along the wall, not a lot of clinical action going on but some staff and people looking a little disorganized and one nurse around my age was looking a little overwhelmed.

I was aware of someone saying, "His wife is here."

The young, nervous nurse simply said, "Over here," and walked me to a treatment room off to the side. We followed. I just kept walking. No sense putting it off. I was as mindset-ready as I was going to be and wanted to get this part over with.

The door to the treatment room was wide open: it should have contained two stretcher beds. The treatment bay as you entered the room was a mess - the stretcher rolled sideways, open gauze packs, stuff on the floor that had missed the bucket, etc. The curtain was partly pulled back across the area of the second exam room, behind which I could clearly see the outline of three men standing and a fourth, a uniformed officer, was also clearly visible also standing with his back to the door. Beyond that I could see the very foot of the stretcher bed: the bottom hem of a pair of police pants and police shoes still on. Beyond that, on the other side of the stretcher and facing the door stood a doctor and two nurses. They were talking and quietly doing something as we entered the room. They stopped and faced me; one nurse left the room as we entered. The nurse who had led us into the room left with her and the room became dead silent. "I'm ready. I'll be good," I said to myself and walked around the curtain.

There was Dana lying on the stretcher. His uniform had been removed from the waist up and he was not covered, but still had his police pants and shoes on. His head was half shaved. There was the usual bedside equipment: IV up and running, blood on the sheet, bloody sponges and open gauze packs all around, the rolling bucket on the floor full of the same.

There, standing at his head, was his partner Bob, who was a tall dark Irish guy in his thirties, with a moustache, always a little rough around the edges and a wise guy - the perfect complement to Dana. But here he stood, white as a sheet and looking like he was in shock, but standing. Next to him were two other plainclothes guys I didn't know, with badges on chains hanging over their shirts and writing stuff on a clipboard. I think the uniformed guy at the foot of the bed was a Sergeant or a Lieutenant, but didn't know him either. I think he was holding Dana's gun belt and gear.

The doctor beckoned me around to the side of the stretcher where he was and I followed, leaving Dave and the Captain. From the lineup on the other side of the stretcher, I heard Dana's voice.

"Did they tell you I got shot?" Dana asked, as he reached out his hand to me.

***WHAT?***

My thought and sensory intake was in overdrive when I became aware of that. All of a sudden, with no explanation, the 'nurse switch' in my brain had automatically turned itself on. Not my regular one, but the switch I threw in my head when I had to work in the ICU and ER. The one that keeps me keen, confident and calm while assessing all observations and constantly triaging them in my head.

Dana continued to speak to me, but it was all "shock talk" - it's not really ragtime, but more like an unfiltered flight of ideas that came out of his mouth as they crossed his mind.

"Did Dave call you first? I made him promise he'd call you first. I told them you were a nurse. I told them you would be good. Bob was excellent! Bob did a hell of a job - Did they get the guys that shot me? Dave and Jerry did a hell of a job. You know how I hate needles...."

I just stood there holding his hand and let him ramble for a minute or two. When he slowed down briefly, he looked at me and said, "They keep asking me if I want to see a priest. Do I need one?"

Without shifting my gaze or skipping a beat, my knee jerk reaction was, "No, you are fine." **WHY** did I say that? I had no information.

The rambling resumed. "Then tell them to get the priest out of here" and a couple of more rants.

The doctor interrupted, nodded to one of the nurses, who left the room (I assumed to let the priest know that Dana didn't want to see him) and spoke up. "Let me explain to everyone what is going on here."

The tension in the room had eased greatly and all became very controlled, factual and business like.

The doctor introduced himself: Dr. Kingsbury, a general staff surgeon who just happened to be doing his assigned shift for the month in the ER, which is how they staffed the small ER there - all staff Docs rotated on turn. I was feeling lucky already. What if it had been an allergist's or dermatologist's turn? I didn't want to go there.

Dr. Kingsbury continued: Dana had sustained two gunshot wounds to the head. One had grazed him but the other had penetrated, resulting in a skull fracture and there were still fragments in there. They had succeeded in controlling the bleeding, but did not feel he was stable enough to ship into Boston. His blood pressure was remaining high and climbing. I knew that meant increasing intracranial pressure likely due to brain swelling. I continued to listen. They had an OR team already called in, were preparing the small operating room there and already had a neurosurgeon on his way from Boston - who was being rushed via police escort. Hey! I was impressed! And this was Winchester Hospital. What a pleasant surprise.

He went on: the neurosurgeon was a Dr. Williams (a pseudonym) who was on staff at a couple of Boston hospitals. Hey! I knew him! He had guest privileges at Malden, too and I'd cared for a few of his post-op patients in ICU, most recently an auto accident victim with head trauma and a young guy with a brain tumor. He was cool, cocky and had a huge ego. But that was because he was a brain surgeon, literally, a damn good one and he knew it. This was REALLY lucky!

The officers at Dana's bedside began their own formalities. Capt. Skopetz shook Dana's hand briefly and wished him well. Then he reminded him of protocol - how they needed to take his weapon, gun belt and badge from the hospital. Bob dutifully produced a bag from behind him that contained Dana's shredded blood soaked police shirt. He still looked like crap. The badge was removed and placed in a manila envelope. His weapon and gun belt were going to headquarters.

I was told that I needed to make the rest of the family notifications because there were reporters there that were starting to get pushy, because neither the hospital nor police had released anything yet and all the press had was what the news-hungry had gotten on their police scanners. That explained some of the people who had been milling around outside the hospital.

The overwhelmed nurse who had not been involved with Dana's care was instructed to take me to a room out of the fray to make the calls. She seemed at ease with this and as she led me to a room off the ER, she chatted away...so, she heard I was a nurse too...where did I work?...that she normally worked on a floor upstairs, but it was quiet and when the chaos had begun in the ER she was floated down to man the desk and wasn't used to this. No wonder she had looked like she did not know whether to shit or go blind. I told her I was used to this stuff and she had done a great job. Everyone had.

In the room with the phone I glanced up at the clock. It was now nearly quarter of ten. My first call would be to Dana's mother. Now here was a woman who had no coping skills whatsoever, was early to bed and an early riser too and I had to wake her up out of a sound sleep and drop this bomb on her.

Next would be my folks. They would be still up for sure and would want to keep me on the phone for every gory detail, especially my mother, who all the while would be calculating how she could get into the limelight somehow.

These were just two of the reasons we'd made it a point to settle down and buy a home just far enough away.

Then, of course, I had to call Miriam. And then as an afterthought, I'd better call my sister myself, so she didn't get some embellished, cockamamie story from my mother.

With the notifications out of the way, I went back to Dana's side. He was ranting to Bob to keep talking to him so he would not fall asleep. The brass had left with the effects they needed, but Bob wanted to stay with him till they took Dana to the OR and Dana wanted him there. The place was still bustling, but it was slowing down.

I had barely reached Dana's side when Dr. Williams arrived. Yep, this was him. Cool and confident as he sized up the situation, he spoke briefly with Dr. Kingsbury, and spoke with Dana.

"You'll be fine. You'll be back to work in a week."

Turning to me - he didn't seem to recognize me - he told me he'd, "Fix him up."

He turned to the staff and said, "Let's get him up to the OR," and sauntered out. Medical colleges call it *Ben Casey Syndrome.*

While I stayed to kiss Dana and reassure him, the staff cut off his police pants, bagged them up with his police shoes and did other bustling preparations. They let me walk along with his stretcher just so far as they began to wheel him up to the OR. He didn't want to go to sleep. I squeezed his hand and told him it was all good. Everything was Okay and he would be fine. As they rolled him through the doors where I had to stay behind I was kicking myself. Why had I let them send the priest away?

The 'floated' nurse, now my buddy, brought me back down to the ER, but off to a side room I hadn't seen before. This was to keep me from the hounding reporters, who now had a story but of course wanted more. There was a TV in there and coffee. Come to find out, it was the break room for the staff. They were letting cops come and go there, too, when they needed a (brief) break, or just to stop by the hospital, or needed coffee or to use the john.

Now I know on TV shows and in movies and novels they all try and show and explain this blue brotherhood cops have, but believe me when I tell you, they don't scratch the surface. To live it was unreal. Cops stopped by that little break room - well over 100 of them. They were from literally everywhere near and far, on duty and off, uniform and plain clothes and had come to participate in the search for these shooters. I didn't know 95% of them, but most spoke to me with some verbalization of support that ranged from a simple nod and a respectful utterance of "Ma'am" to "Don't worry we'll find the bastards and kill 'em when we find 'em." I don't think I have ever been exposed to so much emotional testosterone and adrenaline in my life, before or since.

There was a Red Sox game on the TV that I tried to watch, but really couldn't. It was a long one and running late. I did know that. It was nearing 11 p.m. when a news bulletin broke into the game: "MDC police officer shot and killed in police chase; more on news at eleven immediately after the game." Killed???

I was out of my seat like a shot and out to the desk where my new nurse buddy was and asked why the news bulletin said my husband was killed. She looked shocked and then placed a call up to the OR. I could only hear her side of the conversation (which was brief) and see the look on her face, but the end was that he was in surgery and alive. This was my first exposure to the seedy side of journalism. Now I had to go back to the phone and make those calls all over again and put this new fire out - an aggravation I did not need.

By 11:30 a.m. the whole place really started to empty out and slow down, like someone had pulled a plug. In fact, it became eerily quiet. The shift had changed at the hospital and, out in the cities and towns, the police shifts were changing as well. I suddenly realized I didn't know a soul. The evening events were really hitting me and I was feeling emotional and lonely as I sat there with the TV in the background.

Suddenly, shortly before midnight, I looked up to see a nurse in uniform, who I knew. It was Mrs. Moore, accompanied by a nurse who had come in on 11-7, who showed her where I was. "Mrs. Moore! What are you doing here?" I was surprised and confused.

Mrs. Moore was the 11-7 supervisor at Malden Hospital, where I worked. She was the text book night supervisor: well-seasoned middle aged, very professional and all the staff liked and respected her. She was a great nurse supervisor and a wonderful person and her husband was a Baptist minister in a town north of where I lived. She had come through the dragnet on I-93 and, on her way into work, heard on the news it was Dana who had been shot and knew he was my husband. When she got to Malden she shared this info with the off-going 3-11 shift and the on- coming 11-7 staff. She had gathered several of the staff around the TV in the ER where they watched it on the news. She knew I had no family nearby and knew I was probably alone at the hospital. It had then been agreed that the 3-11 supervisor would stay and cover Mrs. Moore's shift at the hospital so she could come to be with me. I was deeply moved and the timing of her arrival was perfect.

For the first time that evening I let myself cry a little. She hugged me as she conveyed her own well wishes, as well as those of my colleagues at Malden and told me her husband was praying for Dana. I needed this and it felt good.

We sat and talked about the evening's events, but the time still seemed to drag on. 1:00 a.m. ...1:30 a.m. ...If this was so simple, why was it taking so long? Even Mrs. Moore was trying not to, but still looked concerned.

After what seemed like an eternity, Dr. Williams appeared where we were waiting.

He recognized Mrs. Moore and asked, "You work here now?"

She explained to him briefly but he didn't seem interested - but then did seem to acknowledge by facial expression that I did look familiar too.

He turned to me in his cocky and matter-of- fact manner, and said, "I fixed him. He's all better."

Then, in brief business-like medical terms, now that he knew I was a nurse, explained what he had done, that there was no recovery room there at night so they were bringing him from the OR to the ICU and that when he was settled, someone would come and get me. He'd tell them that, seeing as I was a nurse, I'd probably be Okay to see him immediately post-op. Then he left.

Mrs. Moore and I exchanged glances and she flashed a little smirk - what an arrogant SOB. Dana had been lucky to have him.

Eventually, someone did come to get us and brought us up to the ICU. There, standing in the hall outside the ICU, was a reporter. How the hell had he gotten up there? Strike two for the press.

In the ICU I saw it was pretty small, quiet and not busy at all. Dana may have been the only one in there. I don't recall. There were two nurses working at his bedside. One cautioned me he was not really out of the anesthetic yet. I was Okay. I had worked the Recovery room as a student and knew what to expect.

He was out cold but everything was white and clean. That alone made it all look better. He had a huge bandage on the front of his head, and had IVs running, oxygen, and a catheter. I noticed bloody urine. This was new. I touched his hand and spoke quietly to him letting him know I was there and Okay. There was no indication if he heard me but I remembered being taught in nursing school that even in a coma, people can hear.

We kept the visit brief and returned to the ER, where the 'how to get Sandy home' discussion came up. There had been an officer assigned to stay at the hospital - protocol - and others still drifted in and out. Mrs. Moore said she would be happy to drive me home. After all, Mrs. Whittier the 3-11 supervisor was covering her shift all night if need be. But I felt she had already done more than enough. I'd let the department take care of getting me home. It was the wee hours of the morning by now. The officer on duty at the hospital radioed the station to advise them I was ready to be taken home. I was told Eddie McLaughlin would be there to drive me. He had a lot of health issues and had been in the hospital a few times. I had cared for him as a patient and had gotten to know him since he worked with Dana. He was the nicest guy Dana worked with, bar none. Middle aged, but not old enough or with enough years on to retire, he no longer worked the street but did the desk on the day shift. The girls loved to visit him when we had to go to the station when Dana picked up a check, or had to drop something off. He loved them, too. Our oldest had called him "Officer Eddie" and that name stuck. Like everyone else who was home when he heard the news of the shooting had aired, Eddie had gone to the station to be there and wanted to do something. He not only drove me home that night, but to and from the hospital every time I went to see Dana for the duration of his inpatient stay. This was something Eddie wanted to do.

When I stepped outside of the hospital it was the first time I had been outside in hours. The warm evening breeze had been replaced by cool night air, cold in fact. I hoped Miriam had closed up the house but at this point I didn't even call her to let her know I was on my way home. I didn't want to take any chances of waking up the kids. If I was lucky, by the time they would wake up, I'd get a maximum of two hours sleep - and I'd have to break the night's events down into four and six year old terms and tell them. I couldn't think of that right now - just SLEEP!

Eddie waited to make sure I got in Okay before driving off. Miriam, in fact, had closed the house up, but the cold had gotten in. That was Okay I thought, good for sleeping.

She was asleep on the couch, covered by an afghan. I quietly woke her up. We exchanged a few words, barely talking above a whisper. I thanked her profusely and told her I'd catch up with her in the morning. She left, still wrapped up in the afghan as she walked down the street into the cool night air. I watched her disappear while I quietly closed the door. I noticed the sky was just starting to get the slight purplish orange color it gets just before the sun starts to come up and I heard the loud pre-dawn chirping of birds.

Once back in the house, I was aware of the radio that Miriam had obviously turned on, playing softly in the background. The last thing I did as I tiptoed down the hall to the bedroom to collapse on my bed was click the radio off. They were playing Cat Stevens' *Morning Has Broken* with lyrics by Eleanor Farjeon:

"Morning has broken, like the first morning
Blackbird has spoken, like the first bird
Praise for the singing, praise for the morning
Praise for the springing fresh from the word."

Sandy's 1968 Nursing School Graduation

# CHAPTER FOUR
## *The Emergency Room*

A steady stream of medical personnel poured in and out of the small Emergency Room. The pain from the bullet wounds had become worse, and for the first time, I was aware of my mortality. I tried hard to stay awake and focused on my wife's arrival. I couldn't wait to look into her eyes. She was an ER nurse. I would be able to tell how bad-off I was by the way she looked at me. No doubt, she knew her expression would give away my condition.

A hush fell over the small emergency room when my wife walked in. She looked at me and grasped my hand. The nurses left the room. I stared into her eyes - they were loving and kind and I saw no fear or tears. My spirit was lifted 100%. I knew the injuries were serious, but I would be Okay...eventually.

I found I could not stop talking. In fact, my words were coming out in such rapid fire I wasn't sure if I was asking questions or making statements.

After several minutes, she kissed me and said, "I will be here. You'll be fine. Let them work on you. I will see you in Recovery. You may be groggy and not remember, but I will be there."

She told me she would call our mothers before they saw it on the news. I agreed but had a hard time letting go of her hand.

The newly appointed Commissioner of the Metropolitan District Commission, William J. Bryne, came in to see me. He had just been appointed, replacing John W. Sears, who headed the MDC from February 1970 to April 1975.

He held my hand and said, "You did a great job, Officer. We are very proud of you and you are in very good hands. Don't worry about a thing. You just get better."

He told me our Superintendent of Police was away on vacation; otherwise, he would have been there, too. I felt honored but at the same time I knew it was a photo op, as the press took pictures of us. I was uncomfortable with the photographers taking my picture without asking me - my trust in the press was tenuous, at best.

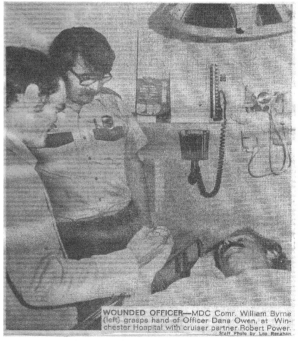

WOUNDED OFFICER—MDC Comr. William Byrne (left) grasps hand of Officer Dana Owen, at Winchester Hospital with cruiser partner Robert Power.
Staff Photo by Leo Renahan

Newspaper photo of Dana in the hospital

There was a news bulletin on the tiny black and white TV: "MDC Police Officer shot and killed in Winchester. Details to follow at 11:00 p.m."

Dr. Kingsbury, the ER doc, smiled and said, "The reports of your death have been greatly exaggerated!" Great line, but I knew he stole it from Mark Twain.

> *Meanwhile, my Mother, who had been a widow*
> *for twenty-five years and lived alone, heard* **that**
> *news broadcast at her home...and fainted.*

The neurosurgeon, escorted from the Beth Israel Hospital, had arrived and was looking over my X-rays. He was discussing the results with the Emergency Room Physician.

The next thing I knew Sergeant Frank Thorpe appeared, holding a shotgun and wearing a bandolier of shotgun shells over his big gut.

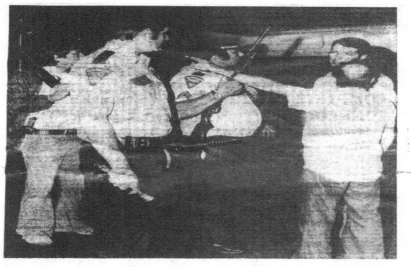

(Times Photo, N. Barbas)
A FRANCIS CIRCUIT RESIDENT shows MDC police the direction four gunmen took after they abandoned their car in Winchester last night. Then men left their car on the Winchester dead-end road after being chased by MDC Police following an aborted hi-jacking.

Thorpe was the shift commander that night at the Fells Station, named after the Middlesex Fells Reservation, which included parts of Malden, Medford, Stoneham, Melrose and Winchester. Thorpe was a larger than life character. He was famous or infamous, depending on who said it. I had worked for him on many shifts. One thing I could say about Sgt. Thorpe was he took care of his men. Despite his unorthodox ways, I liked working for him. The Sergeant told me there were over one hundred officers involved in the search.

He announced, "Dana, we'll get the bastards and we won't take them alive!"

At the time, it sounded good to me, but the neurosurgeon was not happy. He said to the Sgt., "So, I will have others to patch up. Is that what you're telling me?"

Thorpe did not answer. He looked over at the surgeon with disdain, shook my hand and went back out to search for the four suspects. Other MDC Officers I knew came by to tell me to hang in there and then went back out to join the massive man hunt. Many had been off-duty in civilian clothes, carrying their own handguns, hunting rifles or shotguns. The rules of the police game had changed. A brother officer had been shot.

Before I was taken into surgery, there was one more person waiting to talk with me. He was Captain Skopetz, the Watch Commander from Headquarters in Boston. I'd never met him before.

He was holding my service revolver and said, "Officer, I have to ask you if you fired any shots during the pursuit."

His question puzzled me because I had not fired a single round.

"No, Sir. I never got the chance to."

The Captain told me a woman bystander had been shot at Swanton Street where the chase ended. I watched as he smelled the barrel of the gun. Without opening the cylinder, he pointed the business end of the revolver at his nose, I guessed to smell for gunpowder. Because I was a 'gun guy,' I was shocked at his lack of firearms-safety skills - he should have opened the cylinder to make sure the revolver was not loaded. He decided my gun had not been fired.

"How is the woman, Captain?" I asked. It was the first I'd heard a civilian had been shot.

"She is here, in the hospital and fine. They removed a bullet from her hair and scalp. We think it was one of the hijackers' bullets that must have ricocheted," he responded.

I knew he was only doing his job, by asking me these questions. It also affirmed he had to talk to me before the surgery...just in case. He turned out to be a sincere man and would become supportive of my family and me during my recovery.

Next, the neurosurgeon turned to me, and said, "I am going to clean the bullet fragments and glass out of your wounds. Just try and relax," he said in a confident tone.

"Do you want a priest?" he asked, reading my chart which showed I was Catholic.

"Do I need one?" I asked.

"Do you want one?"

"Do I need one?" We went back and forth several times.

"Am I going to die?" I finally asked.

"No, I am going to fix you," he said assuredly.

I decided if I had the last rites of the church, called extreme unction at the time, I would be giving up. I didn't want any unction, extreme or otherwise.

"No priest, then. Thanks."

My thoughts flashed back to when I was thirteen and confirmed by the Catholic Church. The name I took was Michael, a name I just liked when I chose it and a Saint's name, of course. (The selection of a saint's name is required for confirmation.) At the time, I did not know St. Michael was the patron saint of police and warriors.

I started to pray to St. Michael. I felt only he could understand my plight. As they wheeled me into the surgical theater, I was making deals with God. If you let me live, I will... I imagine most people near death make deals. Keeping them is another matter, if they live. Something else was on my mind. I could not die on my daughter's birthday and have her relive it each year, on the anniversary of her birth.

I prayed to St. Michael, "If it is my time, please let it be *after* midnight!"

The lights in surgery were blinding and the room was freezing cold. All I could smell was the antiseptic odor.

The nurse asked, "Do you remember what you ate for dinner?"

"Yes…I had a half a fried chicken, mashed potatoes and peas."

"Anything else?" she inquired, writing down what I had eaten.

"Just a few rolls and strawberry shortcake with vanilla ice cream."

"Okay, thank you," she replied, but had a look of concern on her face.

> *I was later informed if I threw up after intubation (tube inserted into the throat for breathing) I could have drowned in my own vomit. They had waited as long as they could for me to digest my food but the pressure caused by the fractured skull had to be relieved on my swelling brain.*

As the anesthesia mask was about to be applied to my nose and mouth, I saw a fly. It was a big, nasty, black fly, circling around the high intensity lights. The last thing I needed was a fly landing on my exposed skull or brain lining. I told the surgical staff, but they thought I was hallucinating.

I fought the mask and said, "Look! It's a damn fly!"

It was almost like a comedy watching the staff spraying a fly in a 'sterile room.' I remember a male technician standing on a stool trying to exterminate this winged intruder. They told me they got it. I always wondered if they really did.

Things were out of my hands. I would either wake up, or... . I didn't want to think about the alternative.

Someone said, "Count backward from one hundred."

The mask was over my face. "One hundred, ninety-nine..."

It was morning when I awoke in what I thought must have been the recovery room. It was a stark place with no clocks and no mirrors.

There was a tall man in a suit and tie standing at the foot of my bed. He looked vaguely familiar. Maybe he was a cop.

He said, "Hi, I am Dave Rodman from Channel 7." (Channel 7 was a major Boston TV news station).

"How did you get in here?" I groggily asked.

A nurse standing beside him said, "He told me was an FBI Agent."

"Get him out of here!" I growled my voice raspy from having been intubated. The nurse told him to leave and he did, but reluctantly.

Still confused and weak from the anesthesia, I told the nurse to get the MDC cops. I was sure there were still some in the hospital.

The nursing supervisor came in and asked me, "Is there a problem?"

My wife, waiting at my bedside, averted my wrath by pulling her aside to huddle for a conference. It had been obvious this community hospital was not used to reporters trying to get a scoop - or cops getting shot. Later, I demanded a MDC cop stand guard at my door and got it.

# CHAPTER FIVE

## *The Hospital Stay*

They kept me in the hospital for two weeks. The headaches were unbearable and dizziness, nausea and other complications had set in. I had been assigned a semi-private room, even though I asked for a private one. I didn't want to talk to anyone.

It was a typical hospital room with a sliding curtain between the beds. My bed was adjacent to the door; my roommate had the window. He was a retired dentist in his sixties, in for prostate issues, or 'prostrate' as most of us cops mispronounce it. We ended up talking quite a bit, mostly about life in general.

During our first conversation, he said, "Just remember - if you don't have your health, you don't have anything."

The phrase really struck home for me. He was a calming influence, in this drama. In hindsight, it was good for me to have someone to talk to. I later found out my wife, the nurse, wisely insisted I had a roommate.

The hospital room smelled of fresh flowers sent to me from well-wishers, and cards came in from all over the country, many from people I didn't know. These people had read the story about my shooting and were very supportive of law enforcement officers. There were many handmade cards from my daughters' classmates. I had to laugh at the cards the kids made in school, mostly of me as a stick figure. The girls usually showed me with bandages on my head, the boys with stick figures of cops and robbers shooting it out. They were precious and I saved them all.

On the afternoon of June 17, the first and only reporter approved by our public relations officer came to interview me. He was Ron Gollobin with WCVB-TV in Boston. Ron appeared to be in his early thirties. I had never seen him on TV before our interview. He had a thick southern drawl. Ron's hair was reddish brown in what I would call an 'Afro.' He seemed friendly and confident, had the gift of gab, and the distinctive voice a reporter needed.

Ron said, "I just want you folks to know this will be my first on-camera interview. I have been an investigative reporter up until now - avoiding the camera - undercover, so to speak."

I agreed to do the interview for that night's news. I liked Ron's easy and professional manner. On my bedside table were pictures of our daughters in their ballet costumes, which Sandy had brought in for me.

Ron asked. "Do you mind if we show the photos of your children during the interview?"

Sandy jumped up and shouted, "There is no way we want anyone to see our children."

In a calmer tone, she said firmly, "We don't even know who shot Dana, so they are still out there."

Ron replied, "I fully understand and to be safe, why don't you put the photos in the drawer."

Physically, I was weak, felt like crap and looked hideous with my partially-shaved head and full moustache. I never saw the interview on TV, but a lot of my friends did. They said I did pretty well, under the circumstances. I don't remember anything about it. I was on heavy pain medication and it *was* a head wound.

On day three, the nurse told me, "If you don't urinate we are going to have to insert a catheter. Do you think you can go on your own?" She was holding some weird medical jar for me to try and pee in.

"I will try but I can't with you watching. Can I go in the bathroom?"

"Yes, but make sure you go in the jar. We have to test your urine after surgery. If you need me, just ring the buzzer," she said.

So in I went, jar in hand, to try to pee. The thought of having a tube inserted was a huge incentive. Finally, I was able to go, but instead of urine I was peeing dark, almost black, blood. I panicked and rang for the nurse; in fact, I almost passed out.

As she opened the door, I said, "I'm hemorrhaging!"

She tried to calm me down, "There is nothing to worry about." But I was rushed in for tests, where they found I had a bruised kidney. The theory was I bruised my left kidney on the door jamb as I fell out of the cruiser trying to return the incoming gunfire.

The next medical procedure was the removal of glass fragments from both my eyes, from the bullet riddled windshield. The eye doctor told me, "We can do this right in your room. I just have to put in a few eye drops to paralyze your muscles and a little dye to see the glass fragments."

"Will it hurt, Doc?"

"No, you just won't be able to close your eyes for a while."

Well, the drops worked. I wanted to close my eyes so badly, but couldn't. It overrode my natural reflex to close my eyes as something was coming at them. He came at my right eye with some sort of long scraper. At one time it must have been some kind of torture device, because I almost puked. It really had been a bad moment.

THE HOSPITAL SEEMED to be adjusting to this event and kept much tighter control and security. Having been given a lot of pain medication, I remembered some who visited, but not everyone.

I don't know whether it was because my wife was a nurse, or because she was a great 'in charge person,' but she kept things under control during my hospital stay.

Captain John I. O'Brien was one of the Watch Commanders who visited me. 'John I,' as he was called, was another larger than life character. He reminded me of General ('Blood and Guts') Patton from World War II fame.

He told my wife, "Ma'am, you will have a cruiser available to take you to the hospital twenty-four hours a day. If you need help, someone will baby sit as well."

Later, during my hospital stay, two other from the Boston Police Department came to visit me. One had been shot, and the other had shot a suspect in a shootout. I found they were bitter about how they had been treated by their department. The MDC treated us like family.

A close friend of ours, Paul Atlas, who had a bread delivery business, told me the story of how he heard the news. He had been on his route at 3:00 a.m. on June 17, the morning after I was shot. He was driving by the Boston Ski Hill on Route 125 in North Andover, MA, when on the AM radio, he heard, "MDC Police Officer shot last night in Winchester, MA." Paul told me he thought, "It couldn't be Dana." There were about 650 MDC cops in 1975, but he knew I patrolled that area. When the news came back on and he heard it *was* me, he later told me, "I was so upset, I had to pull over. I almost threw up." He called his wife Bette from the nearest payphone. Once she found out I had survived, they came to see me in the hospital.

The first few days in Winchester, I was so out of it most of the time, I vaguely remember their visit. But I clearly recall Paul came to our house after I was released. He brought us enough bread, hotdog and hamburger rolls to last a year.

DURING THOSE WEEKS in the hospital with nothing but time on my hands, my mind went into overdrive. I thought back on how my father had landed on Omaha Beach on D-Day, along with my godfather. My Dad died in 1950 at age thirty-two of a service-connected illness. I was only three. I was granted 4A status in the draft, the 'sole surviving son.' It probably kept me from getting shot up in Vietnam.

Although I decided not to go into the Service, I felt the weight of guilt on my shoulders. Some of my friends had died in Vietnam. Others came home but were screwed up mentally and/or physically. My mother had been classified as a 'War Widow' at age thirty. I was the only child. I felt an obligation to take care of my mother in my father's absence, yet at the same time, wanted to serve my country. I had to prove to my Dad and to my friends that it was not cowardice that kept me out of the service. Instead of military service, I joined the police force to serve my country. I was not a coward and felt my actions during the pursuit when I was shot proved it.

THE BEST THING anyone did for me during my hospital stay was to bring in several scrap books and newspaper articles of the incident. Of course, my wife was the one who thought to clip the articles and make the books for me.

"You will want to save these and look back at them some day," she wisely said.

> *As I sit here writing my story, the scrapbooks full of clippings spanning an eleven year period are at my side. Little did I know this case would take up the next decade of my life, but maybe she did.*

During my stay in the hospital, the surgeon who saved my life would come in and tell me to get up and walk - which I did, of course. His tone had been harsh and he often seemed angry and frustrated. His attitude toward me was demeaning. When I tried to stand to walk, I got dizzy, and several times I almost fell. The nurse would come in and yell at me for trying to walk, as did the other doctors who had seen me. There was an obvious rift between the surgeon and the other doctors and nurses. To me, it had been apparent from that night he operated on me, this surgeon had no love for cops.

One of my doctors said it best, "Neurosurgeons are used to unconscious patients; they are not good at dealing with those who are awake."

Sleep did not come often during my stay in the hospital and when it did, it was filled with flashbacks. It got so bad I did not want to sleep.

Just before I was sent home, about 2:00 a.m. one morning, two of my fellow MDC cops came in with a frappe (milk shake with ice cream).

Bill, one of the more veteran officers, said, "Here, kid. I know you probably can't sleep," and handed me the ice-cold, thick coffee frappe.

He was quite the character who had seen much in his time, first as a cop with the Boston Police Department and then working with the MDC. The nursing supervisor, who looked like the starched Nurse Ratched in *One Flew over the Cuckoo's Nest,* came in and told my brother officers, "You will have to leave." It was way after visiting hours.

Bill, with his police hat cocked back on his head, calmly and confidently told her, "Honey, I have been thrown out of better barrooms than this." They stayed a few more hours.

*Some years later, Bill took his own life, succumbing to the demons many cops face.*

# CHAPTER SIX
## *The Search at the Scene*

My partner, Bob Power, stayed with me the night I was shot until I was taken into surgery. When he came back to the hospital to visit a day or two later, we talked about the events of that night.

We felt the reason the two police dispatchers did not take us seriously, at first, was because of the situation in the radio room.

> *The job tried to take care of folks, mostly veteran officers near retirement, who had some kind of personnel issue. They were usually assigned to the Radio Room.*
>
> *Later, when I asked to listen to the tape of radio transmissions of the chase, I was told the two cops on dispatch duty that night at Met Control had forgotten to turn on the recording system. The oversight would be a hindrance in the initial stages of the investigation. It was also a huge disappointment to me. I really wanted to hear what the pursuit sounded like.*
>
> *Not long after my shooting, younger and sharper cops were assigned to the dispatching duties. It was a change for the better and long overdue.*

It had been a long night for Bob. He told me most of the night he had been transported back and forth from the scene where the chase ended to the hospital. He was asked to describe all the details of the pursuit and shooting, but he wanted to be with me at the hospital. In newspaper photos, he seemed to be in shock, as I had been.

Officer Robert Power, left, discusses shooting. At right, officers search area. (George Rizer photos)

Bob told me the Massachusetts State Police helicopter had flown overhead, to follow the movements of the getaway car as it careened through Winchester. After the car fled the scene of my shooting at Washington and Swanton Streets, it had turned onto Francis Circuit, a dead end road.

The Staties in the chopper radioed the location of the dead-end street as the four suspects bailed out and fled on foot. With each police agency on a different radio frequency, the messages had to be relayed separately. This delay gave the hijackers the time they needed to escape.

Bob told me that after searching the area, they determined the driver and occupants of the Ford had discarded their disguises, gloves, jackets, and the surgical tape they had used to distort their facial features. The suspects left the sawed off shotgun and a handgun in the car and tossed another gun into the bushes a block away.

The following is an excerpt from the report of U.S. Postal Inspector W. J. O'Leary:

*"Found in the abandoned car were the following items:*

1. *Sawed off 12 gauge Ithaca shotgun.*
2. *Colt .38 caliber Police Positive revolver*
3. *Light colored trench coat containing what appeared to be blood stains on the inside lining of one sleeve.*
4. *Bolt cutters*
5. *Two pairs of sunglasses*
6. *Two cloth hats*

*A 'house to house' and search of the immediate area by MDC, Winchester Police, Massachusetts State Police, other nearby community police and Inspection Service personnel during the night and the following morning, utilizing K-9 dog units and State Police Helicopter, disclosed the following items in the areas of 3 and 9 Hillside Ave., Winchester, one and a half blocks from the abandoned car.*

1. *Rohm .38 caliber Police Special revolver*
2. *Black ski mask*
3. *One pair brown cotton gloves with red lining*
4. *One pair brown cowhide gloves, size medium*
5. *One black knitted stocking cap*
6. *One denim jacket*

*The four men who fled from the abandoned Ford sedan on Francis Circuit were not found and the manhunt was terminated at 7:00 a.m. on 6/17/75.*

*Over 100 officers from the MDC, State Police and several surrounding towns took part in the all night search."*

WINCHESTER LT. WILLIAM HAGGERTY places two weapons — a handgun and a sawed-off shotgun — in a cruiser. The armament was abandoned by fleeing suspects after they ran into the woods off Francis Circuit, Winchester.

Sawed-off Shotgun and revolver in Lt. Haggerty's hands

Bolt cutters and watch cap abandoned by the hijackers

THE ONE THING I remembered vividly was when Bob said, **"Stay with me and fight!"** It was the perfect thing for him to have said when I had all but given up and was readying myself to die.

Bob and I were total opposites in many ways. He was brought up in the city and I was a small town boy. Our opposing personalities made the partnership work. I could not have asked for a better partner. Here's why we were such a perfect team.

One night at the beginning of a 4:00 p.m. to midnight shift, I was partnered up with Bob. It had already been a long day. I had worked a midnight to 8:00 a.m. shift, and then worked all day in court. I was in desperate need of a cup of coffee. Just as we were pulling out of the station yard to start our tour, a red van came flying though a red light in front of us.

Bob said, "Let's get him."

I had never looked the other way when someone violated the law, but I really needed that coffee and knew how often a simple traffic stop could lead to a bigger deal. I protested, but went after the speeding van. We managed to stop him on the Fellsway, a major artery leading into Boston.

He said, "I'll handle this. You wait here." This was not the way to do a traffic stop. Both officers were supposed to get out of the car. It was only a red light and I was tired and grouchy. I stayed in the car.

Suddenly, Bob was yelling at the driver and waving his arms. Things were going downhill fast. All I could think about was this would mean no caffeine! Bob's face was beet red as when I stepped up to the van.

"Bob, let me show you how do to this," I announced, in a condescending tone.

"Let me see your license and registration, Sir, and let's everyone calm down," I continued in my most professional tone.

The irate driver's response was very clear, "F*** you, a**hole!"

My resounding reply was, "You're under arrest!!!"

It had become a 'contempt of cop' situation. He had refused to produce his driver's license on request, which is an arrestable offense. Maybe it was the lack of sleep, but I reached into the window and grabbed the driver by his shirt, with both of my hands. He was going to jail.

The strength I could muster was amazing when I was angry. As I hauled this motorist out of the driver's window of the van, there was a problem. He just kept coming and coming. Soon I realized this guy was big - really big, like 6' 3". After I wrestled him to the pavement, I attempted to handcuff him. Getting one handcuff on a suspect was easy. The trick was to pull the wrists together and get the second cuff locked down. I had gone through this type of struggle before and the only way to get that second handcuff on was with another cop's help.

I yelled, "Bob, give me a hand!"

Of course his response was, "You wanted to show me how to do it...Show me!"

I was not surprised by his comeback, which I was sure I deserved, but I needed help.

"Come on. Help me cuff him!" I pleaded.

In the same condescending tone I had used, he replied, "Nope. Do it yourself."

As I rolled around on the street with the uncooperative red light runner, a small crowd of bystanders pulled over to watch. One middle-aged gentleman stood next to my partner and said, "Aren't you going to help him?"

Bob calmly said, "Nope, he can do it himself. He is showing me the right way to do it."

I think the struggling violator became so confused by these two 'professional policemen,' he stopped resisting and gave in, so I was able to cuff him. I am sure the people who stopped felt they had seen two highly trained professional policemen in action!

Now, *I* would have to write the reports and go through the booking process, while Bob went for the coffee, with a smirk on his face, I should add.

AFTER MY SHOOTING, Bob's best story was of the 'Monday morning quarterbacks.' Several of the MDC cops at the Fells Station were doing the 'if only I was there' crap and he told me what happened:

> *"One of the cops asked me why you were shot twice and I wasn't injured.*
>
> *I answered, 'But I was. I had bad cuts behind both ears.'*
>
> *'From the shattered windshield glass?' the puzzled quarterback inquired.*
>
> *'Nope, it was easy to get my head into the glove compartment when the shooting started, but it was a bitch to get it back out!' I said."*

LITTLE DID WE know a tenacious pursuit of those responsible would be triggered when the first shotgun slug cracked my head open. It would not take long to identify three of the four people (and have a good idea about the fourth) in the stolen car, nor would it take long to identify the guns, the disguises and the guy who provided them, along with the 'hot' car. Unfortunately, learning the identities of criminals and wrapping up a case with the evidence needed for convictions lay at the opposite ends of the law enforcement spectrum. I did not know back then it would take the next eleven years to pursue and prosecute the men who shot me and left me for dead, bleeding on a Winchester street. And perhaps those responsible should have killed me in the first place, because it's exactly what they would have to do to shake me from their trail.

My head is thick, literally and figuratively. The bulldog/bloodhound in me had the scent. I was not going to let it go as long as I lived. I would hunt every one of them down and see them either dead or in court. It was a commitment that I obsessed over for more than a decade of dogged pursuit.

# CHAPTER SEVEN
## *Back at Home*

I desperately wanted to be released from the hospital. The medical staff had done all they could and now I just needed to rest and get my strength back.

In the hospital, sleep was hard to come by. It was either interrupted by my vitals taken in the middle of the night, nearby patients, or 'screamers' yelling for a nurse all night long. It was time to go home.

After a two-weeks stay, they let me out early because my wife was a nurse. I was still in rough shape, but needed to be home in my safe haven. The steady stream of visitors had ended. I found cops and cops' wives did not want to face the reminder of how easily and quickly we could be taken from them. For many, it was easier not to think about the dangers of the job. The common attitude was 'it will never happen to me.' I never thought of the job that way, but I understood it was a coping mechanism for them.

On the day of my release, I was given quite the sendoff by the staff. It seemed I had become a bit of a celebrity in the quiet, suburban hospital. One of the nurses, who had cared for me, presented me with a small grey plastic specimen cup with a cover on it.

"We thought you might like this as a memento," she giggled.

I opened it to find the piece of my skull the surgeon had to remove, about the shape and size of a dime.

"Gee, thanks," I said, laughing to myself.

It was a short wheelchair ride to my car, where my wife was waiting behind the wheel. We headed home, at last, where my wife could care for me and our two young kids without having to hire a babysitter.

The first thing I wanted to do was really look at myself in the mirror, alone. I had only glanced at my reflection in the bathroom of my hospital room. The face I was studying had aged ten years in just a few weeks. There seemed to be deep lines where there used to be smooth skin and dark bags hung under my eyes. I examined the stitches on the red, raw wound on my forehead. Dried blood clung to the black stitches - there were too many to count. Topping off the Frankenstein face was my bizarrely shaved head, stained yellowish orange from antiseptic slathered on it. My kids looked at me, this stranger who was their father, with disbelief.

They asked, "Why does Daddy have the sun on his forehead?"

My friends had taken it all in with compassion, but some with pity. But the person I saw in the mirror was not me. My wide-brimmed, khaki colored fishing hat was the solution. No way did I want to explain to the general public how I had received the head wounds. The hat hid it all and was always on my head. My wife washed it only when I was sleeping and could not object.

ANOTHER REASON FOR the hat was embarrassment. I felt I had '**the big pinch**' in my grasp, but it had slipped away. It was hardly rational, but the last thing I needed was someone asking, "So what happened to the guys who shot you?"

Paranoia set in and I was afraid to go out of my house. It was a devastating feeling. I felt too weak to defend myself or my family.

Not long after my release from the hospital, there was a ballet recital for my four year old daughter. The thought of being in a crowd was more than I could handle. It was the first special event for my kids I ever missed. Things were spiraling downward.

At home, a full night's sleep didn't come often and when it did, my dreams were filled with repetitive nightmares of the gun falling 'slo-mo,' from my hand. My outstretched hand would almost catch up to the falling revolver. But I would awaken from each dream, soaked in sweat, without ever catching the gun. Many nights I would wake up yelling and my wife would comfort me and ask what was wrong.

"You were yelling something, but I could not understand what you were saying," she would say night after night.

"It's nothing. Go back to sleep. I'm fine." Of course, I wasn't and she knew it.

The nurse in her was amazing. From the first moment she looked in my eyes as I lay on the stretcher, she focused on my care and was professional and compassionate. She was a commanding force and respected by the medical staff and my fellow cops. If the crew in the emergency room was expecting a hysterical wife, they didn't get that. What they got instead, was a professional force of nature dedicated to one thing - getting me well and back to normal. My wife was amazing and cared for me physically and emotionally to the best of her ability.

But I was fighting an internal battle. I was one of the good guys and the good guys in the 'White Hats' were supposed to win. As a cop, I was committed to protecting the innocent and catching the bad guys. But here I was seriously injured, young, and scared, yet furious the battle was not finished. This would fuel my drive to pursue the people who shot me. In fact, I recall saying to my partner after the first shotgun slug hit me during the pursuit, **"If it's the last thing I ever do, I'm going to catch these guys."** That was a commitment, not just words of anger.

I wanted to be involved in the case, but it was 1975. There were no cell phones, no text messages, no Facebook, no email. The telephone was my link to those who wanted to contact and support me. When my phone finally did ring, I did not get the calls I had hoped for. I wanted support from my fellow police officers, their understanding about my physical and emotional state. When those calls didn't come, I assumed they felt I needed more time to 'recover.' At least, that was how I explained the lack of communication to myself. The silence from my fellow officers had been, in fact, deafening and deadening.

The feeling of isolation was gnawing away at me. A few of my real friends kept in touch, but that was it.

> *We now know isolation is the worst thing for someone who has experienced a traumatic event. Post Traumatic Stress Disorder was just starting to become better understood at the time I was shot. Unfortunately, I was victim to all the myths and mistakes made back then. A cop who feels like a victim is not a good thing. Looking back, I exhibited many of the symptoms of PTSD.*

Loud noises startled me. And any strange sounds in the middle of the night would cause me to grab my gun and flashlight to go investigate.

In the midst of my struggle with demons, real and imagined, there was a scary moment that makes me smile to this day.

At 3:00 a.m., my phone rang.

"Dana? It's Mrs. Sweeny across the street. I think someone is breaking into my house. Please come over!" she whispered into the phone.

"I'll be right there. Just stay calm," I reassured her.

Grabbing my snub nose, a flashlight and, of course, my fishing hat, I went across the cul de sac to investigate, barefoot and in my PJs. She pointed to the side of the house on the second floor, where the sounds were coming from. I took cover behind a large oak tree and scanned the area with my flashlight in one hand, revolver in the other. Hearing a sound from the chimney, I saw the burglar wearing a classic black mask over the eyes. He was climbing out of the chimney! I held my position and waited for...a fifteen-pound raccoon.

> *Before I was shot, no one in my neighborhood knew I was a cop. I almost always went to and from work in civilian clothes or had a jacket covering my police shirt and never talked about my job. That's just how it was in the 1970s. A lot of people did not like cops in those turbulent days of protest and demonstrations against authority.*

I told Mrs. Sweeney to call the North Reading P. D., and tell them to cancel her call. I was sure she had phoned them first, before calling me.

"I never called them, just you. I didn't want to wake them up at this time of the morning," she said in all seriousness. Unbelievable! She was a very nice lady, but like so many, had no idea or concept of what cops do: protect and serve the public.

MY WIFE COULD finally go back to work on the 11:00 p.m. to 7:00 a.m. shift. She would get the kids tucked into bed and all I had to really do was just try to sleep and respond to the girls, if they needed something.

Sandy would call at about 11:30 p.m. to let me know she got to Malden Okay and to check on how I was doing at home. The phone was always on the floor on my side of the bed (a habit I still have to this day). I could easily grab it when she called. I was still getting dizzy when I stood up and I could answer it without getting out of bed.

One night she did her check-in and I was in a deep sleep, unusual because of my sleep issues. I dropped the phone when I was hanging it up. Standing up, I reached down to pick it up and I cracked my head on the sharp corner of our bureau. A direct hit to the wound on my forehead, I was TKOed and I fell onto my knees, dazed. It was the only part of my body I needed to protect, and I had managed to hit it dead center. Staggering into the bathroom, I put a cold cloth on the swollen wound. I decided not to call my wife and lay awake all night afraid if I slept, I might not wake up. The next morning, I found I had not done serious damage to the wound.

WE LIVED IN the last house on a dead end street, with nothing but woods behind us. Many of the newspapers printed my exact street address, adding to my fears and paranoia. I could not believe how incredibly stupid and insensitive it was on the part of journalists to put me in such jeopardy! The hijackers were on the loose and maybe they thought I could identify the guy in the cab of the hijacked truck. I had once felt safe in my yard, but now my S&W snub nose .38 caliber was tucked in my belt, just in case.

Ironically, my source of information was still the newspapers and TV reports, which faded in time, as the event became old news. Scouring the newspaper articles, I noticed everything seemed to connect these guys with organized crime. For extra safety, I kept my Remington 12-gauge shotgun loaded in my work area of the basement. If I needed it, I would just pump a round in the chamber and it would be ready to go. It was a gun I used to hunt with. Now it was for protection. I was taking no chances and was armed day and night.

One day a florist's van pulled up in front of my house. I answered the door cautiously.

The poor delivery boy stared at the gun in my waistband and stammered, "Flowers for the Owen family."

I felt badly that I scared the crap out of him, but could not take the risk. I gave him a ten-dollar tip out of sympathy.

AS LATE JUNE rolled around, I was slowly getting stronger, but the headaches were intense. When a headache got severe, it was accompanied by nausea and vomiting. "A great way to diet," I would joke to Sandy and friends, but I was steadily losing weight. When I started to get my appetite back, I began to cook outside on our grill. In fact, I was a pretty good cook with hotdogs and hamburgers, but that was the extent of my culinary skills.

Wednesday, June 29 was hot and humid, like most of the summer had been. It was peaceful, with only the sound of a few peepers (small frogs) and the occasional buzz of a mosquito.

As we sat in the dining room, eating the burgers I had grilled to perfection, I started sweating profusely in the stifling summer's heat. We could afford only one air-conditioner and it had been installed in our bedroom. Wiping my forehead, I saw a red color on my hand instead of sweat. Ketchup was my favorite topping on a burger and I always used too much, but this was not Heinz. It was blood. Doctors at the hospital had warned me of the possibility of a hemorrhage, long after the wound healed. I was bleeding pretty heavily from the wound in my forehead. Panic quickly set in! I knew a subdural hematoma (bleeding under the lining of the brain) was usually fatal. I could not grasp I had survived the shooting and now might die from a brain hemorrhage, after cooking and eating a burger.

Facing death so soon after surviving the shooting, I was as scared as I had ever been in my life. In fact, more so than the night I had been shot. My wife held a sterile gauze pad over the wound. She tried to stop the bleeding, but was unable to. She told me to relax. She said it just needed to be cleaned out at an ER. She calmly told me she had seen this happen with head wounds many times.

We loaded the kids into our green Plymouth Satellite station wagon and Sandy drove to Malden Hospital. She felt the best option was a place where she knew most of the medical staff. An ER physician she really trusted treated my wound.

"What type of skull fracture did the surgeon who operated on you say you had?" he inquired.

"Linear," I answered. I thought I had the least severe of the different types of skull fractures, when in reality I had one of the most serious types.

The Doc assured me I would be fine. After giving me a local anesthetic, he started to cut away the old stitches and push on the wound to clean it out. I heard him say, "Whoa! What's *this*?"

"Is there a problem, Doc?" I asked - very scared.

"Not really. But I want to give your surgeon a quick call."

I could overhear the phone call turn into a yelling match. The ER doc seemed concerned. Maybe I misunderstood what the neurosurgeon told me but it seemed he had not completely explained the severity of my type of skull fracture. As the ER doc had been debriding, or squeezing, on the fracture, a substance other than blood was forced out. It was the gel foam the neurosurgeon had inserted as protective filler - like a little flat piece of sponge that absorbs the blood and at the same time cushions and protects the fracture. This ER doctor didn't know the gel was part of the initial surgery. The bottom line was it was risky to put pressure on a depressed skull fracture, which was what I had. This was a very unsettling situation for me.

Shortly after the bleeding incident, my wife and I went to the neurosurgeon for a follow-up exam, where the issue came to a head. We sat in the crowded waiting room for about two hours, typical for a doctor on call for emergencies. I think I had finished reading every old *Time* and *Newsweek* magazine when my name was finally called.

In his office, I told him I had severe headaches, nausea and vomiting. We briefly spoke about the hematoma, but he seemed unconcerned. He had no bedside manner and was arrogant and condescending.

"Do you think I will have to take a disability and retire?" I asked sincerely.

Infuriated, he answered, "**And become a malingerer like the other cops?**"

"I told your wife I fixed you. And I did." His tone was cold, curt and, in fact, rude.

"But look at me. I am a mess and the headaches are blinding and I can't keep food down," I pleaded.

"I told you. I fixed you. You should not have headaches or side effects."

"Doctor," Sandy interjected, "you're not listening. I am taking care of him at home and his recovery isn't going well at all!"

We were both stunned and I felt betrayed by this cocky bastard. He basically refused to debate the matter any longer. Instead, to my amazement he completed my LOD-1 (line of duty injury form), giving me permission to return to 'full duty' in two weeks. The same guy who saved my life was now acting like a total ass.

My wife said, "Calm down. We'll get a second opinion."

"Do you have any idea what full duty means in police work?" I blurted out.

He would not answer, but turned his back on me and picked up the next patient's folder.

My wife and I got up and left the room. Slamming his office door as hard as I could, I saw the look of confusion and maybe fear on the faces of those in his waiting room. I quickly covered my head with my fishing hat, my face bright red in anger, and we headed to the parking lot and got into the car.

On the way home I ranted about 'suing the bastard,' but knew it would be useless. If I went ahead with it, my wife would be blackballed in the health care profession and we both knew it. I had just lost my second battle.

IT WAS TIME to regroup. In fact, it was time to get my life back together and stop feeling sorry for myself. Luckily, my wife guided me through this medical maze. My family doctor had been following my case and had been in to see me in the hospital a few times. We made an appointment to see him the next day.

Dr. Myer Feingold was older, wiser and had a great bedside manner. We discussed the visit to the neurosurgeon and I gave him my filled-out LOD form.

He calmly said, "You're twenty-seven years old. How do you feel and what do you want to do?"

Down from 185 pounds to about 155 and with continuing debilitating headaches, I had lots of doubt about continuing to work as a cop. This was the job I had worked so hard for and now it was in jeopardy.

"I want to get rid of these headaches, put some weight back on and maybe go back to work. I have to be honest Doc, I am really afraid to even leave my house."

"That's normal, after what you've been through," he reassured me. "I have guys like you who have come back from Vietnam and they have the same fears," he said in a very calming tone.

"But I was not in a war like those guys were, Doc."

"No. However, you just survived gunshot wounds and the effects are the same," he replied.

What he was saying made a lot of sense and I felt he treated me like a human being. A huge weight had been lifted off my shoulders, just knowing he understood what I was going through.

"The way I see it you are too young to retire. You can hang around the local gin mill and tell people how you got shot, or go back to work and prove to yourself that you can do the job again. I want you to give it a try for a year. First, we need to get you better. I am sending you to a neurologist who specializes in these types of head wounds," he advised.

To his credit, he never bad mouthed the surgeon; he just said what he felt was best for me. My doctor told me I had some damage to my brain from the trauma.

In his unique style, he said, "I have good news and bad news about the damage to the right frontal lobe. The bad news is you may have severe headaches for years. The good news is you will be a cheap drunk - it's the area of the brain alcohol affects."

He was right on both counts!

I left his office with a whole new outlook. He did more for me in that one visit than he could ever understand. Or maybe he knew how he helped to heal me. He was a credit to his profession and in my mind one of the good guys.

# CHAPTER EIGHT
## *Thinking Back to a Deadly Decade*

My recuperation at home was slow and painful, but it gave me time to think back on events that left a mark on me, during my first years on the job.

On September 24, 1970, Boston Patrolman Walter A. Schroeder had been gunned down by Susan Saxe, Katherine Ann Power, William 'Lefty' Gilday, Stanley Ray Bond and Robert Valerie. They were part of a larger group of anti-Vietnam War activists. It was an odd mixture of ex-cons and Brandeis University intellectuals, who decided to fund their anti-war activities by robbing banks. Officer Schroeder was answering a silent alarm at the State Street Bank in Boston's Brighton neighborhood. As he got out of his cruiser, Gilday shot Schroder several times with a .45 caliber semiautomatic rifle. He died about twenty-four hours later. The total take of the robbery was $26,585.

> *The bank where he had been killed would again be robbed, years later, this time by the Ten Hills Gang, as part of their criminal acts to gain notoriety.*

Officer Schroeder had been the father of nine children. Somehow, I felt a connection to him. The details of the funeral were read to us at roll call. This would be the first of many police funerals I would attend. To me, it was my duty to attend such events. In those troubled days, cops had to stand together and support each other.

I watched as politics prevailed, even at a police funeral. We assembled in a Brighton shopping mall for the march to St. Anthony's Church. Position in the funeral procession indicated status, size or importance in the Commonwealth. The Boston Police were first in line. Schroeder was one of their own. Next in order was the Massachusetts State Police, an agency made up of twelve hundred troopers. The MDC Police, with six hundred and fifty officers, should have been third, but were placed farther back in the procession. Sergeant Frank Thorpe, our squad leader that day, marched us into the number-three slot. He convinced the 'political' number-three department the MDC belonged there.

We each wore a small black band of mourning over our chest badge. Blue police raincoats, Class A or dress uniforms were the uniform of the day. Our boots and shoes were spit-shined. The sounds of the bagpipes and muffled drums filled the air, along with officers calling cadence. Nearly one thousand cops tried to stay in step during the rain-soaked march to Officer Schroeder's home parish.

We had been there to show our support and respect for the family and for the Boston Police. In a sea of blue uniforms, it had been inspiring to be a part of a team...a family. Yet, as I was learning fast, politics was a way of life in law enforcement - inseparable from the badge and gun.

At the time of Schroeder's funeral, I had been on the job only five months. Seeing so many police officers together and becoming part of this tight-knit group felt like my destiny. The death of a police officer, not far from my home, hit hard. Like so many others, I had been too busy with my own life, before I took my police oath, to pay attention to such tragedies. This could have happened to any of us. It was not a good feeling and after Schroeder's funeral I no longer felt as indestructible as I once had.

IN MY THIRD year at the Fells District, I was still considered a rookie, so I was assigned to work with one of the veteran officers. On the evening of August 25, 1973, we had been patrolling the Medford area. That night, we received a radio call about an armed robbery at the Meadow Glen Drive-in Theater (now the Meadow Glen Mall). We quickly covered the few blocks, with blue lights and no siren. Turning onto Locust St., we saw a car smashed into an aluminum light pole. The robber, who reportedly stole the getaway car must have had hit the pole head on, while fleeing. Examining the inside of the car, I saw what looked like bloody dentures on the dashboard on the driver's side.

My partner said, "He shouldn't be hard to find."

The Medford Police arrived at the same time we did. Soon, eyewitnesses provided a description of the suspect. We were looking for a young, white male about 5' 6", with long, black hair. He was dressed in black and bleeding from the mouth. He was armed, dangerous and he had already fired a shot during the robbery attempt.

Witnesses pointed to the marsh across the highway, adjacent to the Mystic River. He was on foot in an area from which it would be hard to escape. We were familiar with this area, which was only a half a mile from the MDC Fells Police Station. It was a marsh with high grass and reeds, often the scene of brush fires in dry weather. If he was in there, he would be hard to locate in the dense undergrowth. On this hot summer night, the swamp would be loaded with mosquitoes, ticks and leeches, and all kinds of nasty critters.

More and more police units streamed to the scene and set up perimeters. This multi-agency response was always a communications nightmare. Each agency was on a separate radio frequency. Remember, this was the early 1970s.

The big issue was 'who's in charge?' The robbery happened in Medford, so the city cops showed up. The marsh and roadway belonged to the MDC, which is why we were there. Units from the Massachusetts State Police also arrived because they had state wide jurisdiction. Everyone was there but no one took charge. It was rapidly becoming a disorganized and chaotic cluster.

*I imagine they had the same problem at the 'Watertown shootout' with the Boston Marathon bombers on April 19, 2013.*

Darkness fell and the hours slipped by. I was standing across the divided highway as officers arrived with shotguns and rifles. All we could do was seal off the area and wait for daylight.

Then, one of our MDC K-9 units arrived. The dog sniffed inside the crashed car to get the scent of the armed robber. The problem was many cops had searched the car before the K-9 arrived. However, the dog seemed to pick up a scent and the MDC handler let the German shepherd go off his leash. There was a lot of barking and the sounds of reeds breaking as the dog charged into the marsh. Then, we heard loud growling and what sounded like a struggle as the tall grass shook and moved violently. The cruiser spotlights and headlamps illuminated the area. I drew my service revolver and took cover behind a vehicle. We all waited with guns at the ready in case the robber decided to shoot it out, or tried to escape from the police dog. It was a tense moment when anything could have happened. Minutes later, the dog appeared from the marsh, proud as a peacock…with a skunk in his mouth. It was still alive and spraying his predator with a pervasive, choking and nausea-inducing stink.

We all burst out in laughter as the tension subsided, except for the K-9 Officer, who loaded the stinking dog into his station wagon cruiser and rushed off to get as much tomato juice as he could find. Tomato juice was supposed to neutralize skunk odor. It surprised me how often police work veered from a life or death moment to the absurd in the blink of an eye!

The night dragged on and I was having a coffee on the far side of the divided highway with a few other cops. We were relaxed but watchful. It seemed we would be there all night, when across the highway, out of the marsh, a white male appeared. He had long black hair, was dressed in black and sported a bloody mouth.

A Medford cop who was closest to him yelled, "Hey!"

The bloodied robber, who appeared to be surrendering, raised his right arm from behind his back and fired a shot with a .32 caliber revolver at the Medford cop who was only yards away. The officer grabbed his stomach and fell forward. His partner and many other cops returned fire. I guessed the robber knew it was over and he was trying 'suicide by cop.' He would have been hopelessly outgunned.

With a group of several other officers, I ran across the divided highway as the suspect fled back over a tall bank and into the thick marsh. We ran to the wounded cop and rolled him over.

He checked his chest and stomach with his hands, then said in total amazement, "He missed me!"

I couldn't believe he had not been hit, nor could the cop. I think the gun must have misfired. The not-so-wounded cop stood up and, out of anger and probably embarrassment, emptied his service revolver towards the long-gone shooter, firing all six rounds.

His bullets hit against the rocks and dirt on the hill. They made small sparks and looked like gunfire coming back at us. The cops behind us opened fire, thinking we were being shot at!

A shotgun-toting cop yelled, "Where is he?"

"There! There!" Several cops pointed to the eight foot hill.

"Shoot! Shoot!" They screamed at the young MDC cop who was aiming the shotgun. With bullets coming from behind us, we quickly took cover. We were lying face down on the street behind a curbstone, trying not to get hit by friendly fire. The young Met cop let three blasts go from the shotgun. It took down several branches and initiated more gun fire from other cops. The trouble was, all the shooting was done by cops. It was a fusillade of bullets and nearly impossible to stop.

Finally, someone yelled, "Cease fire! Cease fire!"

After several minutes, the gunfire stopped. We had no way of knowing if the suspect was hit. Thankfully, none of us were.

One of the MDC sergeants decided to form a human chain to locate the gunman in the dark. We lined up, flashlights and guns in hand and stepped slowly through the high, thick ground cover. Just a few yards into the marsh, I heard someone shout, "We got him!"

The suspect, not hit by all the gunfire, was roughly dragged out by a group of cops. A local newsman took a great photo as the toothless gunman was pulled out, blood running from his mouth and a defiant look on his face.

It was the first time I had been under fire, even if it was friendly fire from my brother officers. Confusion was the biggest enemy.

I thought, "This is what my buddies must have gone through in Vietnam."

I wondered if there would be more incidents like this. I also wondered about the lack of leadership and discipline, which could have been deadly. All of us, including the hapless robber, were just plain lucky that night.

**Finally Seized in Mystic River Marsh**

8-25-73

# Gunman's Night Got Off to Bad Start

By BERT MacNEIL
and ARLENE DAVIGNON

A gunman who began his evening with a car crash last night went on to rob a Medford open-air theater, traded shots with police and was finally captured in dense marsh along the Mystic River.

According to police, Richard G. Evers, 22, of Wafford Way, Charlestown, smashed his car into an aluminum light pole on his way to the Meadow Drive-In on the Mystic

Valley pkwy. in Medford.

Although deprived of his car and suffering a few broken teeth, Evers continued on foot to the theater where his first encounter was with usher Paul Sweeney, whom he knocked down, police said.

Then, he allegedly forced Sweeney into the ticket booth, pulled out a .32 caliber revolver and demanded the day's receipts from seller Patrice Boudreau, 18, of Medford.

Interrupted by a customer, Evers sold him a ticket. Then,

interrupted by another employe, Arthur Garland, who drove out from the office, Evers allegedly fired a shot at his car and then ran off down the parkway.

Medford officers Stephen Cullen and Paul Alpers, dispatched to the scene, said they spotted Evers walking toward Malden. They said that when they got out of their cruiser to approach the suspect, he turned and fired at them.

They said Evers fired about four shots and they dropped to the ground and fired back. No

one was hit, and the suspect ran into the marshy area.

Thirty-five state troopers led by Lt. Dets. John Donovan and William White, and police detachments from Somerville and the Metropolitan District Commission came to the aid in the capture.

Evers was trapped between the river and the parkway with truck-mounted searchlights seeking him out. Medford Police Lt. Harold White ordered the more than 100 of-

ficers to form a skirmish line and close in.

Evers was captured by Medford Ptl. Frank Randazzo who said he spotted the suspect curled upon the ground. Randazzo said he jumped him and held the struggling Evers until more officers arrived.

Evers was charged with armed robbery and assault with intent to murder and is scheduled for arraignment tomorrow morning in Malden District Court.

A SUSPECT identified as Richard Evers, of Charlestown, is apprehended after he allegedly robbed the Meadow Glen Drive-In in Medford. He was captured by Medford, M.D.C. and State police officers.
Staff Photo by John Gilmore, Jr.

Suspect, with bloody mouth, dragged out of swamp

# CHAPTER NINE
## *The Seventies*

On Friday, November 30, 1973, Boston Police Detective John D. Schroeder, the brother of slain Patrolman Walter Schroeder, was shot and killed, when he surprised three men robbing the Suffolk Loan Company.

The members of the Boston Police Department and the wider law enforcement community were in shock. How could a tragedy like this hit one department and one family a second time? How could criminals coldly take a man's life? I realized this was truly the good guys vs. the bad guys. They were the enemy, plain and simple and I was prepared to do my part in this struggle.

Another fallen hero...another funeral march. There was a call for the reestablishment of the death penalty. It was debated for months in liberal Massachusetts. Emotions ran high. Politics, of course, entered the equation and the death penalty failed to become law in the Commonwealth of Massachusetts.

> *Did I support the death penalty for the killing of*
> *a police officer? Absolutely and I still do. So did a*
> *large majority of the general public, but it was the*
> *liberal politicians who had the final say.*

LONG BLUE LINE of policemen marches up Cambridge st., Brighton, to funeral home and wake of slain Boston detective John Schroeder.
Staff Photo by Leo Ranahan

## Police to Insist Sargent Sign Death Penalty Bill

Incredibly, the next day, three young black males held up the A&P Supermarket on Jersey Street in the Back Bay neighborhood of Boston, near the Fenway. A Boston P. D. cruiser on routine patrol spotted three black males coming out of the store with bags of money. The robbers, armed with two handguns and a shotgun, saw the cruiser and opened fire on the two Boston Police officers inside. The cops ducked under the dashboard of their cruiser as the windows were shot out by the robbers. Then, as the trio fled into the swamp, known as the Fens at the Muddy River near Kenmore Square, the cops returned fire.

Our two-way radio bristled with the information of the hold-up and shootout. Boston Police called for assistance to set up a perimeter to seal off the marshy area before the robbers could escape.

Descriptions of the heavily armed men were broadcast and my unit was ordered to report to the Fells Station. We were in Saugus, about four miles north of our station and another mile or so from the active scene in Boston. We responded with blue lights and I activated the siren as my partner Frank flew towards our station, our speed often reaching 80 mph on the residential roads. I switched the radio back and forth to hear both dispatch and the responding units and occasionally could hear shots fired in the background. I hoped Boston P. D. or any of us would take down the bad guys before another cop was killed.

My partner that night was a member of our sniper team, so our first mission was to go back to the station and get equipment. Frank got his gun case, which kept his Remington .308 caliber rifle with a telescopic lens clean and safe. I was issued a 12-gauge shotgun from the station gun locker. I grabbed two bandoliers - one of double 00 buck and one of rifled slugs - and threw them over my shoulder as we scrambled back into our cruiser. The slugs were about 1 ½ ounces of lead, with a range of about one hundred yards. It had stopping power like no other.

We flew through red lights and intersections. We could hear gunfire continuing over the radios of units at the scene.

"All units responding to the Fenway use caution. Shots are still being fired," the dispatcher blurted over our radio frequency.

The adrenalin rush made it impossible not to physically shake, as the blood rushed to my extremities. Frank and I talked about how we both needed to calm down, especially if my sniper partner was to be called on to take a shot. A sniper usually only got one shot and it needed to be a good one. That called for a steady eye and hand. The shakes would be a hindrance.

Nearing the location, the road was gridlocked. Onlookers always pose a problem at a wild scene like this.

Riding shotgun, I worked the siren back and forth between wail and warble, and ordered cars to pull over using the P.A. system. It was obvious some of these Boston drivers were not going to move. My partner started to hit the rear bumper of the blocking civilian cars with the front bumper of our cruiser. The hard thumping motivated them to get out of our way and yield. We inched through the heavy traffic at the scene, driving on the sidewalk as stopped cars blocked the roads.

Once on scene, we were given instructions by a Boston Police Officer. Frank was sent to a bridge over the Muddy River to set up his sniper post. I was assigned to a group of cops on the bank of the marsh. Cruisers, headlights and spotlights were positioned behind us to illuminate the tangle of high grass and reeds. There were about fifty officers from Boston, MDC and State Police. The Muddy River, a glorified creek, lived up to its name. The stench from the swamp was sickening and the smell of cordite from the gunfire filled the air.

The mood of the Boston cops was grim and determined. They had just lost the second Schroeder brother the day before and had nearly lost two more tonight. The look on the cops' faces had been unforgettable, perhaps the look of revenge.

The area was near the Museum of Fine Arts, not far from Fenway Park and was full of college students.

A group of hecklers, I assumed were college students or anti-war protesters, began shouting, "I hope you pigs die. You pigs couldn't find a needle in a haystack," and other incendiary remarks.

I was near a Boston cop, a huge hulk of a man with a big belly. He was obviously an old timer who had seen much action in his long career. He wore his police hat tipped back on his head, and the stump of a cigar was clenched between his teeth.

A young Massachusetts State Trooper, about my age, walked up to us. He was all spit and polish, with a high and tight military haircut, jodhpurs and polished high field boots. He was equipped with a shot gun, tear gas grenade launcher and a tactical vest with a bunch of tear gas grenades attached to it.

All the while, the students were taunting and yelling, "Die pigs. Die!"

I watched as the old timer said to the Trooper, "Hey, kid. You got any of those tear gas grenades that break into three pieces?"

The trooper replied, "You mean a triple chaser?"

"Yeah, that's the one."

"Yes, Sir. Right here," he said, pointing to a grenade on his vest.

"Can I see one, kid?" the old timer asked.

"Yes, Sir. Here you go," he replied, handing the triple chaser to this veteran Boston cop.

The big fellow did not look at the hecklers and he seemed oblivious to their loud taunts. "What do you do, kid? Pull this pin?" he asked, as he yanked the pin from the triple chaser grenade.

The Trooper shouted, "You need to throw it, Sir, before it explodes!"

With that, the old timer turned and tossed the grenade into the crowd of 'peaceniks.' I watched as it exploded into three distinct pieces, looking a little like fireworks on the Fourth of July on the Boston Esplanade. Each piece released a cloud of gas into the group. Unlike Independence Day fireworks celebrations when onlookers said "oohh" or "ahhhhhh," the hecklers quickly dispersed away from the triple chaser, yelling, "F***** pigs!" No longer laughing, they were coughing and choking as they retreated.

The old timer turned back to the trooper and said, "Thanks, kid," as he lit his victory cigar. By his facial expressions, I could see the trooper was wracking his brain. All ordnance had to be accounted for after a scene like this. I knew what he must have been thinking: how was he going to explain the missing triple chaser in his report?

I had never seen so many cops with weapons: Thompson sub-machine guns, shotguns and M1 rifles. Some cops on the far side of the dried up swamp lobbed tear gas into the air and a grass fire broke out. As one report in the Boston Globe said in a masterful understatement, *"Tear gas was lobbed into dry grass, which burned..."* I could see the silhouettes of several cops standing in a police rescue boat, essentially a rowboat, outlined by the light of the grass fire. They were using the oars to pole through the shallow, filthy water. It reminded me of a painting I had seen once of General Washington crossing the Delaware. The Fens was hardly the mighty Delaware, though.

It was about to get even better. Some of the tear gas fired on the opposite side of the marsh was blowing into our faces.

"Hey, you're gassing us!" someone yelled.

When that did not stop the incoming barrage of gas, some of the cops near me responded with some of their own gas grenades. Unbelievable! In the midst of a serious hunt for armed robbers who shot at cops, it seemed like a football scrimmage had broken out - the skins against the shirts, cops against cops.

Heavily armed Boston police officers crouch in tall grass along banks of Muddy River in the Fens as they seek to rout men who fired at cruiser after robbing nearby supermarket. (Globe photo by Tom Landers)

Tear gas, police dogs used in search

# Holdup suspects elude police in Fens

Despite the absurdity, distractions and occasional humor, this was deadly business. It had been at least an hour since the initial call and the small marsh was now totally surrounded by cops.

Then someone yelled, "There they are!"

I strained to see the suspects, but could not from my vantage point. Nor could the cops lying beside me on the bank we used as cover. But all hell broke loose. A few cops fired, more joined in and then even more fired their various weapons. Even the cops behind us were shooting over us. I was more afraid of the cops behind us, than the robbers. The sounds of bullets whizzing over our heads kept us pinned down, hugging the ground.

> *This type of shooting, in cop parlance, is called 'sympathetic shooting.' One cop shoots, then others join in, even without a target. I refer to it as 'oh-shit shooting.' Although we train officers not to engage with this reaction, there is probably no way to prevent it.*

Two suspects popped up and started shooting, or so the story goes. The cops...lots of cops, returned fire...lots of fire. I never saw the robbers, so I held my fire. It looked more like a one-sided military battle. The gunfire went on for several minutes and then subsided. I was never able to see the armed robbers and had no way of knowing if they were hit by the barrage of handgun, shotgun, rifle fire and the *rat-tat-tat* of the Thompson sub machine guns. After the shooting stopped, there was a long stretch of silence. We held our positions for what seemed like an eternity. Then the search was called off by the Boston Deputy Superintendent in charge.

The next day, after an extensive search and dragging the Muddy River, it was reported in the Boston newspapers the holdup men had vanished. Those of us at the scene could not believe they could have managed to slip away.

Sometime that following spring after the ice melted, I read in one of the Boston newspapers, the bodies of two of the three robbers were found. The third man was never located. The cause of death of the two who were found was reported to be from natural causes, drowning. I always wondered if the drowning was due to lead weighing them down.

I had only been on the job for three years and had experienced *two* police shootouts. Afterward, I reflected on how, at the scenes of major police shootouts, I had maintained my calm and discipline. This was a job I could do, I told myself, maybe even one I was well suited for. The adrenaline rush and excitement far outweighed my fear. Under fire, I had done my job in a professional manner, even in the midst of the chaos around me by fellow officers and in the face of taunting by unthinking kids. I knew then, I was a capable police officer who would not knuckle under fire or pressure. It was a good feeling. I had found my place in the world. I tapped my badge with pride.

# CHAPTER TEN
## *Christmas, 1974*

On a cold night in December 1974, I had been assigned the selective enforcement car. My job was to issue traffic tickets. This was a one-man patrol and a nice break after the early fall and the tactical duties during this forced busing era in Boston. Reporting for duty at 4:00 p.m., I stood roll call and went to Mr. Donut for my first coffee of the evening. The snow was falling lightly and Christmas was only a week away. Even the city looked peaceful with the fresh, clean coating of snow. It was a weeknight, so I expected a quiet shift, but the Christmas season was also a time for armed robberies. The registers were often filled with the cash of holiday shoppers, a tempting target.

Just after 6:00 p.m., I saw a young boy, about age six, with a woman who was most likely his grandmother. They were at a bus stop at the block of stores not far from my station at Wellington Circle. Like I said, it was cold and snowing and I thought they may have missed the last bus.

I thought to myself, "I am not a taxi service, I am a cop," and headed up the Fellsway on patrol.

Then the strangest thing happened. I flashed back to my childhood when I was a boy his age. My grandmother, a Scottish woman originally from Halifax, Nova Scotia, would take me Christmas shopping in Boston. My grandmother did not drive, so we took the train from Abington, on the South Shore, into Boston.

I remembered how cold I was but my grandmother made sure I could shop and see the Christmas lights in the big city. She made sure I had a cup of hot chocolate with whipped cream to warm my insides. My fondest memory was of the Enchanted Village at the Jordan Marsh store. It was a wonder of mechanical figures and lights in an old time village, with twenty-eight holiday scenes and two hundred and fifty magical animated figures. The highlight for me was an electric train running through the entire village. It warmed the heart of anyone my age.

With those pleasant Christmas memories in mind, I took the first turn I could and drove back to the bus stop and asked the woman and her shivering grandson if I could help them.

In a heavy Irish brogue, she said, "I'm feared we missed our bus, Officer. Could ya give us a ride to Charlestown?"

Remember, this was the same area we patrolled during bussing and cops were not well liked in the oldest neighborhood in Boston.

I said, "Sure. Hop in," and opened the back door of the cruiser.

The young freckle-faced boy in his winter coat, tiny Scally cap with ear flaps and mittens, was freezing. I turned the heat up to full and his grandmother directed me to their apartment on a hill in Charlestown. The boy never said a word, but was listening to the squawk of the police radio and looking at all the switches and gadgets in the cruiser. I remembered how I looked in awe at the Christmas lights in Boston when I was his age.

After a silent five-minute ride, she pointed out the three-story brownstone they lived in.

She told her grandson, "Johnny, thank the nice policeman," in her rich and sweet brogue.

The boy said nothing, but leaned over from the back seat and kissed me on the right cheek. He had stopped shivering.

That simple little kiss brought tears to my eyes. Without a word, he thanked me in his own way and made me glad I came back to the bus stop for them. It is one of the nicest things that happened in my twenty-seven years on the Police Department. It was a true Christmas story I will remember to the end. I often wondered if Johnny grew up with a better understanding of who a cop was. That young boy taught me more about compassion and how to treat the public than any class I ever took.

# CHAPTER ELEVEN
## *The Photo Spread*

In the summer of 1975, the feeling of isolation had become unbearable. I wondered if I would ever be contacted by the investigators. The two MDC detectives assigned to the case had interviewed my partner the night I was shot. They told him they would be in touch with me, but I never heard from them.

What had seemed like months were, in reality, just a few weeks when I finally got the phone call I was waiting for. It was MDC Detective Sergeant Tom White.

"We want you to look at a photo spread tomorrow, if you feel up to it."

"Sure, Sarge. I feel fine. What time should I be there?"

"Dana, be here at 10:00 a.m. and the Postal folks will be here as well."

I had to try and pick out the robber in the Postal truck from a group of photographs. I had caught a glimpse of him before he covered his face in the cab of the TT unit and again when he ran to the getaway car. The second time, I was focused on the gun in his hand and not his face.

The pressure was on. Someone had to identify the hijackers. I was the only one able to put one of the bad guys at the scene of the crime. Would I recognize him? Eyewitness testimony was crucial and I knew it. It was that simple.

The following morning I drove down to the MDC Detective Bureau. The police building overlooked Carson Beach in South

Boston, not far from the John F. Kennedy Presidential Library. It was an old brick building circa 1959, which would become the scene of race riots in 1977. As I walked up the steps to the entrance, I noticed the calm summer day around me, with the taste of salt water in the air and the constant cry of seagulls. But I was anything but calm.

The Detective Sgt. introduced me to the United States State's Postal Inspectors. After some small talk about how I was feeling and how good I looked (which was so untrue), we got down to work. They informed me how this procedure would work. I would be shown a spread - several photos of the suspects and other men who resembled the prime suspect.

I felt the main suspect had to be in the spread, or they would not have called me in. Detective Sgt. Tom White was all business. So were the Postal Inspectors. If I picked out the bad guy, my identification would be fought, dissected and argued in court. We all knew it. That's how the game was played.

They had laid out the photos like a deck of cards on an old wooden table. Each picture had a number on it. Some of them had tape covering mug shot numbers and dates.

Hoping I would instantly recognize him, I looked at the ten photos. Facetiously, I hoped there would be nine guys that looked nothing like the real suspect, but this was not the case. My heart pounded as I scanned the photos. I stopped and stared at one photo, then continued scanning. I stopped at a second one. There were two different photos that looked like the hijacker I saw that night!

Detective Sgt. White said to me, "Take your time and relax. If you are not sure, say so. Do you recognize any of these photos as the man you saw in the truck on the night of June 16?"

I took photos labeled Photo #2 and Photo #10 out of the spread and put them next to each other on the table in front of me. I felt strongly he was one of the two.

"Do you need a few more minutes?"

"Yes, Sir. I do."

I wanted so much to 'make the identification' but also knew picking the wrong guy would damage the case and give the defense attorneys plenty of meat to chew on in court. The pressure was intense. A few minutes passed in silence.

"Do you feel it is one of those two?" the Detective Sgt. asked, as he pointed to the two photos I picked out.

"Yes, I do."

"Can you positively identify the man you saw that night?" the dreaded question was asked.

In a defeated tone, I said, "No, Sir. I can't."

Oddly, I felt relieved. I had been completely up front and could not make a positive ID. I knew I had to be sure, for me and the case. Since I wasn't, I had to tell them I didn't know.

The detectives assured me it was better to be honest. We all knew it was a long shot, but it had been worth the try. They asked which of my two finalists I would pick, if pressed. I pointed to the one on the left, Photo #2.

"No. That is not our suspect."

"Sarge, can you tell me, off the record, which one of the ten is the suspect?" I asked.

He pointed to the other photo I had narrowed it down to. It was James Hackett, the prime suspect in four bank robberies.

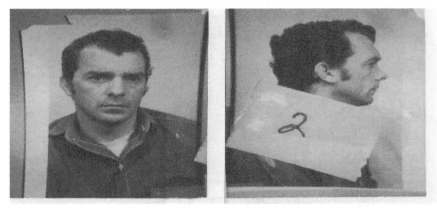

Photo Spread – Photo #2

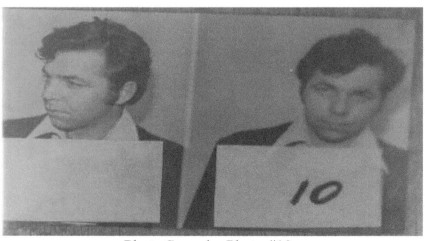

Photo Spread – Photo #10

# CHAPTER TWELVE
## *The Investigation Begins*

The hijacking officially became a federal crime once it was discovered the truck was carrying U.S. Mail. The investigation, headed by federal authorities, began in earnest. A conviction carried a ten-year minimum mandatory sentence and the statute of limitations on the crime was five years. Five years seemed plenty of time for us to get our ducks in a row, I thought, but the days, weeks and months slipped by quickly, pushing us up against that timeline.

The lead investigators assigned to the case were United States Postal Inspectors William (Bill) O'Leary and Frederick (Fred) Ricker. They had been partners for some time and each complemented the other. They investigated robberies, burglaries and internal thefts of United States mail. These two seasoned detectives were in their late forties. Fred had worked a nationally famous 1962 case, 'The Great Plymouth Mail Robbery,' the largest U.S. cash heist ($1.5 million) to that date.

A joint task force was set up utilizing federal and state agencies, because a cop had been shot in the mail hijacking case, with Bill in charge, and Fred assisting. Bill was an average-sized man with a stately manner and a shock of white hair. His Irish heritage showed clearly on his pleasant face. In all of the years I knew Bill, I never saw him without a smile. He had the gift of laughter. It put people at ease, even the bad guys.

Fred, on the other hand, was a tall, balding, former United States Marine with a more serious demeanor. They made a great team and I liked them from the outset. I never saw either man without a suit, white shirt and tie. Fred was always smoking a cigar. In local law enforcement circles, they were known as 'suits.'

Postal Inspectors drove brand new, unmarked cars. Their cars were not the police standard issue: four-door, solid color Fords with police radio antennas showing. Their cars were usually Fords or Mercurys, but two-tone in varied colors, many with vinyl roofs and fancy hubcaps, but with no antennas showing. Most of our unmarked police cars were easy to spot. Their cars blended in.

THE DAY AFTER I had been shot, North Reading Detective Edward Hayes and Detective Sergeant Henry Purnell read a teletype item from Met Control. There had been a list of guns, including serial numbers, recovered in the abandoned getaway car from the hijacking the day before. Detective Hayes was amazed to find three of the same guns were on another list given to him by an informant, he referred to as T-1, a month before the hijacking and my shooting. Detective Hayes told me he called the MDC Detective Bureau to tell them about the guns.

A series of strange events followed. Hayes called the MDC Detective Bureau on the phone. MDC Detective 'Blue' (pseudonym) answered. As Hayes related his information about the list of guns, he was suddenly cut off and heard a dial tone. Thinking he had been inadvertently disconnected, he called right back. Two more calls were disconnected.

The disconnection came exactly at the point in the conversation when Hayes said, "Hey, listen, I have a list of guns used to shoot one of your officers who lives in my town."

But three times, the response was a *loud click,* followed by a dial tone.

A suspicious Hayes then called Lou Tomasillo, Special Agent with the Bureau of Alcohol, Tobacco and Firearms. Hayes relayed the information to this agent he knew and trusted. No hang-ups this time.

Agent Tomasillo notified the Postal Inspectors about the list of guns Det. Hayes' informant had seen before the hijacking. The informant also supplied the name of the person who had 'hidden' the stash of guns. The informant said there was a parcel of disguises cached along with the firearms in a horse barn, not far from North Reading. The disguises were hats, sunglasses, fake facial hair, a trench coat and gloves. Bingo!

The Postal Inspectors called me soon afterward to tell me leads had been pouring in from the United States Bureau of Alcohol Tobacco and Firearms, the Massachusetts State Police and the North Reading Police Department. I felt sure with that kind of progress, the investigation would be quickly wrapped up and the suspects arrested. If only!

The suspects were alleged to be a gang of bank robbers based out of Somerville's Ten Hills Café, just north of Boston. This gang was made up of a group of men in their thirties. Most were unemployed roofers, carpenters and painters. Many shared an Irish heritage and were rumored to be part of the well-known, much-feared and infamous, Winter Hill gang, headed by Howie Winter, a notorious reputed mobster.

After looking into it, law enforcement thought the rumor connecting the gang at the Ten Hills Café with Winter had been started by the gang itself, to elevate its status in the underworld. It had been untrue, complete bologna, according to Howie Winter, himself.

Howie Winter and Dana Owen - April 2010

To keep this group separate from the Winter Hill gang and other Boston area crime organizations, we labeled them 'The Ten Hills Gang.'

The Ten Hills Gang was 'organized crime,' based on a loose interpretation. Word on the street was they planned to take over the territory of Howie Winter's activities in Somerville after removing the leadership, in what today might be called a 'hostile takeover.' When I asked Howie Winter if he was worried about being done in by the Ten Hills gang, Howie Winter smiled enigmatically, showing plainly he had no worries whatsoever about any threat from the Ten Hills crew. Winter obviously considered his rivals to be amateurs and minor league players at best.

Most of the Ten Hills crew grew up in the projects of Somerville, not far from the Café they would later use as their headquarters. They were known to be very dangerous and unpredictable. Informants said drugs were always mixed with the beers at the hangout.

The Postal Inspectors set up surveillance of the Ten Hills Café only days after the hijacking. Unmarked cars and vans were utilized. It was not easy to find a good spot for taking the needed photos, so they would switch off vehicles of different colors and makes as often as possible. Inspectors O'Leary and Ricker were the team leaders and Inspector W. R. (Roger) Hunt was the camera guy. He used a Japanese 35 mm camera with a long telephoto lens. Everyone entering or leaving the Café over a period of several weeks was photographed. The inspectors logged over a hundred hours just watching and photographing.

The black and white shots were then shown to Detective Lt. Jack Dwyer of the Massachusetts State Police. Jack, a former Somerville sergeant, was also an expert on the Somerville mob. He could identify the players.

James Hackett (left) at the Ten Hills Café

One of the Inspectors told me, "We didn't go to the FBI in those days." I asked why.

He lowered his voice and said, "Let's just say we have been burned too many times in the past in dealing with the Bureau."

*Later, I would have my own experience with FBI treachery on this case and would come to better understand what they meant about being burned.*

The inspectors also told me, "Every now and again, a car would pass by us with two guys dressed in suits and they'd give us a look." I guessed we weren't the only cops watching the Ten Hills Gang and Café.

Most of the prime suspects were photographed in the first week or so. The surveillance was called off when Jimmy Hackett, the alleged gang leader, was photographed smiling, looking at the van and giving the Feds the middle finger.

*Hackett was believed to be the one who hopped in the truck's cab that night and held a revolver on the driver.*

By then, the Postal Inspectors had more than enough photos of the gang members. One of the photos showed Hackett wearing sandals, which was the same footwear worn by the man who held a gun on the truck driver during the hijacking. These were little details that might prove important later in the case.

The investigation of the Ten Hills Gang showed clear modus operandi in the hijacking and prior armed robberies. The gang preferred the 4-door Ford LTD, probably because of its resemblance to an unmarked police car. The crimes had been spaced about a month apart. They needed time in between jobs to plan and rehearse before the next robbery. The guns and disguises had been rented. The car, for each job, cost the gang a standard $100, according to informants. It had been stolen-to-order by a local, young car thief who lived two streets behind the Ten Hills Café. His name sounded familiar to me. In fact, after checking, I had arrested him in another stolen Ford LTD a few months prior to the mail hijacking.

This gang had been named as suspects in the following bank robberies:

- BANK ROBBERY
  March 4, 1975
  SUBJECTS (3)
  State Street Bank and Trust Company.
  Brighton, MA
  Vehicle used: 1970 blue Ford hardtop
    Stolen from a bank guard a .38 caliber revolver recovered and used in the Mail Robbery. This was the same bank where Boston Police Officer Walter Schroder was slain in 1970 by machine gun fire, by a gang composed of Brandeis University students (Susan Saxe and Kathy Power) and other ordinary criminals.
  Robbers obtained: $3,853 in cash and no bait money

- BANK ROBBERY
  March 20, 1975
  Messenger robbed by 2 armed men leaving bank
  The Century Bank and Trust Company
  Somerville, MA
  SUBJECTS (2)
  Money taken: all cancelled checks and unusable food
  stamps

- BANK ROBBERY
  April 4, 1975
  SUBJECTS (3)
  Century Bank and Trust Company
  Somerville, MA
    Vehicle used: 1970 4 Door Ford LTD Blue (stolen
    at Federal Street Garage, Boston, MA where the car
    thief who supplied the cars worked as a parking
    attendant).
  Suspects shot at by bank guard fled.
  Total loot taken: over $17,000

- BANK ROBBERY
  May 9, 1975
  SUBJECTS (4)
  Newton-Waltham Bank and Trust Company
    All the money discarded when red dye security pack
    exploded in getaway car

- U.S. MAIL TRUCK HIJACKING
  June 16, 1975
  SUBJECTS (4)
  Vehicle used: 4 Door LTD Ford brown
  No money taken

At the end of June 1975, after five armed robberies and the attempted murder of a police officer, the gang had netted $20,853. Split five ways, that made $4,170.60 for each guy, and over a four month period, each member took home a little over $250 a week. They easily could have made more money working at a legitimate job. But that's who they were robbers.

Two crimes in Somerville, less than two blocks from the Ten Hills Café, pretty much proved the mail robbery was not the work of the Winter Hill Gang. Somerville was 'off limits' to the notorious Winter Hill Gang, headquartered in that city. Winter Hill did not commit crimes in their host city.

The focus of the investigation now turned to informants. The police agencies hoped some people would find themselves in a pickle with the law and roll over to rat out the gang in exchange for a free pass. Detectives from various agencies pressed their informants for any information. The word about the hijacking spread fast among the criminals, far faster than the same info reached law enforcement. Someone awaiting trial might be willing to trade info about the crime for a lighter sentence. This was the way it usually played out. Informants had a vital role in solving many crimes.

We felt we had identified the gang members responsible for my shooting and the other robberies. At this point, it was up to the investigators to put together a case solid enough to hold up in court. The Inspectors felt confident they could, which meant I could concentrate on my recovery.

MSP Detective Lieutenant Jack Dwyer's help was crucial in this case. He was a gentleman and a true professional, and well respected by those on both sides of the law. Jack was a contact of the Postal Inspectors and had informants throughout Somerville, including two in the Ten Hills Café. They were so reliable they knew almost every move the gang made. The information had been invaluable and Jack never had to reveal their identities.

Without a doubt, the lives of the informants would have been in jeopardy if the gang knew they were informing.

It appeared arrests would happen quickly. But, appearances can be deceiving sometimes. Things took a turn for the worse as a familiar problem in law enforcement cropped up. Fierce competition among the different police agencies got in the way of the investigation. The credit for solving the crime overtook the race to bring the offenders to justice properly. This was a sad fact of life in police work and always will be. Jealousy ran high in police circles. As a result, information was being withheld, and not shared, for fear another agency would swoop in to make the arrests and get all the credit. If only the public knew. It sickened me how competition trumped cooperation. For God's sake, a police officer was nearly murdered in a violent crime, one of a series of them. Why couldn't we all work together on the case instead of acting like children?

Sometimes, the obstacles were not related to jealousy, but could be chalked up to lack of diplomacy. Here's a case in point. Postal Inspectors Ricker and O'Leary went to the North Reading Police station to talk to Detectives Hayes and Detective Sgt. Purnell.

Fred said to Detective Hayes, "We need the name of your informant on the guns."

"We don't want to give this guy up unless we have to. It will ruin his life and put him in danger," Hayes replied.

The conversation quickly became heated.

Fred told Detective Hayes, "You either give him to us, or you and your partner will face federal charges for obstruction of justice!"

The inspectors were asked to leave the station immediately. More to the point, they were thrown out.

Fred called me the next day to say, "Hey buddy, can you go into North Reading P. D. and smooth things over? We had a little misunderstanding with their detectives."

"I guess so, Fred," I replied. "I live in the town, but don't know any of the cops."

With my tail between my legs and totally unsure of what to say, I went down to the station and met Detective Hayes and Detective Sgt. Purnell the next day. They invited me into their office for a cup of coffee and explained the informant was a former North Reading cop, who married into the family of the guy who supplied the guns and disguises to the gang. The atmosphere was tense as Hayes and Purnell glanced back and forth at each other as I made my case for naming the informant.

"I really don't know what to say," I began. I understood their dilemma perfectly, but it didn't change the facts.

"I understand," I told the two detectives, "but let's not forget I am the guy who got shot and I am personally asking you to give him up," I said. It didn't look as if they were going to budge. I reached deeper.

"I don't know if you both have kids," I told them, "but I was shot on my youngest daughter's fourth birthday. I am sure you know these guys need to be taken off the streets. No one forced your informant to give you the info on the guns."

"Dana, give us a few days to talk to him and we will give the Feds his name," they answered. "And tell your buddy Ricker, we don't like to be threatened!"

I smiled and said, "Thanks. I can do that." We shook hands and have remained friends all these years.

A few days later, Fred Ricker called me at home and said, "Thanks, buddy. Hayes gave us the snitcher's name."

It was a strange position to be in, but like it or not, I became the middle man between the North Reading Police Detectives and the United States Postal Inspectors.

The investigation led to an individual in the Somerville projects, David Donnigan (a pseudonym), who had been the owner of the shotgun I had been shot with. He was believed to be an associate of the gang. He bought the Ithaca 12-gauge pump and a Stevens double-barreled 12-gauge on November 9, 1973 in Burlington, MA. Both shotguns were later sawed-off (barrels and wooden stocks cut and shortened).

Donnigan was questioned about this firearm by two MDC detectives and the Postal Inspectors six days after I was shot. He said he gave the firearm to a Michael O'Cruimin (a pseudonym) to keep, as his mother did not like guns around the house.

The investigators then accompanied Donnigan to the O'Cruimin residence. Michael made a show of looking for the guns in a closet. When he couldn't find them, he said they must have been stolen. Donnigan and O'Cruimin then got into a fight over the guns and had to be separated by the detectives. Both were considered peripheral, but integral, players.

The MDC detectives asked Michael what he did for work. He said, "I do odd jobs for Howie Winter," the reputed head of the Winter Hill Gang.

The Feds told me once Howie's name was mentioned, Detective 'Blue' and his partner lost all interest in the case. They quickly closed their briefcases and left the apartment. Such was Winter's powerful and much-feared reputation in Somerville, even among law enforcement.

> *These same two MDC Detectives were mentioned in* Legends of Winter Hill *by Jay Atkinson:*
>
> *"Up on Winter Hill several years later, in front of a used car lot owned by two disgraced MDC cops..."*

It seemed their reputations followed them. Both of these MDC cops were removed from the case at the request of the Postal Inspectors.

> *I later found out more disturbing facts about these two. Detective 'Blue' was the man who hung up on Det. Hayes. In 1987, the other one would*

*pled guilty to fraud and perjury, having cheated on a chief of police's exam in 1976, in the notorious police civil service exam scandal that roiled the Commonwealth.*

# CHAPTER THIRTEEN
## *Back on Duty*

My first time back to the Fells Station was in late August to pick up my pay check. I was horrified, yet strangely fascinated to see the shot-up cruiser I drove the night of the hijack chase in one of the bays of the garage. The garage smelled of oil and gasoline in the hot, muggy weather. I worked my way across the slippery concrete floor to check out the damage and try to figure out how many times it was hit by the gunfire. There was no one around so it was a perfect time to observe it close up. It was surrounded by yellow police evidence tape and showed the scars of the battle, much like I had. The 1974 Ford station wagon was dark green with white doors and roof. The letters 'M.D.C.' and badge decals were on each front door.

There were the two bullet holes on the driver's side windshield. One bullet had entered high and deflected down, hitting me on top of my head. The second one, down low, caught me in the forehead as I ducked to the left. There was a third hole on the passenger's side, on the outside of the windshield post. It was most likely caused by bullet that ricocheted hitting the woman bystander. After the hijackers had disabled me, it appeared they then aimed for my partner.

Both roof-mounted blue lights had also had been hit. There were several bullet holes in the grey plastic grill, one of which had cut the wiring to the headlights. I had only seen black and white photos of the bullet-ridden cruiser in newspapers. The photos were shocking, but the real thing was even worse.

There was powdered glass and dried blood, from my head wounds, on the driver's seat. It was hard to believe how much I had bled. I realized how lucky I had been to survive. After looking at the carnage, I was really unsure if I could, or even if I wanted, to do this job again. Sweating profusely and shaking, I was glad I had been alone in the garage with my thoughts. I could not get over how both bullets had slammed into my skull. Had I ducked right instead of left, the second round would have missed me. On the other hand, had I not ducked, the bullet would most likely have hit me in the chest and I would have been fatally wounded.

My solitary visit with the shot-up cruiser in the garage had shaken me to my core. The difference between life and death for me was literally less than an inch. Seeing the bullet holes, my dried blood, broken glass and shot-out lights had left me feeling small and vulnerable. My thoughts were all over the place. My dad died at age thirty-two and I had almost been killed at age twenty-seven.

I'd seen enough of that cruiser. With well over 100,000 miles, it was at the end of its life. It had done its job that night and it would be retired and used for spare parts. I knew in my heart, it was not yet my time to retire. I had to see if it was in me to go back to duty.

The longer I stood there the vulnerability hardened into renewed conviction to slap the cuffs on those who had such disregard for human life, including mine. I suddenly realized I had been looking at the shot up Ford for half an hour. I shut down that line of thinking and went in to get my check.

BY EARLY SEPTEMBER, it was time. I knew the first night back would be a roller coaster ride. I almost called in sick several times during the day. I was really unsure if I could do this job again. Even my deodorant wasn't doing its job and I had to wash up about five times.

Arriving at the Fells Station, an hour before my 4 p.m. to midnight shift, I took the time to see if the shot-up cruiser was still in the garage. It had been about a month since I viewed it, but it was no longer there. I walked into the station, which had no air-conditioning, and the locker room and attached shower stall area still smelled musty. No matter how often the janitors scrubbed the ceramic tiled walls in the summer, the smell was overpowering.

I made sure I had all my gear. I had a freshly cleaned and starched uniform shirt from home. My wife always ironed the shirt with the military creases. Pride and command presence were paramount to me. I was not a sloppy looking cop.

In the guardroom, my police hat lay upside down on the top shelf of my locker. The gun belt and revolver were still in the paper bag they had been placed in, at the hospital. For the next fifteen minutes or so, I cleaned my .38 caliber S&W model 64 revolver, my handcuffs and all my leather gear.

I put on my bullet proof vest under the short sleeve uniform shirt, which helped to hide how much weight I had lost. I had decided the vest belonged on my body, not in the back seat, no matter how uncomfortable it was. My wife had given me a St. Michael's medal to wear on a silver chain around my neck. It had been blessed by our parish priest and it was there to protect me. I had prayed to St. Michael the Archangel after I was shot. Now I prayed he would keep me safe.

It was a good thing we were still in short sleeve summer uniforms. A long sleeve shirt and clip-on tie would have hung off of my skinny torso. I made a mental note to go to the rag shop (supply section) to get some long sleeved uniform shirts at least one neck size smaller.

The scar on my forehead was still visible. It had some peach fuzz growing back, but still looked red, raw and nasty. I reached up and grabbed my police hat. As I put it on top of my head, powdered glass from the shattered windshield ran down the back of my neck. Goosebumps ran up my spine and I broke out in a cold sweat. My heart was pounding so fast and I could hardly breathe. My mind flashed back to the shooting. I took deep breaths, trying desperately to slow my pulse before my heart burst open!

Once I was able to calm down and stop shaking enough to undo the buttons, I took off my bullet proof vest and shirt. I tipped my hat over and shook all of the glass out. Using a towel, I wiped most of the powdered windshield glass off my sweaty body and got dressed again.

Looking at myself in the full length mirror, I combed the glass out of my hair and tried to regain my composure. This was not the way I pictured my first shift back on the job. Not really liking what I saw in the mirror, I looked away and I took the long walk down the hall to the rotunda, where Roll Call was about to start. It was time to find out what I was really made of.

Roll call was a formal procedure. We lined up in the uniform of the day. The duty sergeant inspected our appearance and revolvers. Then he read off the cruiser and route assignments and announced recent crimes in our district. The Shift Sergeant made a point of welcoming me back and then began to read the assignments.

For weeks, I had worried about being assigned to desk duty. I needed to be on the street to find out if I could do this job again, not sitting behind a desk. My fellow officers may have felt the same way, may have had the same doubts I had.

They shook my hand, and said "Welcome back," but I could feel the tension in the air.

The doctors, at my request, had checked off 'Full Duty' on my LOD (Line of Duty) forms. At the time, my biggest fear was not a gunfight or getting shot again. I feared I might overreact and shoot some poor slob reaching for his driver's license.

The duty sergeant read off the assignments and my mind snapped back into focus.

He was speaking, "...and Officers Gately and Owen. You're the 301 and take the 6F car" (plate number of the cruiser).

The sergeant seemed to know what I needed on my first night back. He had assigned me to ride with Jerry, who had driven me to the hospital, often on two wheels around the corners, that Monday night back in June.

The Fells District in Medford was designated as '300s' call signs. Each was a certain area or sector. The 301 car covered greater Medford, Stoneham, Melrose and Saugus. To me, it was the best first assignment back I could have hoped for.

Jerry was the senior man and he drove. That was fine with me. I was content to do the passenger duties. The first priority at the start of a shift was coffee. My FTO (field training officer) told me back when I came on the job "Kid, we get coffee first. It may be the last time we get a chance all night." Often, it proved true. Wise words.

Walking into what was then a Mr. Donut at Wellington Circle, it felt good to be back in uniform. One of the ladies, who worked at the donut shop, had sent me a get-well card when I was in the hospital. Now she told me how glad she was to see me, but said she thought I was foolish to come back to work so soon. That was one vote against my decision to return, but so far, the only one.

We parked in front of Anderson-Little, a well-known men's clothing store of that era. It was a favorite place for us to shop with our 20% police discount. The store had a glass facade with mannequins in the huge windows. The style of the time was wide striped ties under the sport coats on the dummies. The store was between the donut shop and Howard Johnson's, the orange-roofed ice cream shops, restaurants and hotels. Established in Quincy, the chain stretched from Maine to Florida, famous for 28 flavors of ice-cream. We always backed in so we could watch the traffic at Wellington Circle and we could throw the coffees out the window if we saw a speeder or red light violator.

Howard Johnson's in Wellington Circle

Wellington Circle was a tangle of intersecting arteries leading into Boston from the east, west and north. It was a nightmare for traffic cops. To us 'working cops,' the circle was like a freshly stocked trout pond, full of 'good stops.' A motor vehicle was used in about 90% of crimes. Wellington Circle was a great place to fish.

"How does it feel to be back, kid?" Jerry asked as we settled into the seats of the cruiser to have our coffee.

"It's a lot better riding up front than on a stretcher in back," I quipped.

"You need some of those 'sinkers' (donuts) to put some weight back on," Jerry laughed.

Jerry was a former US Marine and one of the street cops I looked up to. Since my first days on the job, I had been assigned as a 'tactical' cop right out of the Academy. I liked the action of the street and hoped I could get back in the swing of things.

Jerry must have sensed my misgivings and doubts. "You're going be fine. Be strong!" he said, encouragingly.

I tore a small hole in the cover of the coffee cup. We called it the 'truck driver tear,' so the coffee would not spill out, even on the move. That was before the 'to go' covers of today. I barely had three sips of the strong black coffee, when the police radio crackled, "Any unit in the area of Wellington Circle?"

Grabbing the mic, I answered, "301 car is at the Circle."

Dispatch then responded, "301...silent hold-up alarm at the Kappy's Liquors at the Circle...Medford P. D. notified."

Kappy's Liquors in Wellington Circle

We were parked about 45 seconds away from the liquor store. It was just on the other side of the circle. The coffees went out the window and we responded with no lights or siren to the silent alarm. A silent hold-up alarm meant either an armed robbery was in progress or someone had hit the button by mistake.

"Any units in the area to back up the 301?" Met Control inquired.

I excitedly radioed Met Control, "301 will take the front!"

"10-4...301 has the front. We need a unit to cover the rear."

As I switched from Channel 1 to Channel 2, I heard, "305 will cover the rear."

"All units responding to Kappy's Liquors use caution. The suspect may be armed!"

This was my first call since getting shot. I had been on duty for about ten minutes. Maybe the counter lady at the donut shop had been right: I had been foolish to come back to work so soon.

As we skidded to a stop at the liquor store, the clerk was in the doorway signaling to us for help. So, in we went, with guns drawn. My heart was pounding so fast I hardly heard the clerk say, "That's him over there!"

This is how police work is sometimes. There was no time to wait for backup, just time enough to act. We ran in and took the suspect at gunpoint. He was a drunken shoplifter who reeked of booze. He obviously had no money, no weapon and needed some cheap wine.

I doubt he ever knew how close he came to dying. I thought to myself, "God has a strange sense of humor." But in many ways, this was an answer to a prayer. With my gun hand shaking from the adrenalin rush, I tried to calmly and casually holster my service revolver. I didn't remember drawing it. I just reacted and reverted back to my training. Reflexes did the rest.

I had done it! When I went through that door, gun in hand, all my training came back to me. I did not over react...I could do this job!

Jerry smirked at me and said, "Welcome back, kid."

"Thanks," was all I needed to say.

I was a cop again. Not quite healed, but with all the right responses appropriate to the situation. Nerves were not a problem. My biggest question about myself in the wake of the shooting had been answered in the best possible way. I did not over react and was back on the job I loved.

# CHAPTER FOURTEEN
## *Superman*

As a joke gift, just before I returned to duty, my wife bought me a dark blue T-shirt with a huge red and yellow - *S* - Superman logo on it. I liked the shirt so much, I wore it all the time. It was a color match under my blue uniform shirt. For a guy who survived two gunshots to the head, it was the perfect present and it got great laughs from the guys at my duty station. Laughter helped me handle the incident and its aftermath.

A few weeks after returning to work, I had taken off my uniform shirt and bullet proof vest and was wearing the Superman T-shirt. 'Choir practice' had been scheduled at the end of our PM shift. Cops just getting off duty would have a couple of beers together behind the Fells Station. We called such get togethers 'choir practice', after a term used in *The Choirboys*, by Joseph Wambaugh, a former Los Angeles police officer.

The area in back of the Fells Station could not have been better suited for these gatherings. The Mystic River was behind the area where we had our beers and told improbable stories to one another. Marshland, with tall swamp grass, blocked us from public view and the station yard was restricted to police vehicles only. Most of us came to choir practice in civilian clothes, a few in police pants and a tee or civilian shirt. Usually, there were a couple of big buckets filled with ice to keep our beers in. They ***had*** to be ice cold. If it was going to be a long choir practice, we'd bring folding lawn chairs in the trunks of our cars.

Mosquito repellant was the only other necessary piece of equipment, but free pretzels and potato chips from the Cain's factory on the Medford Vets Highway, just a block away, were welcome additions.

It was a great way to unwind from a busy shift. Back in those days, there was no late night television. Instead, we came up with our own badly-needed entertainment. During the summer, most of the shifts were busy and stressful.

A key part of choir practice was drinking a few beers. The guys would either chip in on a case of beer, or some thoughtful teenager would 'donate' the beer as we broke up under-age drinking parties in one of the parks. It saved us money and the teens didn't go to jail. Seemed like a nice compromise back in the 1970s.

Choir practice was a safe place to vent steam, debrief and unwind. It was important to laugh and tell stories to people who understood the high stress of the job. It was better to let off steam amongst ourselves behind our station, rather than elsewhere. It was not a good idea to hit a barroom at closing time. It would make other bar patrons uncomfortable if we did. We 'choir boys' were a tight-knit group and this routine was our safety net. We all looked forward to these sessions at the end of our workday.

At these bull sessions, we would exchange war stories with each other about what had happened on the prior shift. Someone might talk about a grotesque call or weird fatal accident. Other times, one of the guys would describe an arrest where some fool literally talked himself into jail. The stories were endless, as were the laughs, as we competed to outdo or top the previous story teller.

On this warm, fall night, about fifteen of us guys gathered in the small clearing behind the Fells Station. It was about 12:30 a.m. and the mosquitoes were not that bad at that time of night.

As often happened, the direction of the stories turned to the one who could out-gross or top the last story. I was one of the better story tellers, I felt. Previously, I made the mistake of telling a few of the gross cop tales in mixed company at a party. That was a serious no-no and I almost made a few of our civilian friends sick. Most folks have no idea of the horrors we saw on a daily basis. So, those stories were saved for choir practice.

After the silence following my war story, you could hear a few mosquitoes buzzing around and not much else. I had put a big, cold, damper on our little party. It was time to wrap it up.

Not the first or last time, a story made our stress worse. Sullen and deflated, we picked up the empty beer cans and headed home. I felt mental exhaustion, but at least I was getting tired and hopefully I could sleep.

*Looking back at all the choir practices, I realized I never talked about the night I was shot. I felt it was a taboo subject: our mortality was never on the conversation agenda - it was too close to the bone.*

About 1:30 a.m., when the choir practice broke up, I'd had no more than my usual two beers. After I had been shot, my family doctor told me, "You'll be a cheap drunk, due to the trauma to the right frontal lobe." That is where the second bullet struck and his diagnosis was on the money. Two beers gave me quite the buzz. Consequently, I never had more than two. Three was simply more than I could handle.

On my way home that night, I decided to drive by the Ten Hills Café before closing time. I did this twice a week, on average. It was a warm and lazy night and it seemed like a good idea at the time to do a drive-by and check the bar room to see who the lookout was. No matter what time of day or night, there was always a lookout posted to watch for cops. I was still depressed from the story I told, but the warm buzz from the two frosty brews kept my energy level up.

I was driving my Dodge Dart with a 'cold license plate' attached. (A cold plate was an abandoned one left at the station.) Any time I staked out the Café, I had a cold plate on my car. I kept a bunch in my trunk.

As I took the shortcut down Shore Road, I slowed down as I came to the intersection approaching Mystic Ave. I was under the overpass of I-93, a block from the Ten Hills Café. Just then, a car came screaming out of the darkness towards me, headlights blinding me. It slid sideways around the corner onto Bailey Road, tires screeching and smoke pouring from them!

As my eyes adjusted, I saw two young guys in the stalled Ford similar to the one I chased in the U.S. Mail Truck Robbery. But they were most likely a couple of the Memorial Road project kids out for a joy ride in a stolen car, a common occurrence.

The Ford missed my car by inches and slid sideways onto the street parallel to Mystic Ave., where it stalled. The near-miss scared the hell out of me and I sat for a minute trying to regain my composure. Maybe it was the two beers or my frustration over the lack of progress in the robbery and my shooting, but I got out of my car and headed towards what I was certain was a stolen vehicle. In the back of my mind, I knew it had been a dumb move. I should have listened to the voice in the back of my mind.

As I walked up to the car, I had no plan, no idea of what I was going to do or say. I had no handcuffs or radio, so an arrest was out of the question. I knew young car thieves always ran like the wind and were almost always juveniles. Almost no punishment would result, even if they were caught. These kids usually graduated to bigger crimes when they turned eighteen and would face jail or prison time in adult court.

On that warm night, dressed in my Superman shirt and jeans, I had my .38 snub-nose tucked in the waistband in the small of my back.

So, there I was at the window of the still smoking, stalled stolen car. I was just going to give them a piece of my mind.

I could still smell the burning rubber as I went to the driver's side. That's when, just like during the hijacking, events began to happen in slow motion. The driver, a teen with a screwdriver stuck in the popped ignition, was trying to restart the stolen car.

He was a baby-faced, redhead and he looked at me like, "Who the hell is this guy?"

Another boy, about the same age, was in the passenger seat. They both were focused on restarting the stolen car and were ignoring me, but not for long.

"Hey, boys. You almost hit my car. You ought to be more careful," I said, looking at the driver.

"F*** off! Who do you think you are, Superman?" the young car thief yelled.

He took the large screwdriver out of the popped ignition and pointed it at me in a threatening manner. "Screw!"

So, this little punk thought he was going to scare me off with a screwdriver? I felt the anger flooding my system. In one motion, I reached behind my back with my right hand and pulled out my snub-nosed .38 caliber revolver and pointed it at Mr. Screwdriver.

The two teens saw the gun at the same time and both faces changed quickly, going pale and wide eyed. In unison, they yelled, "Shit!!!"

In one sudden motion, they bailed out of the passenger's side and scrambled over each other and ran down the street. I fired two shots straight up in the air, even though I knew the only thing warning shots did was make the fleeing car thieves run even faster. But with anger and frustration rushing through my brain, that's what I did. I let two rounds go in the quiet, early morning darkness, echoing through the residential area.

The gunshots put both teens in overdrive, and they never looked back. Like scared rabbits, they scampered between some houses, falling over each other along the way. For some reason, I felt better and even smirked as I walked back to my car.

I have to credit the residents of Ten Hills. Not a single light came on and no one came out. That is just how things were. You minded your own business in those days in Somerville. Stolen cars and late night gunshots were not uncommon in the Ten Hills area.

I went back to my car, trying to act like nothing had happened. I re-tucked the revolver into my waistband. Shifting my car into drive, I headed up onto I-93 at Mystic Ave., the same ramp where Bob Power and I had first spotted the hijacked truck on the night of the hi-jacking. Inside my head was a jumble of thoughts, ranging from accusations to excuses. On my way home, I methodically tried to go over what had just happened. I had come close to crossing a line, and once crossed, there was no return. I am sure the beers didn't help my judgment that night but the main reason behind my response to the teens had been my pure frustration at the lack of progress in the Mail Truck Robbery.

The car the kids had stolen for their joyride was so similar to the getaway car in the hijacking and the area where they almost hit me was only a few hundred feet from where we spotted the hijacked truck. One incident mixed into the other even though there was no real connection, except in my head. In my mind, I tried to justify what I had done. I had scared the crap out of two punks, but it had gone much further than that...much further.

What if one of them had a gun and I shot him? I could see the headlines: "Off duty cop shoots teenage joyrider." "Cop kills youth, claims self-defense."

The press would have a field day. My mental stability and suitability for duty would be questioned, and the beer on my breath would not have helped my case.

How ironic! My biggest fear about returning to duty had been whether I would over-react in a tight situation. This had been my first altercation. Had I over-reacted? I had to figure out why I did what I did with the two youthful joyriders. I knew I had been lucky to escape serious consequences. I tried to calm down and sort things out. My mistakes and misjudgments were apparent.

I never identified myself as a police officer to the car thieves. No one had been hurt, but I had acted recklessly, violating our policy on discharging a weapon and was not sure exactly why. Was I, in fact, a loose cannon, out on the streets with a gun and a badge?

I made a decision not to say anything about the incident to anyone, not even to my wife, to whom I usually told just about everything. The stolen car would be found sooner or later. I was sure no one saw me. If someone did and wrote down my license plate number, it was one of the cold ones, which I would swap for another.

Sitting in my car, I thought, "How could this have happened?"

I had been swapping war stories, at a routine choir practice with fellow cops. Then driving home, I was thinking about my shooting and the scene suddenly turned chaotic. I had been nearly hit by a stolen car and then confronted by an arrogant 17 year old, wielding a screwdriver. And it had ended with my firing shots in the dark, which was completely against protocol and procedure.

That night at home, I couldn't sleep. I wanted to punch a wall. I had to do something...anything. My head was pounding and I was sure my blood pressure was sky high. How much of it was due to the shooting a few months before? Could I trust myself out on the streets again when things got tense? I had heard and read about other cops getting screwed up after being shot or shooting somebody else. Had I become one of them?

Maybe it was time to take a disability pension and give up the job I loved. I lay awake all night trying to hash it out and make sense of it.

The next morning as I sat with my mug of strong, black coffee, my wife asked, "How was the PM shift?"

"Quiet for a change," I lied.

Sipping my coffee in the comfort of my kitchen, I thought of how lucky I had been to have survived being shot. I had been lucky a second time, that night before.

I chalked up the event to anger, maybe even fear, but part of it was righteous indignation. These kids had no regard for their lives or anyone else's. I had wanted to teach them a lesson, dole out some street justice, but it was the wrong way to do it. I had acted unprofessionally and I was ashamed and baffled about why I had acted that way.

In the future, there would be plenty of young car thieves to chase and arrest while on duty. I vowed from then on to let the courts dish out the punishment. I would just be a cop.

With the cool weather approaching, choir practice would soon end until next summer. For me, that was my last one of the season. Maybe for good.

After breakfast I went down to my workbench in the basement. I felt as if someone was watching me, like I was doing something wrong. My hands were shaking a lot as I cleaned my off-duty pistol. I had a hard time inserting two fresh rounds into the open five shot cylinder. I stuffed the spent shell casings in my pocket, for later disposal. I could not believe the guilt and worry I was going through. I promised myself this was the only time I would ever have to cover my tracks like a criminal.

Next on the agenda was to put a fresh cold plate on my car. I kept a few in my trunk, in case I thought one of the lookouts at the Ten Hills Café might have jotted down my plate number. On route to work that night I tossed the empty brass (shell casings) and license plate into a dumpster.

It was time to regroup and go back to being the person and the cop I was meant to be. Looking back, this was a major turning point and it set the stage for how I would conduct myself in the future. I would keep my promise to myself to catch the guys who shot me. But I knew I could only succeed if I did it without emotion and as a professional.

I have always wondered if those two joyriders ever told the story of how Superman chased them with a gun and fired shots into the air, or if they kept their mouths shut like I did. I also wondered if those two ever stole another car.

A part of me hoped the story got around the nearby Ten Hills Café, but I never found out if it did. Maybe all three of us kept it secret for very different reasons.

# CHAPTER FIFTEEN
## *The Hilltop Steakhouse Affair*

I had worked the case on my own, off and on since July. When I was home, my mind was miles away. How would life be if the good guys did not win? I could think of nothing else. I had to catch them. I was obsessed with the situation at this point and my family life was suffering. It had not been a great time in my life.

I consulted with the Inspectors to find out what I could do to help. We agreed my main task would be to identify the type of cars the gang members drove and to jot down the license plate numbers. Their headquarters was the Ten Hills Café in Somerville, so that would be the place to start. I informed MDC Detective Sgt. Tom White of my plan to help the Postal Inspectors in the investigation. I told him they were short on man power. Most of what I told the Postal Inspectors and Detective Sgt. White were half-truths, so each one would think I was 'needed' by the other. They probably saw right through the scheme. But they knew I wasn't going to let two bullets to my head go un-pursued. So, I tracked license plates. I had hoped this tedious, leg work would lead to, well, leads.

On these surveillance forays, I would use my own car, a non-descript 1972 Dodge Dart. I used cold plates because the bad guys could get a listing on a plate as fast as I could. Organized crime reached into many areas of law enforcement and the Registry of Motor Vehicles was no exception.

There were lots of abandoned license plates (tags) packed in cardboard boxes at the Fells Station. Lost tags were piled up in storage. They would sit there for a year before they were destroyed. I kept my real license plates in the trunk of my car, in case I was stopped by a local cop or, God forbid, I was involved in a motor vehicle accident. If that happened, I would have a lot of explaining to do.

I also kept a Remington 12-gauge pump shotgun, which I originally bought for duck hunting, in my car trunk. I always kept it loaded with double 00 buck - the same rounds I was shot with. These guys were bad actors and I knew there was always the possibility they could spot me and want to take me out. I did not want to be caught unprepared in their territory. They were always on the lookout for cops.

This type of 'leg work' investigation often paid off down the road. I would sit on the Café from different vantage points. As soon as I saw a car starting to move, I would jot down a plate number and then follow the car to its destination. A pattern developed as they went from gin mill to gin mill. Most of these establishments were in the Winter Hill section of Somerville. The Paddock and Pal Joey's, a.k.a. the Back Room, were regular haunts. After watching them for a while, I knew what car would be in which place at what time, like clockwork. During the day they hung out in a barber shop up on Winter Hill.

I slowly gathered this info. I met with the Postal Inspectors and handed over the information I had collected and they would update me on the status of the case. It may have just been busy work, but I needed to do something and was happy to contribute in any way I could. We needed someone to roll over, or a witness to identify the bad guys involved in my incident or in one of the bank robberies. We did not have that.

The Ten Hills Café was a perfect location for the gang's base. It was on Mystic Avenue with limited parking. It was a red, brick building with few windows. You could not see inside the place from the street. The front of the entrance was L-shaped and the guys could duck in and out to look for cops, which was a full-time job for these men. I never went by the place without seeing a lookout posted at the front entrance. I wondered which one of the bastards I saw from my vantage point had tried to kill my partner and me. Without a doubt, they were in the barroom, sucking down beers, snorting cocaine and planning their next job. Would I be able to stop them before they shot another cop? I sure as hell was going to try.

We had weekly meetings and MSP Det. Lt. Jack Dwyer would tell me if I was headed in the right direction with those I tailed. One afternoon I followed a car from the Café to a lumber yard. I think the vehicle I followed was a Ford Thunderbird. I do recall the listing coming back to a Salvatore Sperlinga. The name meant nothing to me and he was a generation older than the guys I was looking for. He didn't seem to fit in with the crew that hung out there, but it was worth a peek. I met with Dwyer that night to show him my daily list of cars and owners.

Jack said, "Dana, you're going in the wrong direction with this one. Sal Sperlinga is the bookkeeper for Howie Winter and The Winter Hill Gang and would never be involved in a crime like the mail robbery."

We went over the information on the other guys I had followed, and found a few were likely part of the Ten Hills crew.

Whenever I was in uniform on duty, I would drive by the Café, nice and slow, in a marked cruiser so the lookout could see a cop. I didn't want them to waste their paranoia. It was a foolish game on my part, but seeing them out front, free, smoking and joking, really pissed me off. I still had crippling headaches from the bullets to my head, probably from the guns of the same men laughing together outside the Café.

One night in late September, as I was watching them during off-duty hours, I noticed a lot of activity at the Café. Three men came out and piled into a car. They seemed to be on a mission.

The car belonged to Roy, one of the suspected wheelmen in some earlier robberies. I had done my homework well and felt something was up. But I had no portable police radio and was not on duty.

As the car took off, I followed from a safe distance. It was about 8:15 p.m., the same time of night I had been shot. Darkness had fallen, which made it much easier to tail them. If something big went down, I worried I might be in over my head. But there was no turning back.

They led me to a well-known restaurant where I often dined, called the Hilltop Steak House. It was just north of Boston on Route 1 and had a huge artificial cactus and a herd of life-sized plastic cows out front. The place was noted for excellent steaks and was always packed, with a two hour wait-time standard. It looked to me as though the men I followed were going to have steaks, so I was ready to head home, when something unusual happened.

Their car pulled into the parking lot but instead of finding a space, they immediately swung out again and roared south on Route 1 in Saugus. I followed as the car accelerated southbound at a fairly high rate of speed. Maybe they spotted me tailing them, but I didn't think so.

About twenty minutes after retracing the route, they pulled back into the Ten Hills Café. To me, this was either a rehearsal or a 'timed run.' Something was definitely going on. I parked down the street to get a better look, but still could not see the faces of the three men who had been in the car. Because of the distance and darkness, I couldn't identify anyone.

The next day I reported the incident to our Detective Bureau. I was told it was 'good intelligence info' and they would make a note of it. I stood there for a minute or so, but noticed nothing was written down. For the first time, the tone of voice of the Detective Lt. seemed condescending. I was sure they thought I was grasping at straws and they were humoring me. They had been rude to me and it was shocking to think people on my own job were kissing off valuable 'intel' about a potential impending robbery. It took the wind out of my sails. I doubted myself and wondered if I was just wasting their time and mine.

Had my tip been heeded, a person's life could possibly have been saved. Unfortunately, it took a tragedy to prove I was on the right path and my cop instincts had been correct.

## CHAPTER SIXTEEN
### *The Holdup and Murder*

On Friday, October 3, 1975, two men held up the Hilltop Steakhouse in a brazen daytime robbery. A Wells Fargo Guard had received a mortal wound while collecting money bags, containing cash and checks, from the owner's office. One of the robbers had been shot and badly wounded, and the pistol he dropped had been recovered at the scene. This occurred only a few days after I had tailed the car, containing the three men from the Ten Hills Café. I was certain it had been a timed run to the Hilltop as a rehearsal for this robbery.

Adding to the series of coincidental events, the victim, Louis Silva, had lived in *my* town of North Reading and had *also* been married with two kids. The morning after the Hilltop Steakhouse robbery, North Reading P. D. Detective Hayes had been reading items coming across the old noisy teletype machine, a part of his daily routine. To his amazement, he read a Walther PPK pistol had been recovered at the holdup and murder. This pistol had been on the list of guns and disguises the informant had given him back in May, the same list which included the guns recovered in the mail hijacking.

I had hoped the Ten Hills Gang hadn't pulled off the robbery and the murder. But my worst fears had come true. It appeared the same guys who shot me had senselessly killed Guard Silva. If only my agency had believed me, the Guard may not have been killed, but I knew this was wishful thinking. Still I wished we'd been able to take the gang off the street, before the murder. It took me a long time to let the feeling of guilt go.

Detective Hayes alerted the Postal Inspectors the gun used in the Hilltop robbery had been on his list. Just as I thought, the suspects in the Hilltop robbery were, in fact, the same suspects we chased back in June.

The Postal Inspectors told me what they knew about the holdup. Bleeding and near death, the wounded robber, John Grider, was thought to be a hindrance to the gang and had been dumped on the street in Somerville. Grider, found by a passerby, had been taken by ambulance to Somerville Hospital. Although he had been listed in critical condition, he would survive the gunshot wound. When he recovered, he was taken into custody and formally charged in the robbery and the murder.

> *There had been erroneous newspaper reports, just as there had been in my shooting. In one article, Grider was reported to have been killed and his body dumped on the street.*

Years later, I spoke with Captain Albert J. DeRosa of the Massachusetts Port Police, a close friend of Louis Silva's and a fellow Wells Fargo Guard at the time of the Hilltop holdup. When his friend got him the Wells Fargo Guard's job, Capt. DeRosa said Silva wisely advised, "If you get held up, give them whatever they want."

He went on to say, "It's only money and it's almost always insured."

Al DeRosa had not been with Silva on that fatal Friday, but relayed these details as he had heard them.

"The other armored truck guard sat locked in the vehicle, which was standard operating procedure. Silva walked into the restaurant and over to the office of the owner, Frank Giuffrida, to pick up the money bags, containing $57,682 in cash and checks. Silva walked through the unsecured area in this huge, bustling steak house, and past a man who had been standing against a post, reading a newspaper. This was not unusual in this busy open area."

The captain went on to say, "Silva picked up the two bags containing the money, as he had often done. He was not wearing a bullet proof vest. He said he didn't like them."

*I felt the same way before I was shot. In 1975, the vests were hot, heavy and bulky.*

"He also never carried the shotgun, stored in each armored truck. He was just not a gun guy. As Silva headed out of the office carrying the money bags, the man pretending to read the paper outside the owner's office put his gun against Silva's back and pulled the trigger, without saying a word."

The shooter had been James Hackett.

It had been a cowardly act and completely unnecessary. The word on the street was the shooter was always 'coked out' in order to get up the courage to pull a heist. The bullet he fired passed through Silva's heart, mortally wounding him. Silva somehow found the strength to drop the bags, draw his own revolver and return fire. One of his rounds hit Hackett's fellow gang member John Grider in the stomach, who was holding a Walther PPK pistol, according to witnesses.

The Wells Fargo-issued round that hit Grider was a hollow point bullet, which mushroomed once inside the body. It had been designed to do extensive damage, to neutralize the threat.

The police report read, *"The bullet shattered his large intestine, small intestine, part of his spleen, and a part of his colon."* Grider dropped his Walther PPK pistol and grabbed his stomach. Hackett fired more rounds. At least two more bullets struck the already mortally-wounded Guard. Hackett grabbed the money bags and helped his wounded partner to the waiting stolen getaway car, allegedly driven by Richard Murnane. Newspaper reports at the time stated at least four people were involved in the robbery.

The Captain and I sat drinking coffee at a local shop as he related the details of the fatal day, thirty-seven years later. I could see Al choke up as he told me more.

After the shooting, Silva's young son would often ask him, "Uncle Al, when you go to work, can you please bring my Dad home?"

I thought back to how close my daughters came to losing me, and I fought back tears, too. Neither of us said another word, we just sat together and finished our coffee.

ON OCTOBER 27, James Hackett was arrested at his home in Arlington, MA and charged with the first degree murder of the Guard Silva. I was asked by the investigators on my case to attend a probable cause hearing of Hackett, for the Hilltop robbery and the murder, at Lynn District Court.

The Postal Inspectors asked me to let them know if I recognized Hackett, the suspect in the hijacked truck. Even if I could have, it would be inadmissible in court because I had been unable to pick him out of the photo spread. They also wanted me to see if I could recognize any other suspects in the courtroom.

*"On December 9, and December 29, 1975, the two witnesses (the Edison company employees) to the June 16, 1975 hijacking as well as the two M.D.C. Police Officers, were brought to Lynn District Court where a probable cause hearing was scheduled. The probable cause hearing involved suspects in the robbery of the Hilltop Steak House and murder of a Wells Fargo Security Guard at the Hilltop Steak House on October 3. Only one of the prime defendants in the murder case, James Hackett was present. However, on December 9, David Toppi, one of the*

*four suspects in the mail hijacking case was present as a spectator. All four witnesses viewed Hackett and Toppi, but none could state that either Hackett or Toppi were the persons they saw on June 16, 1975." [Report of W.J. O'Leary].*

The Ten Hill's Gang had been in their heyday and well organized. About a dozen members were in the courtroom to intimidate the witnesses - several cooks and waitresses who witnessed the Hilltop robbery and the murder. It worked exactly as they had planned. The defense lawyer, Harvey Brower, asked each witness, on the stand and under oath, for a home address. He would then ask each witness to repeat the address several times and the bad guys would boldly write down where each witness lived. These were big, intimidating guys and I couldn't blame the witnesses for being scared. It was a circus and I was totally disgusted.

Hackett looked familiar to me, but that was probably because I saw his mug shot in the photo spread. He was the only one I got a glimpse of during the hijacking, so there was no way I would recognize any of the other hijackers, even if they were in the courtroom.

Hackett had been in jail on $50,000 bail since October 27. Grider had turned state's evidence in return for a plea of second degree murder. Even though Grider testified against Hackett, Harvey Brower, the defense lawyer (who later went to jail for another crime), managed to get Hackett found *not guilty* on January 29, 1977. Most of the eyewitnesses had been either scared off, or they changed their initial testimony. The case was badly handled and a critical mistake had been made during questioning about the gun recovered at the scene.

*"Joseph Capone and David Donnigan were included among those called as witnesses before the Grand Jury. As mentioned in prior reports,*

*Joseph Capone was identified as the person who allegedly stashed five firearms in the barn of (name deleted) in (town deleted) MA during the month of May 1975. Three firearms recovered in or near the getaway car after the hijacking on June 16 and one firearm recovered at the scene of the robbery and murder on October 3, 1975, where four of the five weapons observed by "T-1" in the barn. David Donnigan was the person to whom the shotguns were traced. It was reported that both witnesses were evasive in their statements before the grand jury and no incriminating information was provided by them."*

Joseph Capone and David Donnigan denied any knowledge of the guns and crime, of course. Detective Hayes and his partner, Detective Sgt. Purnell, were never called to testify about the gun. He could have testified about the list of guns from his informant, T-1, and the fact Grider's Walther PPK pistol was on the list.

The informant and the owner of the barn, where the guns had been found, were both asked a question during the trial: "Had they seen a stash of guns at a certain address?"

Unbelievably, when the prosecutor asked the question, he somehow got the *number* in the address wrong. Both witnesses were able to answer "No," truthfully. This basically excluded linking the guns to the gang. It also put 'reasonable doubt' in the mind of the jurors. The prosecution had made a game-changing mistake.

Richard Murnane, also the suspected wheelman in my case, fled before the trial. Hackett's finding of *not guilty* was a huge miscarriage of justice. Capone, the guy who allegedly supplied the guns, was never charged. Grider was the only suspect in the mail hijacking who would go to jail for the crime in the Hilltop incident. In exchange for his testimony against Hackett, Grider had been promised he would be released in fifteen years. His sentence for testifying, issued by jury of the Gang, was a contract that was put out on his head.

The trial had been a total disaster and all involved in the mail robbery investigation felt the same way. This was supposed to have been our big break. The gang members on trial could have faced life imprisonment. But due to inept prosecution and simple carelessness, it had gone down the toilet. We were back to square one.

During a meeting with the Postal Inspectors, I said, "We are going to get these bastards one way or the other. I can't let this go and neither can you."

They agreed.

# CHAPTER SEVENTEEN
## *The Awards*

I thought back to when I was in the hospital. I had wanted nothing more than to recover, heal and get home to my wife and kids. As I lay in my hospital bed, I understood why people lauded for bravery would say they did nothing heroic. I simply did what I had been trained to do. It was my job. The logic and training instilled at the Academy guided my actions during the real life incident.

There had been a quiet moment at my hospital bed when my patrol partner, Bob, and I were the only ones in the room.

The Vietnam combat veteran said, "That was the bravest thing I'd ever seen."

He was talking about how, even after I was shot, I threw the cruiser into a skid. The car swung sideways and my side was facing the blocked getaway car, exposing myself to gunfire. He told me he knew I used the car as cover for him, disregarding my own safety. I did not look at it as a heroic act or even a particularly brave one. After the second bullet hit me in the forehead, I knew I was out of the fight. But my mind still worked methodically. It had been the only logical thing for me to do. I knew Bob was the only one who could continue the fight for both of us, by shooting back at the fleeing felons.

It had taken me a while to piece together the full story of exactly what had happened. Even as I heard myself telling the story, the whole ordeal seemed like a nightmare. There were parts

I remembered so clearly and gaps that were filled in from information I had collected from the newspapers, television, fellow cops, and friends and family. The front page of the Winchester Daily Times had a photo of a detective holding up a revolver and the sawed-off shotgun I had been shot with. Next to it was a photo of our cruiser with the two bullet holes in the windshield. The article said I *"was hit in the head by one of the two bullets that penetrated the windshield"*, when, in fact, I was hit by both.

MDC POLICEMAN Dana Owens was hit in the head by one of two bullets that hit and penetrated the windshield of their cruiser. Owens, who is reported to be in good condition today, and another MDC officer were chasing a car containing four armed suspects in an aborted hold-up attempt. The suspects had smashed out the rear window of their vehicle in order to fire at the pursuing police.

After I got back to work, my brother cops seemed very interested in the whole episode. Some asked lots of questions and wanted to hear every last detail, and others, who probably didn't want to pry, welcomed me back and just let me talk. The more I talked about it, the more it began to sink in. I began to realize just how close I had come to dying.

Each time I told my story, my brother cops told me I should get a medal or commendation. I began to think maybe I *should* be cited for something. I certainly laid it all on the line in trying to catch the guys. After all, we did stop the robbery and gave them a pursuit for the ages. But then again, I was just doing my job.

At the time, I didn't know Sgt. Frank Thorpe, the Fells Supervisor, had submitted a report, the morning after I was shot, recommending a Class A commendation for my partner and me. Class A was the highest of the written commendations awarded for an armed encounter or other actions that were 'beyond the call of duty.' When I found out about his recommendation, I felt proud the Department considered us for a commendation. The MDC Police had a history of acknowledging generations of cops for their efforts.

Thorpe's recommendation slowly wound its way up the chain of command through the bureaucracy, and to the Commendations Committee, a board of high-ranking police officials who decided who should be rewarded.

At a Committee meeting, one of the captains, referring to Bob Power and me, said, **"They shouldn't get a thing. They didn't catch them, did they?"**

A friend of mine on the board told me about the Captain's opposition. The awards were put on hold, thanks to the 'good captain's' resistance.

I was crushed and, at the same time, absolutely furious. The objecting captain was known as a 'Desk Jockey,' a derogatory term for a ranking officer who sat behind a desk his entire career. In addition, working inside the station, he had time to study for promotional exams. He was a paper pusher who could not handle the stress of the street. Even though I had no respect for the man, I could not get his words out of my mind. It made me wonder if others on the job felt the same way about the two of us.

During the chase that night, we held our fire to protect innocent bystanders, as we had been trained to do. We did

The Awards ◆ Page 137

everything right, everything by the book and this test taking excuse for a cop, who never laid it on the line himself, had taken it upon himself to decide *not* to recognize us for what we had accomplished. So we hadn't caught them, but we *had* intercepted an armed hijacking, saved the U.S. Postal Service somewhere between $100,000 and $150,000, and probably saved the life of the kidnapped truck driver. This chair-borne Desk Jockey had the audacity to judge us harshly.

My friend on the commendation board, who was powerful in our union, called one day to say, "Just keep your mouth shut and let me work this out."

Hopefully, someone higher up than this pathetic Captain, someone with common sense, would intervene. Clearly, I could not go over his head and say to his superior, "Hey, we almost died out there." It was just not done - a patrolman could not go over the head of a captain, jumping over the chain of command. I was sure his higher ups had no idea he had interfered with the awards. I had to accept this: my fate was in the hands of Capt. Desk Jockey.

In early November, something amazing happened. A friend tipped me off the United States Postal Inspector down in Washington, D.C. had been informed about us stopping the robbery. Then I heard the Inspection Service had contacted my police agency. The U.S. Postal Service was going to present each of us a citation for our actions that night. In addition, we would each receive a check for $250. The MDC Police had a rule against taking a gift of over fifty dollars. A written order had to be issued to waive the rule for us to accept the financial award. Ironically, the rule was instituted to prevent corruption.

The Feds had acknowledged our significant effort, even though we didn't catch anyone. But my employer, based on the spiteful Captain, rejected my Sergeant's recommendation? Captain Desk Jockey, suddenly found himself in a bit of a pickle. After sniffing the wind, the Captain realized he had put himself in an embarrassing position. Ever mindful of his next promotion, he wouldn't want to lose face with the Feds or, even worse, his own higher-ups. Thinking only of himself, he made a decision and…reversed himself. Remarkable!!!

MDC Police citations were quickly made up to be presented at the same time as the U.S. Postal Service awards. The citations were printed and framed, but the medals would take a week or two to be delivered, even as the Captain pushed to rush the job along.

During this time, I had been hospitalized with complications stemming from some of the medications. Just two days after I had been admitted, the phone next to my hospital bed rang at about 4 p.m. It was Capt. Desk Jockey. He officially told me the Postal Inspectors from Washington, D.C. and Boston were going to present citations to my partner and me.

The Captain said, "Owen, I need you at headquarters in uniform at 10:00 a.m. tomorrow."

I replied, "Captain, you're calling me in my hospital bed."

In a very condescending and sarcastic tone, he said, "If you can't make it, we'll put the **shit** they are giving you into a paper bag and we'll ship it up to the hospital."

I paused, took a deep breath and said, "See you at 10 a.m., Sir."

To hell with him, the sniveling suck-up. I would get my citation and I'd enjoy every minute of it. I was never sure why this Captain treated me this way. Perhaps he knew which one of us was the real cop - but I decided it really didn't matter. Things were looking up.

I called my wife and I told her the whole story. She pulled a lot of strings to convince the medical staff to let me out of the hospital. She got them to recognize how important this was to me, especially for my emotional and mental well-being. She brought in my freshly-pressed uniform and I was let out on a day pass stamped 'Against Doctor's Orders.'

So, the next morning, my partner Bob picked me up. Wives were never invited to any police activities in those days, a foolish departmental policy. Wives and families were excluded from almost all police ceremonies, except for a cop's funeral. Instead, my wife had to stay in my hospital room and try to smooth things over there.

We drove to MDC Boston headquarters, to the little, ornate, stone dungeon on Somerset Street. We were taken to the MDC Conference room on one of the upper floors, where my partner and I received the citations. It was called a 'Special Citation' from the United States Postal Service out of Washington, D.C. I looked as if I was wearing a much larger person's uniform, after losing so much weight, but I managed a smile for the photos.

The award plaques and checks were presented to us by F. J. Nemic the assistant in charge of the U.S. Postal Inspectors in Boston, MA. Also, Inspectors O'Leary and Ricker attended proudly, with the MDC Commissioner and our Police Superintendent.

The Special Citation read:

> *For conspicuous performance of duty, heroic contribution to the public welfare and distinguished adherence to the finest traditions of law enforcement in preventing the hijacking of a U.S. Postal Service mail truck at great risk to your personal safety and well-being on the night of June 16, 1975 at Boston, Massachusetts.*
> *at Washington, D.C.*
> *Neil Benson*
> *Chief Postal Inspector*

(Left to right) W. Snedeker, F. Nemic, D. Owen, R. Power,
W. O'Leary and L. Carpenter

The MDC captain who called me in the hospital, the one who
wanted "to put my **shit** in a bag and ship it up to my hospital
bed," was not present. And honestly, he was not missed by
anyone.

# CHAPTER EIGHTEEN
## *The Medal of Valor*

My spirits soared when I was formally notified by the commendation committee my partner and I were going to be presented with the Medal of Valor at the annual MDC Policeman's Ball. This was the highest award in police work and only a select few had been given the award in the long history of the MDC Police, dating back to 1893. The definition of valor from Merriam-Webster states it best: 'strength of mind or spirit that enables a person to encounter danger with firmness: personal bravery.'

The Policeman's Ball, a gala event, was held every year in November at the Prudential Center in Boston. Fifteen hundred cops and guests usually attended the affair. I really needed a haircut, but I was afraid to have it cut. I still had a few dissolvable stitches in my scalp. My fear was most likely unfounded, but the last thing I needed was another trip to the hospital. The phrase "like I need another hole in the head," took on new meaning for me. Luckily, long hair and sideburns were the style for policemen in 1975.

The night before the Policeman's Ball I had watched a TV police show called *Adam-12*. I had been released from the hospital a day or two before and was just relaxing. I loved anything Jack Web produced and also never missed *Dragnet*. *Adam-12* featured two Los Angeles policemen, Jim Reed and Pete Malloy. Reed was the veteran, and Malloy was the rookie of the team. In the episode I watched, Reed was presented the Medal of Valor for foiling an armed robbery. Reed and the other recipients were standing on a stage and in uniform when they were presented the medals. About ten minutes after the show ended, my phone rang at home.

It was my Police Superintendent, Laurence J. Carpenter. I only met the "Super" once, after I had been shot. A patrolman almost never had occasion to speak with the highest ranking uniformed officer in the department.

The Superintendent said, "Officer Owen I want you and your partner in full uniform tomorrow night at the ball."

I thought, "He must have watched *Adam-12*, just as I had."

I said, "Super, I was planning on wearing a suit and my wife will be with me."

I thought my plea would work. The Policeman's Ball was always a formal affair and a few guests even wore tuxedos.

"You can wear your civvies, but bring your uniform. You and Officer Power can change in my suite." Then he said, "Call your partner. I want you both in full uniform when I present the medals."

Before I could answer, he hung up. It was not a request, it was an order. The phone call to Bob went as expected. He was against the uniform idea.

I said, "Superintendent Carpenter said it's an order. See you tomorrow night," then I hung up, avoiding the useless exercise of arguing a directive from the top brass.

All I really cared about was to be there with my wife and to be presented with the highest award of the Metropolitan Police Department. My weight and strength would come back in time and hopefully, so would the hair on top of my head. Wearing my uniform would not be that big of a deal.

We arrived at the Prudential Center in Boston with our uniforms in garment bags and our gun belts and revolvers in our duty bags. Many of my fellow policemen saw me for the first time since I had been shot. They shook my hand and told me I looked great. In reality, I looked like I had just been released from a concentration camp. I had lost about 30 pounds and was as white as a ghost. My suit hung off me and I knew my police uniform would look two sizes too big on me, as well.

Bob and I were shown to the suite where the high ranking police officials had a bar, hors d'oeuvres and other amenities. It was my first glimpse of what is was like to be a politician or top police brass. The fancy finger snacks consisted of things like scallops wrapped in bacon, jumbo shrimp cocktail and what looked to me like black fish eggs…it must have been caviar. I wished I had felt better. My stomach was already upset from the new medication I was taking and food of that nature would not settle well, for sure. We stowed our gear and went back down to dinner.

After the meal of roast beef, Bob and I were told to go up and change into our uniforms for the awards ceremony. Once again, our wives were not included and had to stay at our table. In fact, they were not even in the first row, always reserved for politicians, and high ranking officers. In my opinion, spouses were part of the team. Put the members of the team in front! I always felt the law enforcement community made a huge mistake by overlooking the entire family. Sadly, this would not change for many years.

As we put on our uniforms in the Presidential Suite of the swanky hotel, we were both nervous and hoped we would not have to speak on stage. Bullets didn't bother me as much as the mere thought of standing in front of all of all of those people and trying to sound intelligent. Just the idea was terrifying.

I happened to overhear an interesting discussion about who would be on stage to give out the medals. The exchange was between the Police Superintendent and the new MDC Commissioner John F. Snedeker. The Commissioner had been appointed after I was shot and was the head of the entire Metropolitan District Commission, including roads, parks and beaches, and our police agency. He was a politician, not a cop.

The commissioner felt he should also be on stage to present the awards. The conversation went something like this:

"Larry, I will present one of the medals after we do our speeches," the Commissioner said.

"I'm doing this by myself," the Super shot back.

"I am your boss and we will do this together," the Commissioner replied.

They talked as though I wasn't there. And yet I was standing right next to them.

"You're a politician. I am the highest ranking uniform cop on the Department and I worked my way up through the ranks. These are my guys and I will present the medals myself," Supt. Carpenter asserted.

It became a heated exchange and the Superintendent won out. He would be on stage with us, but without the Commissioner. It was just shocking to watch at close hand, the role politics played in police work. The fact I was being awarded the medal seemed unimportant. The politics of it trumped all.

In full uniform, we waited anxiously for the word to go downstairs and take the stage.

"Have a drink and relax, guys," one of the captains said. "It will be a while and we will give you a five-minute warning."

The Chivas Regal looked inviting, as did the Irish whiskey. But, I passed on a drink. Discretion was the better part of valor.

Bob had a scotch, a second one and then a third. I had a wicked headache and was worried I was going to puke my guts out any minute. My nausea got worse. After excusing myself, I went to the bathroom to throw up. Then, I felt better.

So, down to the event we went. Bob was red-faced, but relaxed from the scotch. I was white as snow and I looked like a little kid wearing his father's uniform.

OFFICER ROBERT M. POWER
OFFICER DANA C. OWEN
*Medal of Valor Recipients*
SUPERINTENDENT LAURENCE J. CARPENTER

Superintendent Larry Carpenter, dressed in a tuxedo, read off our citations and described what we had done that night. I really never heard exactly what he said, because I was thinking about what I would say, if I had been asked to speak.

I looked at the huge ballroom from the stage and out at the hundreds of guests. I focused on my wife's face, as she sat at our dinner table, which was several rows back. The look of contentment and of pride on her face kept me going, as it had throughout this whole event. Her knowing smile had such a calming effect on me, even at this distance.

Supt. Carpenter took my medal out of its box. It was multicolored and had the Metropolitan Police logo and state seal in the center. It was on a red, white and blue ribbon, which I could see would not fit over my size 7 5/8" police cap. So, I had to take it off and show my half shaved head, the stitches, and the stubble growing back. At first I was embarrassed, but then, after thinking about it for a moment, I felt I should wear the scars with honor. After all, I got them in the line of duty.

When he placed the ribbon and medal over my head, I beamed with pride. So much so, I stood as tall as I could and felt shivers run up and down my spine. After the medals were placed around our necks, the crowd gave us a standing ovation. Not like the ovations I had seen at plays or concerts. It was spontaneous and was from my peers. It gave me a feeling I had never experienced before. I was on top of the world and never had to speak.

Then, as if to spoil my own enjoyment of the moment, the words of Capt. Desk Jockey popped back in my head. **"Why should they get anything? They didn't catch them."** Those words echoed in my mind and burned even more. As foolish as it seemed, those words from someone I had no respect for just burned and burned like a hot poker revolving inside. Maybe he had a point after all. Maybe others felt the way he did, but I hoped not. I reassured myself with the thought, "It isn't over yet, Capt." I was determined to keep the vow I had made to myself when I had been shot. I would - somehow, someday - catch the bad guys.

After the award ceremony, we went back downstairs to our table. Several of the cops, my closest friends, came over to see the medal and congratulate me. We shook hands and talked for a few minutes and then as the music began, I got up to dance with my wife. That night was the time to savor the moment with my wife and fellow officers and friends.

Monday morning would be soon enough to redouble my efforts in the investigation and ask the Postal Inspectors to do the same. I swore to myself I would make Capt. Desk Jockey eat those words someday. What neither of us knew was the chase was not over. It was just beginning.

# CHAPTER NINETEEN
## *Motorcycle Patrol*

The investigation into my shooting was slipping away as the months came and went with no progress. The Postal Inspectors went to the U.S Attorney's Office for the second time asking for the case to be presented to a grand jury. For the second time the request was denied due to a lack of evidence. We still needed someone to put the perpetrators at the scene of the crime.

We had hoped Grider might testify, but he had been reluctant to do so. Grider told the Postal Inspectors, FBI and the Massachusetts State Police he "had information on the mail hijacking and several bank robberies." He had been sentenced to life in prison after pleading *guilty* in the Hilltop Steak House robbery and the murder. In Massachusetts, that meant a life sentence, but he would be eligible for parole in fifteen years. He was obviously shopping for a better deal.

In June of 1977, a new policy called 'redeployment' had been initiated by my agency to avoid overtime and to fill vacancies in a district. Because Bob Power and I were the junior men on most shifts at the Fellsway District, we would be assigned to work in a different district almost every night. We had been redeployed fifty-six shifts in a row. The 'Fells' was a popular District and we could be the junior men for years to come. It was the most sought after assignment for any MDC cops who lived on the north shore of Boston, because of the short commute to work.

After the shooting, some of the shift supervisors simply wanted us out of their hair. We had done everything by the book during the mail robbery, yet some were uneasy we might 'get involved in something' on the street.

A few of my brother officers told me, "They think you're crazy and they want you out of here."

Other bosses liked us and fought to keep us in the Fells on the shifts they supervised. But our lack of seniority at the Fells Station made the situation hopeless.

Forced Boston School Busing, ordered by a Federal Judge to help desegregate the public schools, was in full swing and there had been a ton of federal overtime money to be made in South Boston and Charlestown during the racial clashes. One night while redeployed to the Old Colony District, a door opened for us.

The Old Colony was on Day Boulevard, in South Boston and also housed the Tactical Squad and Detective Unit. One day a lieutenant from the tactical unit, who often saw us when we were redeployed, said, "Why don't you two transfer to the Tactical Oriented Patrol Squad. I need some young workers like you guys."

We took his advice, requested it, and got the transfer. TOPS was originally called the Tactical Oriented Patrol Squad, but once forced busing started, it was given a new politically correct name - the *Traffic* Oriented Patrol Squad. It contained the same cops, same riot equipment, same tactical vehicles and motorcycles, but a kinder and gentler name. To the press and pro-busing movement 'tactical' was too military. So the name changed, but nothing else.

The unit consisted of all new cruisers and tactical vans, along with twenty five motorcycles. At one time, the bikes (motorcycles) had been assigned to the geographical Districts, a few allotted to each. Once busing started, they were all sent to South Boston and became part of the newly formed TOPS unit. If there was a major disturbance, the unit was the first one sent in. It was viewed as an elite unit and most cops in the MDC patrol districts felt the TOPS officers were prima donnas.

Two motorcycle positions opened up and went out to bid under our union contract. It was not something I had been really interested in, but Bob and I talked of maybe putting in for the job. One of the duties included escorting black students from Roxbury to a previously all-white school in South Boston. Finally, we had seniority over most in the TOPS Unit, which consisted of younger cops with only a year or two on the job. I was a firm believer in seniority. I had paid my dues as a junior man at the Fells for the last eight years. Besides, the motorcycle squad always had the most federally funded overtime and I could use the extra money.

I thought the motorcycles might be a diversion from my obsession with the mail hijacking, but in the back of my mind I also knew how dangerous they could be. I had promised my wife and myself two things after joining the force: I would never be a motorcycle cop and I would never work undercover. I was about to break the first promise.

My wife reluctantly supported me, but had great reservations about my being a motorcycle cop. But she knew how miserable I had been, getting redeployed night after night.

She had one valid point, asking, "What about the other idiots on the road?"

I promised her I would be extremely careful. The bid was supposed to be awarded strictly by seniority, but the agency had become very political in those years.

When I first asked about openings on the motorcycle unit, my lieutenant told me, "Forget it. They already know who they want."

So, of course I applied and lied on the application about my riding skill. Neither Bill nor I had any experience at all, but we both claimed we had been riding since shortly after birth.

Our brother officers who had seniority on the motorcycle squad gave us a crash course in motorcycle riding. On quiet nights, we practiced in the MBTA parking lot on Revere Beach. Officer Jimmy Bruce, one of the more senior cops, had been a motorcycle cop for years. He liked us both and felt the same way most of us did about seniority. Jimmy taught us how to ride. The goal, he told us, was simple: don't crash into any parked cars in the huge lot. Easier said, than done.

We passed the bike road test at TOPS and were assigned to the squad. I guessed the political higher ups did not want to fight the grievances if the senior 'qualified' guys did not get the posted contract jobs.

Dana Owen – 1977

My first bike assignment was to patrol an MDC beach. It was in Quincy, MA, just south of Boston, and was the perfect assignment. If I drove east, I could keep the ocean on my left and only make right turns. I had really not mastered left turns yet. I was not sure if it was my old head injury, but I felt unsteady turning left. Training wheels were not an option on a police

Harley Davidson. As luck would have it, we were assigned to a two-week police motorcycle safety school and thus became decent riders.

Summer had passed and it was Thursday, October 12, 1978. That night was cool and I was working Team-Policing with three other MDC motorcycle officers. We had finished a sweep of the Nahant Beach parking lot, which closed at 8 p.m. We were wearing black leather jackets and gloves and woolen breeches, the fall uniform.

As we headed down the Lynnway (a highway connecting Revere to Lynn, MA), I was the last bike in the line of four. It was a three-lane, divided highway and we were heading back to South Boston. We were in the left lane approaching a cut-off to the Carlton Hotel. I glimpsed at a bill board across the highway, "WELCOME CREW OF USS BIGELOW," which I assumed must be a navy ship.

Suddenly, in my peripheral vision I saw a blur coming at me from my right rear. Then, everything went dark. Awakening from what I thought was a dream, I heard an unfamiliar voice. It was an EMT and...I realized I was on a stretcher again...in the back of an ambulance.

Pontiac driven by the drunken sailor

The pain in my left shoulder was so intense I could feel the slight bump, bump, bump of the broken white lines on the road.

The voice was saying, "You're Okay, but you have some broken bones." There was no sense in asking what happened. I had obviously been hit by the blur.

*As it turned out, a drunken sailor from the USS Bigelow and his fellow seaman were in the car that hit me. His buddy said to the inebriated driver, "Make a left here, or you're going to miss our exit!" As he turned, he slammed right into my motorcycle. The sailor, who was later convicted of drunk driving, made a foolish decision and tried to flee with the Harley locked under his left front fender. He did not get far, dragging an 850 pound Police Harley down the highway with sparks flying. Based on this information, any sympathy a jury might have had for a sailor, disappeared.*

Downed 1973 Police Harley Davison Lynnway, Lynn, MA

Unlike the time I had been shot, this time there was a lot of pain. My neck was immobilized in a Thomas Collar but I could look down at my hands. They were both badly broken. My right index and middle fingers were swollen and dark purple, and looked and felt as if they would explode. My pinky finger on my left hand was bent backwards, almost touching my wrist.

The fingers on my right hand had been crushed between the accelerator handle and his car. Witnesses said I was ejected from the bike and slid on the left side of my helmet and on my wooden riot baton which was on the left side of my duty belt. Luckily, I was unconscious while sliding over one hundred feet until I slammed into the curbed divider, fracturing my left clavicle. I asked how my legs were.

The EMT said, "You're very lucky. Your legs are fine."

I tried to lift my head to make sure he was telling the truth and could see someone had taken off my high riding boots.

"Where are my boots?" I asked.

"One of your buddies has them."

Our custom made boots were hard to get and were a sought-after item in the bike squad. One of the guys I was riding with had taken them for safe keeping. Of course, like me, he was a size 10D. I didn't expect to see those boots again.

Both my helmet and night stick looked as though they had been ground down by a machine. The stick was flat on the outside and the helmet was down to its last layer of fiberglass. The doctor later told me the stick and helmet saved me from much more serious injuries or death.

Once again my wife was called, but this time she was told the truth. I was in stable condition. My partner, Bob Power, picked her up in a marked car and drove her to the hospital.

We had been told by Dan Rooney, my favorite sergeant at the academy, the second string of doctors and nurses often treated an injured uniformed officer. It was on the job training, you could say, in certain, non-life threatening cases.

Unfortunately, this was the case at the local hospital. A young foreign doctor, who barely spoke English, told me he had to start an Intravenous (IV) drip in my arm. I told him how much I hated needles, but had many IV's when I had been shot. He smiled and nodded. I felt he had no clue what I had said.

I did understand him when he asked if I had good veins. "Yup, they tell me I do," I assured him. He started to insert the IV needle (that looked the size of a needle used to pump up a basketball) into my left arm at the fold in the elbow. All of a sudden he started probing, digging and turning the needle in my arm searching for the vein.

"What the hell are you doing???" I screamed in pain.

In his broken English, he said, "Oh, have bad veins."

"Bullshit. You're killing me!!!"

He repeated his probing and digging with the IV needle on the back of my right hand. I was almost lifting myself off the stretcher writhing and groaning in excruciating pain.

"I need to try other arm."

"You hurt me again...It will be strike three and I'll smack you!" I threatened.

Then he did the same brutal probing. I shoved him with my broken left hand and with all my strength, pushing him into the wall, just as my wife walked through the door to the treatment room.

"What are you doing, Dana?" using the same tone of voice she used when our kids were in trouble.

"He's trying to kill me!" I said in defense of my stupid actions. My hand and collar bone were killing me from bouncing the doctor off the wall, all five foot nothing of him.

The head of anesthesiology came in at about the same time, apparently over-hearing the commotion. He put his hand on the back of my right hand, patting it.

"Officer, you need to calm down," he said soothingly.

I told him what this clown of a doc had done to me.

"Please calm down. He's new. There you are...all set," he reassured me.

I looked at the back of my right hand, the needle inserted and taped in place. While he was talking and patting my hand, he put in the needle without my feeling a thing...so much for bad veins.

My wife had me transferred to the Malden Hospital by ambulance, at my insistence. I painfully signed my name on a form which read 'Against Medical Advice.' I had been transported to a place we trusted, and where I was getting to be a regular. I was kept in the hospital for several days, over the weekend, because the doctors questioned whether I had a broken neck and wanted to wait until Monday for the orthopedic specialist. Once it was determined my neck was Okay, they set the broken and smashed fingers, and I was released with casts on both hands, my left shoulder in a harness for the fractured clavicle. I was told 'No Duty' for at least six months.

As I began Occupational Therapy (OT) and Physical Therapy (PT), my mind wandered back to the investigation. The OT and PT therapists said the six months could be as long as a year. It all depended on how hard I was willing to work. I had nothing but time on my hands and the fact those guys who shot me were still on the loose was eating away at me.

The therapy was performed at a hospital in Stoneham, MA, a nearby town. It was run by Seventh Day Adventists and had been highly rated. The only thing I did not like about the hospital was...there was no coffee! I took this as cruel and unusual punishment. Caffeine was not allowed. It was against their religious beliefs.

At our first care plan meeting, I was given news I had feared. The chief therapist told me, "You will never be able to ride a motorcycle again and maybe never be able to qualify with your service revolver." I had no strength in either hand and zero dexterity. The road back was going to be a long one.

It was not the thing to tell an iron head like myself, noted for uncommon stubbornness. I was more determined than ever to be able to do both - ride and shoot. Maybe he said that on purpose to inspire me. Who knows? The female therapists were on my side and we got down to work. I brought in my own coffee in a thermos.

Week by week, I slowly improved. The physical therapy was painful and boring. I had ample time to look over my file on the mail case and call the Postal Inspectors. I was very focused on getting back to work. The one thing I did was my exercises at home...religiously. As the months passed, all the hard work I had done showed, and I could see the end in sight.

It seemed I was almost ready to go back to work. At the next monthly meetings with the therapists, it was determined I would need to begin occupational therapy in place of physical therapy, for at least another month.

OT was focused on exactly what my duties would be when I returned to work. I would need to qualify at the range and the therapists wanted to know many details about the motorcycle. Hand grippers with elastics simulated the clutch and brake levers on the handle bars of the bike. This group was so thorough. They had my partner stop by on his Harley to see exactly what it would take for me to operate the bike with my damaged hands.

With the strength in my hands and dexterity at acceptable levels, another meeting was set up to finalize my treatment.

One of the young female therapists asked, "Does a Harley Davidson vibrate? Vibration could affect your hand strength."

I laughed at the question. "Does a motorcycle vibrate while under power?" I asked. "Is the Pope Catholic?"

A 1973 Harley had a tremendous amount of vibration, but I had no idea how vibration could have anything to do with my hand strength. They decided to continue my OT and they would somehow simulate the vibration.

On my next appointment, the young female therapist had a device for me to try. It was a hand gripper with a pink vibrator attached - a.k.a. sex toy. I am not sure who blushed more, she or I, when the rest of the nurses laughed at the homemade contraption.

It showed those therapists knew exactly what they were doing. It also showed their creativity to harness a sex toy as a hand-gripper. When I used the ridiculous looking device, the strength in my right hand had dropped by a whopping eighty-five percent. I was stunned! What if I had returned to duty on a motorcycle without knowing what vibration would do to my strength? Let's not go there.

A few more weeks of occupational therapy and I was released, just short of a year after the accident. I returned to full duty. Going back to work this time was so different from my return after I had been shot. The challenges were going to be all physical. My mind was pretty straight. The only question was whether I could perform my duties as well I had done them before the bike accident.

# CHAPTER TWENTY
## *The Pope in Boston, 1979*

My case was going nowhere, but I still held out hope. We needed a miracle if we were going to catch the gang of robbers who had shot me. We had to indict them before the statute of limitations ran out in June of 1980.

It was 1979 and Pope John Paul II was coming to Boston. It would be an historic event: the first Papal visit to the city, and those of the Catholic faith were looking forward to his visit and so was I. The planning for his arrival had gone on for a year. The MDC Police would be involved in security because the Papal motorcade would pass along many MDC roadways. There would be officers on foot, horseback, cruisers, helicopters, boats and motorcycles. The Papal visit somehow gave me hope that justice in my case would be served.

My wife had been working as a nurse in a nursing home. She told her patients (residents) I would be involved in the security for the Papal visit. I had been assigned to a post on an overpass in South Boston overlooking the Southeast Expressway, a major Boston highway artery that feeds traffic to the South Shore. My job was to make sure the area was secured, as the motorcade passed underneath. Even though I had enough seniority to join TOPS, Bob and I were the junior men on the motorcycle squad. The senior bike officers would be assigned to escort the motorcade and would be sent to the airport to meet the plane. I had no issue at all with that. I was always a strong believer in paying dues. However, a huge part of me would have loved to be in the actual motorcade.

As the date for the John Paul II's visit grew near, the network of elderly Catholic ladies at the nursing facility decided to give my wife rosary beads, relics and other religious items to be blessed by His Holiness. After I explained to my wife I would only see the Pope pass under me, we came up with a plan. We carefully wrapped each item and I put them in the locked fiberglass saddlebags on my police Harley. I knew the Holy Father would bless and wave to the crowd as he passed by, and hoped the blessings would blow my way, onto the ladies' treasures. It was the best I could do.

This would be a once in a lifetime opportunity for these women. Most were in wheelchairs, and could only watch the Holy Father's visit on television. Their excitement grew as everyone hoped I would have their items blessed by His Holiness. These women were precious and nothing got by them. They were focused on a mission, not unlike I was.

With my saddlebags full of the religious items, I prepared my motorcycle for the big day. It was the same 1973 Harley that had been wrecked when I was hit by the drunken sailor. It had been rebuilt from the frame up and looked better than new in the dark green and white coloring. I washed and waxed it, and polished the chrome until it shined. My bike would be spotless, despite the forecast of heavy rain. We were ordered to wear our dress uniform, with a reflective safety cross strap but *no* raingear - we wanted to look our best for this momentous occasion.

The world was watching as the Holy Father landed at Logan Airport in East Boston, on October 1, 1979. He landed in a green Aer Lingus jet with a huge shamrock on the tail.

*I wondered why he used the Irish airline, because I thought the church owned Alitalia at the time. He had flown aboard a specially modified Boeing 747 (EI-ASI or St. Patrick) from Rome to*

*Dublin and later from Shannon to Boston. I learned later Aer Lingus was the only other airline, in addition to Alitalia, John Paul II traveled in.*

He was greeted at the airport by the then First Lady Rosalynn Carter and Cardinal Humberto S. Medeiros, Archbishop of the Catholic Archdiocese of Boston.

The Cathedral of the Holy Cross, the mother church of the Catholic community was located in Boston's South End and would be the first stop for the motorcade. It was the largest Catholic Church in New England, and where the Archbishop celebrated Mass.

The police radio crackled as the motorcade left the airport and wound its way through East Boston, the Italian neighborhood of the city, and then on to the Irish stronghold of South Boston. Both areas were heavily populated with generations of people of the Catholic faith.

I was at my post on the Expressway at Exit 17 - over Columbia Road in South Boston. The route of the motorcade was marked by yellow marine grade rope on both sides of the street. The crowds were huge despite the relentless, pouring rain.

As the motorcade approached my post, I looked down at the long line of police cars and motorcycles. It seemed to go on forever. There were one hundred and fifteen motorcycles assigned to the Papal Motorcade from various agencies. Boston had never witnessed anything of this magnitude, not even when the President of the United States came to town. He had been God's special designee, I thought to myself.

Always keeping an eye on the crowd, I watched as the motorcade passed under my post and then saw the Holy Father's opened-top limo. The Pope was smiling, waving and blessing the wet throngs of spectators. Some of the other cops on the post with me snapped a few photos with cameras they kept dry in the saddlebags of their bikes. I wished I had thought to bring mine. It was awe inspiring to see the leader of my church. My fellow motorcycle officers surrounded the limo along with Boston P. D. and State Police bikes.

As he passed under the overpass, I felt an aura run through me. I had never felt anything like it and was beyond belief. It must have been the field of energy surrounding him. It felt like a statically charged wave of energy sending shivers down my spine and yet it was a very peaceful feeling. It was so powerful, it felt like a strong gust of wind and the power of his presence nearly knocked me over.

Our orders were simple: we were to hold our position until Headquarters advised us to secure. I was just winding down when a general broadcast came over the police radio that changed everything.

"After the motorcade passes by, all MDC motorcycles are to fall in behind the motorcade," Met Control informed us over the radio.

Something was up. The pre-scheduled plans seldom changed. When the call came in, the Papal motorcade was already a half mile past my location.

The radio squelched, "All motorcycles not already assigned to the motorcade are to report to the Traffic Oriented Patrol Squad (TOPS) Commander at the Holy Cross Cathedral."

My heart was pounding as I climbed onto my bike, pushed the starter button and revved up the engine to a deep-throated roar before taking off. I sped down the ramp with blue lights flashing and siren wailing to work my way through the throngs of onlookers. The other three MDC motorcycles with me screamed down Dorchester Avenue, as we tried to catch up and take our place at the rear of the Papal motorcade.

As we drove past the re-routed intersections, more and more Boston and MDC bikes joined in. We had the ambulance and tail car in sight.

*The tail car, a marked police car, is always found at the end of a motorcade and also known as the crash car. If an unauthorized vehicle attempts to interfere with the motorcade, the tail car swings into action and crashes against the intruder, if necessary.*

Arriving at the Cathedral, we were briefed on a situation that obviously had been planned for by Boston and Secret Service intelligence. A large group of protesters on the route across the street were intent on blocking the route, halting the motorcade.

I was assigned to a new position by a Secret Service agent, along with another MDC cop and two Boston P. D. bikes. We were told to hang loose while the Pope said a service for many local priests in the Cathedral. After the service was over, we would take the Pope out the side street exit, then back onto the original roped-off motorcade route. A decoy motorcade would drive towards the demonstrators.

The Holy Father got into the limo, while three Secret Service Agents climbed up and onto the rear of a black, heavily armored 'Presidential' Lincoln Limousine. On the front right fender was the American flag and on the left, the Papal flag.

We were informed there had been sightings of at least two people with guns along the parade route.

The agent addressed our group of four motorcycle cops, "Each of you stay on the limo to cut down the angle of fire. I don't care if the Pope himself tells you to back off. Stay there!"

He specifically told me to stay on the right rear fender of the limo, no matter what.

I thought, 'I would much rather take a bullet for the head of my church, than for most politicians.'

*It may seem hard to believe anyone would try and kill a religious figure, but, on May 13, 1981, just six years after his Boston visit, John Paul II was shot and severely wounded in an assassination attempt. After that attempt, He only rode in the 'Pope-mobile,' a converted Range Rover with a bullet proof clear glass box on the back. The Pope could stand and wave and bless the crowds in safety.*

But in 1979, the Pope still traveled in an open car. I had my bullet proof vest on under my Class A uniform and was ready to do my duty. I also was wearing a Saint Michael medal on a chain around my neck, which my wife had given to me when I returned to duty after being shot. Protecting the Holy Father was a high honor. I had come a long way, having grown up in a small town. I was just in the right place, at the right time...maybe it had been fate.

I was standing down, but had to be ready to go in a moment's notice if something went wrong. I tried to relax, but my mind wouldn't let me. I was on full alert. I could never understand how the Secret Service Agents did it day after day.

When the church service ended, the protesters became very vocal and the protest signs were held up. I stood at parade rest, next to my bike as the other motorcycle cops did. The Holy Father walked out slowly, holding his pastoral staff, followed by a line of bishops and priests. He stopped and gave us, his security team, a special blessing. I couldn't wait to tell the ladies at the nursing home. Their items ***had been blessed*** by the Pope - and not just by a wave in the air as He drove by.

We saddled up and proceeded down the back streets which were not on the marked route. People stopped and waved to the Pope in disbelief. The demonstrators were outsmarted and after a few blocks, we returned to the roped-off, intended route. I doubt the Pope even knew what the Secret Service and Boston Police had pulled off so smoothly.

I stayed on the right rear fender like I was welded to it, almost close enough to touch the Holy Father. We headed to the Boston

Common. There was an outdoor Mass planned and the crowd was one of the largest ever gathered in city history. It was cold. The rain was pelting down and the windshield on my bike was not keeping the rain out of my eyes. I reached into the small bag on the handlebars and slipped on a pair of pilot's sunglasses...all I had to protect my eyes.

Dana Owen assigned to the Papal Limo

The look on the faces of the people as they saw the Holy Father was one of joy. Flowers were thrown at the limo and our motorcycles were covered in blossoms and baby's breath.

*I brought home two of the sprigs of baby's breath. My wife preserved them and put a sprig into each of our daughters' bridal bouquets when they were married.*

The roar of our bikes seemed distant. I sat as tall on my bike as I could, as we wound our way to the Boston Common for the outdoor Mass.

The most striking thing was the contrast of colors. The sky was almost black and a fog hung over the tall buildings, hiding the tops from view. The alternating white headlights of the escort cars and the flashing blue and red lights of the motorcycles pierced through the murky fog. A sea of colored umbrellas and rain gear of the crowds made the scene surreal.

From time to time, I looked to my left at John Paul II. He was wearing a red hat trimmed in gold, known in Italian as a *saturno* because its wide lips resemble the rings around the planet Saturn. He wore a red cape over his white clothing. Looking from side to side, he looked right at me and smiled knowingly. In that brief moment, I felt he looked *inside* me, not just at me. I am sure it seemed that way due to my Catholic upbringing, but it did not diminish the feeling. This was the best assignment I had ever had. Pride was the only word that described how I felt. A deep, welling pride surged throughout my whole being. I was so proud to be there, protecting the leader of my church.

The crowd at the State House was so large, it overflowed into the street and we could hardly navigate the corner on the last leg of the motorcade. Despite the deep puddles and heavy rain, we arrived at Boston Common.

> *Motorcycles did not perform well in water or deep puddles and would break down or stall. But not one of the more than one hundred motorcycles broke down that day. I thought that, in itself, was a minor miracle.*

The motorcade pulled up behind the huge stage on the Boston Common erected for the Mass. We got off the motorcycles and stood at attention as the Pope made his way to the elevated altar on the stage.

The crowd was estimated at over 400,000 people. The cold rain could not dampen the spirits of those celebrating the first Papal visit to the city. The cheers of the crowd were deafening and the flashes of thousands of cameras lit up the sky like lightning.

During the Mass, I stood beside my motorcycle with the rest of the members of the motorcade, waiting to escort his Holiness to the Cardinal's Residence in Brighton. A priest came to our location to offer Holy Communion to those involved in the protection detail. I could not help but think how my Dad had passed away at the young age of thirty-two after surviving the bloody D-Day Invasion. At age thirty-two myself, I had survived two gunshot wounds and a motorcycle accident, and was escorting the head of my church.

BACK AT THE nursing home, the elderly residents had watched the motorcade and the entire event on television. When my wife saw me in the motorcade, she pointed me out to the enthusiastic group. She told me they were thrilled I had been so close to the Pope. When I brought in the items 'blessed' by the Holy Father, the ladies were very low key. They told me they never had any doubt I would succeed in my mission. They had prayed for me to complete the task and told me it was simply answered prayers.

DESPITE THE MANY photographs of the members of the motorcade taken with a dignitary, I never received one photograph. We always had our picture taken by the Secret Service. We had escorted the President of the United States, Jimmy Carter, and photos were taken of us shaking hands with him and other dignitaries at Logan Airport. In fact, I had my picture taken with four Presidents, including Ronald Reagan with his wife Nancy, when he campaigned for President. I never got any of those photos and wondered if there was film in their cameras.

This time, I worked hard to get some of the pictures of me next to the Papal Limo. I was one of hundreds of cops who had the same idea. Bill Brett, a friend to all the cops in Boston, was the photo editor for the Boston Globe. I think Bill knew the first name of almost every cop in Boston. He looked through stacks of photos and found a great shot of the Pope and me, which hangs on the wall of my home office. He also made several copies for my kids and grandkids.

Much later, around Christmas time, my wife and I were doing some shopping at a mall book store. I hated shopping and still do. I was bored and not pleased to be there. Then I saw several photo journals of the Papal Visit. Looking through one of the books, The Pope in America a Pictorial Visit, there, only a few pages in, I saw myself in living color, riding just behind and on the right rear of the Papal limousine. I tried to get my wife's attention without yelling across the store. I was so excited I yelled anyway. Of the 115 motorcycles in the Boston visit, I was the only one shown in the book. Maybe my luck was changing. Maybe I was destined to catch the guys who shot me after all.

Dana Owen turning the corner at the State House Boston, MA

What were the chances I could be shot twice in the head, and survive? Or that I would be hit by a car while riding a motorcycle and my leg would be spared more serious injury? Or that I would be involved in the Papal motorcade? I think there must have been a guardian angel looking over me. I not only thought it - I knew it - and still do. This was my personal belief after surviving events few do. I took the printing of my picture in the book as a good omen. In fact, I took it as a sign from heaven. I bought all three copies of the book they had in stock.

My batteries had been recharged. I felt a state of grace with an inner glow from the Papal visit and possibly intervention from heaven. Now, with the Pope safely back in Rome, it was time to return to the pursuit of the thugs who came close to killing me with their shotgun. I was ready and I felt the Holy Spirit was by my side.

Author's note: Pope John Paul II was canonized as a Saint on April 28, 2014.

My Dad 1st Lieutenant Carlton A. Owen
U.S. Army Corps of Engineers - World War II

My Dad (right) in France - World War II
('Flo' on Jeep's bumper was my Mom's name)

Sergeant Dana Owen Massachusetts State Police
Retirement photo -1997

Front Row: Officer Jack Flynn, Commission William Geary,
Officer James Bruce and Officer Dana Owen
Back Row: Officer William Thompson(with beard) and
Officer William Shanley

Officer Owen ID Folder – 1970

My Memory Book

Dana and Bob Power 2013 MDC Reunion

Bill O'Leary, Dana Owen, Roger Hunt

# CHAPTER TWENTY-ONE
## *Assigned to the Case*

I felt a sense of desperation about the case now. The federal statute of limitations would run out on my shooting case all too soon. We had just about four months to bring charges or the suspects would walk free. I wasn't sure how I would deal with such a crushing defeat. Along with desperation came depression. I still had severe post traumatic headaches from the night I was shot and left to die, and they worsened as the deadline neared. I had to take some kind of action. I tried to think of what I could do to help and tried to come up with a plan...a new idea...anything!

It was February of 1980, almost five years since the hijacking. We had identified the men involved, but still didn't have enough evidence against them to bring a case that would hold up in court. Trying to figure out what we had missed, I would think about it all day long and wouldn't sleep at night. When I did close my eyes, the flashback of the gun falling from my hand filled my mind, something which had not occurred in years. I couldn't believe these guys would skate scot-free of all charges by early summer. This was not the way I envisioned this chase ending.

After struggling with what to do, I decided to call the Postal Inspectors assigned to the case.

"Bill? Could you and Fred meet me for lunch?"

"Sure, Dana. What's up?"

"I want to give this one last shot."

"Meet us at the Howard Johnson's at Wellington Circle in Medford at 11:30 a.m. I'll have Fred with me."

Bill and Fred had never kissed me off in all the years they had worked on the case. They were true professionals and we had become close friends. They knew more about me and my family than most of my friends. I knew they wanted to solve this case as much as I did. It had become personal for them, too.

I met them for lunch and told them we just could not just give up like this. Maybe, I told them, we had missed something. I was willing to go over all the old reports - to take another look.

To my surprise Bill said, "Do you want to work with us full time on the case?"

Trying to seem calm and confident, but with my heart beating hard inside, I said, "Sure."

This was beyond anything I expected. I was speechless. My mind raced with excitement at the opportunity, but at the same time, I wondered if my bosses would let me work full-time on this case. The problem was I was not an investigator, but a street cop. But Bill and Fred told me not to worry - they would make the arrangements.

The next day when I reported for duty at 10 a.m., I was called into the MDC Detective Unit, which was across the hall from the Traffic Oriented Patrol Squad. The two men in charge of the Detectives were sitting in the office. I was told to close the door and sit down. Yes, I was nervous and I wondered what they were going to say. I did not want to get my hopes up and then have them dashed.

The Detective in charge Detective Lieutenant Thomas Keough spoke first, "At the request of the Postal Inspectors, I am putting you on special assignment."

His tone and mood were serious and business-like. In fact, he was so serious, he made me uncomfortable. I wasn't sure if he was angry, or if he felt I had done an end run around him.

Detective Sgt. Tom White spoke next, "You are to report only to me and you're not to tell anyone what you are working on. Is that clear?"

"Yes Sir. But what if my TOPS boss wants to know what I am doing?"

"You tell him to talk to me," he almost barked at me. "No one needs to know what you are doing - no exceptions." The Detective Sgt. made that crystal clear. "You will report to Postal Inspectors O'Leary and Ricker Monday morning in plain clothes. All of your reports will be addressed to me and we will only talk in private about the case, not on the phone. The other detectives in my unit are not to know what you are doing and they will be told not to ask you. Do you have any questions?"

"No, Sarge."

"Good luck - Be careful."

"Thank you - I will," I said, and walked out of their office.

I was both nervous and elated. I could work on the case full time. I was officially assigned to the federal case, a rare opportunity for a uniformed cop.

I had to tell my boss, the TOPS Lieutenant, I had been re-assigned. He was the one who had asked Bob and me to join the unit and was disappointed to hear I was leaving. He demanded to know what I would be doing in the Detective Unit. I asked him to talk to the Detective boss. He told me to wait in his office, while he went across the hall.

He came back and said, "I hope you know what you're doing." I hoped so, as well.

As a parting shot he said, "Of course, I will have to assign your motorcycle to someone else." That part hurt. He knew how much this piece of steel meant to me and how much I loved riding it.

"Yes Sir," I said, trying to conceal my disappointment over losing my prized Harley.

The TOPS clerk who drew up my transfer papers seemed to have a sixth sense about things - he had the ability to know things before they happened, like Radar O'Reilly in the TV show M*A*S*H.

He pulled me aside and said, "I better see your picture on the front page of the Boston Globe."

I just smiled and said, "That makes two of us." I wondered what he was thinking about when he made that comment.

WITH MY NEW assignment to the Postal Inspectors, I faced an important issue. What do I wear for plain clothes? Shiny black police shoes and white socks - my standard - weren't going to cut it. I had been in uniform for five years and had scant civilian outfits. I couldn't be a 'suit' like the Feds. I needed my own look. Of course, I had to look cool like the television and movie detectives.

So, off I went to the local Sears store, charge card in hand to buy a few 'detective outfits.' I asked my my wife to come along, because my taste in clothes was non-existent. Brown was the only color I liked.

We picked out casual slacks, brown of course, and dark colored socks. Oxford cloth shirts in blue seemed perfect to go along with a couple of sport coats in classic tweed and a corduroy blazer (brown, once again). I needed a few neckties and would let her pick those out. If I was going to be a detective, I thought I needed a trademark. Trench coats were the style, but not for me.

After careful consideration, I decided my signature look would be a pair of brown cowboy boots. There were not that many Massachusetts cowboys, but I had seen many detectives on TV shows wearing boots. Besides, Wyatt Earp wore boots and I liked the television show when I was a kid. Did I imagine myself something akin to a western marshal? Yup…afraid so.

The boots were perfect, I thought to myself. Not only would folks quickly notice my distinctive look, but a boot had a practical side too. It was the perfect place to tuck my snub-nose revolver in a special holster. And, boots fit right in with the newspaper story.

> *The newspapers inaccurately labeled it a 'wild west shootout.' Shootout was hardly the right term; it had been more of 'a shot at.' Neither my partner nor I ever fired a shot, for fear of hitting a bystander. We had been out-manned and out-gunned. Those who shot me had no rules whatsoever and only wanted to escape. We played by the rules, which put us at a disadvantage and gave them the upper hand. That went along with the badge.*

The weather was cold, so I would need a hat. No brainer there - it would be a Scally cap, the kind both my grandfathers always wore. It was warm, wool and made in Ireland. A pork pie hat just didn't cut it.

Feeling pretty spiffy and making sure all the sales tags were off my new duds, I reported for duty at the Postal Annex in South Boston. The structure looked like it had huge tailpipes coming out of one side of the building, facing the Four Point Channel. I thought they were air-conditioning vents and maybe they were. I was told one of the bosses of the Postal Service had been an Admiral. He wanted to make the building look like the back of an aircraft carrier.

And, of course, this is where the hijacked truck pulled out the night of the hijacking. The Gang's inside man had worked here. His duty was to mark the truck for the hijackers so they would stop the one carrying the $100,000 cash payroll destined for Vermont.

I was given credentials and a temporary pass to get into the secure Inspection Office. I was even assigned a parking space where the Inspectors parked, inside the security gates. Everything was going great, except my feet were killing me. I had not had time to break in my new cowboy boots. They were stiff and truly uncomfortable. Within hours, I had some nasty blisters on my heels. I wanted to stand tall and look cool. I wondered what my face looked like as I clenched my teeth with each step, trying not to limp.

I met with the Inspectors assigned to the case. Bill and Fred were the team leaders and there were new, younger Inspectors, too. It was a great feeling to be part of a team once more. After the introductions and all the variations of welcome aboard, it was time to get down to work. We were very aware of the calendar's rapid march. I was given several large, expandable file folders full of reports, documents, photos and the case number for the hijacking.

The secretary who really ran the office asked, "How do you take your coffee, Dana?"

"Black, no sugar, please. Is there any other way?" I asked, and started to pore through the huge stack of documents.

The first few days were spent reading, broken up with many cups of coffee and take-out sandwiches from a local deli. As I looked over the reports in my file, I was in awe of the amount of information they had gathered and the professional way the reports were written. There was so much circumstantial evidence. The one thing still missing was a witness, a witness who would put the gang members at the scene of the crime that night. All we had so far was hearsay.

# CHAPTER TWENTY-TWO
## *Tricky Business*

My job was to continue the surveillance of our suspects. I had done it on my own for so many years, but now I could use the Feds' secure radio channels and access many different types of vehicles. They had great toys, like periscopes in vans marked as phone company vehicles, taxis, etc. It was all so hi-tech for 1980. It sure beat the MDC for resources.

Back at the MDC, rumors spread fast. When the word got out I had been assigned to work plain clothes, many of my fellow cops questioned what I was working on and who the targets were. I had to be careful about what I said. It was a good policy to hold important information close to my chest. Loose lips do sink ships and I wanted mine to stay afloat t. I didn't even tell my wife how deeply I was involved.

In the uniformed division, a rumor had been spread I was working for the Internal Affairs Division (IAD), investigating a few MDC cops out of work on suspected phony injuries. How they came up with that one, I never knew. I shared the same distain for IAD as most street cops, but it was a double-edged sword. My shooting had occurred so long ago, I doubted anyone would figure out what I was really doing. Then again, I was sure the cops who knew me would never believe I would work for IAD.

I HAD TO be really careful about how I proceeded. Rumors of corruption inside our agency had been circulating for a few years - investigations involving wiretaps and issues with other federal agencies kept many in a paranoid state. The scandal known as 'Exam Scam' hit the news and made the mistrust in the atmosphere even worse. Many cops, throughout the State, had been suspected of cheating on promotional exams. Chiefs of Police and high brass in many departments were involved. It seemed all of law enforcement was getting a black eye in the media. Suspicion about bad cops was not uncommon in police work, nor was it unfounded. I hoped there were only a few corrupt cops on my job, but even one was too many. Unfortunately, there were more.

I was also concerned about another issue. My fellow cops worked and lived in the Somerville area, and some of them knew and grew up with the suspects in my shooting. I just didn't want them to spoil my case by a simple slip of the tongue to the hijackers.

There had been no real activity from the Ten Hills Gang after the Hilltop robbery. They had gone quiet, either lying low or out on the lam. Grider was in prison for the Hilltop robbery and the murder of the Wells Fargo Guard. James Hackett had been found *not guilty*, a huge travesty of justice. Murnane, the alleged wheelman, had been on the run for four years. He had been captured in Phoenix, Arizona in August of 1979, and then, suddenly, the charges against him for armed robbery and first degree murder were dropped. He walked in and out of the system way too easily. I guess this was how informants were treated.

Then, a ray of hope appeared on the gloomy horizon. I was told by a source an inmate, doing time in New Hampshire, claimed to have information vital to the mail hijacking case. The inmate had ties to the gang at the Ten Hills Café. He was waiting for his upcoming trial and looking at some serious jail time. He hoped to make a deal for a more lenient sentence.

I reached out to my friend and MDC cop, Paul Halpin, who had helped me ID the photos taken by the Postal Inspectors just after my shooting. I asked Paul if he knew a Kevin Trainor, the inmate who had reached out to make a deal. Paul said he not only knew Trainor, but told me he "played Little League Baseball in Somerville with him and he was the best man at my wedding before we both went into the Army and went our separate ways."

Paul had grown up in the Memorial Road projects in Somerville and, if I had to guess, he had been as tough as any kid in the projects. And…he knew many of the players in my case. Back in 1975, Paul had been at the Hilltop arraignments in Lynn at the request of Detective Lt. Jack Dwyer. His job was to identify the gang members who came to intimidate the witnesses. He knew Grider and David Toppi since childhood and could identify the rest of the crew by sight.

I asked my MDC detective bosses if I could include Paul and another MDC cop, Billy Thompson in the investigation. Billy and I had been close friends for years. I had worked with him before and he was a great undercover cop and skilled in the art of surveillance.

Detective Lt. Tom Keough said, "Dana, this is your case. I am giving you free rein."

Trainor had been jailed on bank robbery and the kidnapping charges. He and an associate were accused of kidnapping bank executives' wives and demanding money for their release. It was a great ransom scam, until a victim dropped a note out of the window of the suspects' car. It fell at the feet of an MDC cop on traffic duty at Leverett Circle (near the Science Museum) in Boston. It read - I am being kidnapped. HELP!!! The pair was arrested and faced serious state prison time.

Our potential informant seemed promising. Trainor was a veteran of the system and had been known to associate with the Ten Hills Gang. The big question was whether he had been a participant in the hijacking. His name had never come up in our investigation. He, too, had become a jailhouse informant and had been moved to New Hampshire, probably for his own protection.

Trainor was looking for a deal on his upcoming sentencing. In return, he would tell us what he knew about the hijacking. The Feds told me to be very cautious and promise nothing. This was my first interview and I wanted to get it right. Paul and I went to the state prison in NH. When we met Trainor, he was not happy Paul had come along. I let them size each other up for a little bit, and after they exchanged some pleasantries about the old days, things settled down and I got down to business. I was upfront and told him I could not guarantee anything, but if his information was good, I would discuss his case with the Postal Inspectors. He asked me to name the guys I thought were in the getaway car that night. It was a test to see what I knew. I was not sure if I should lay all my cards on the table, but time was not on my side. With nothing to lose at this stage, I named the four suspects. I was not sure if we had the fourth guy's identity right. I wondered if Trainor would name himself as the other participant.

"Okay, Kevin," I replied, "Richie Murnane was the wheelman, John Grider was in the front passenger seat of the getaway car. In the back was David Toppi, who was joined by Jimmy Hackett, after he bailed out of the hijacked truck."

Trainor laughed and said, "You got three of 'em, but you're wrong on one."

Questions started racing, one after another, in my head, "Was Trainor the fourth guy after all? Maybe…maybe not. Had I missed something? Or is he just playing me?"

"Which one's wrong Kevin? Toppi?" I took a gamble.

We had David Toppi or Peter Hackett as the fourth suspect in the car, but needed more proof.

"Yup, it was Peter Hackett, Jimmy's brother, and he's covering his brother's ass," the experienced inmate smugly replied.

"Are you willing to testify to that in court?" I asked.

"If the deal is good enough," Kevin smirked.

We shook hands and I told him we would be in touch. Paul and I went back to Boston to meet with the Postal Inspectors. We reported our findings, but Trainor's information came from overheard conversations at the Ten Hills Café. The information was third-hand and, thus, would be considered hearsay in court. I had just made my first stumble as an investigator. I hoped it would be my last. Back to square one. Again.

# CHAPTER TWENTY-THREE
## *Immunity*

After pleading *guilty* to second degree murder in the Hilltop Affair, John Grider had been incarcerated at the Massachusetts Correctional Institution (MCI) in Norfolk. Shortly after I was put on special assignment, Postal Inspectors O'Leary and Ricker told me they had interviewed Grider back on September 2, 1977. They had worked hard to get him to testify before the grand jury.

As a participant in the crimes of June 16, 1975 (my shooting), he could place the suspects in the car and describe the conspiracy leading up to the crime. The inmate said he would be willing to talk about the hijacking, but before he did he wanted immunity from prosecution. I had been cautiously optimistic this would be the break we had hoped for. At the same time, I tried not to get my hopes too high.

The Postal Inspectors had agreed to grant Grider federal immunity and formally applied for it on September 15, 1977. It would take a little over two years of red tape before the request was approved.

After the United States First District Court in Boston granted him federal immunity, we had to apply for state Immunity. Without both state and federal immunity, Grider could still be charged with an old crime, a risk he would not take. But even with the protection of both types of immunity, there was a 'Catch-22,' and that meant there was a problem. Bill explained the situation to me. As part of Grider's plea agreement, he would 'not do Walpole time.' MCI-Walpole State Prison had a bad reputation, and Grider felt he would not be safe there. 'Walpole' was a hell-hole maximum security prison. During this period, Walpole had an 'execution squad' going. Tommy Sperraza was killing people inside, sometimes for money, and roughly a murder a month. One inmate was strangled with his bathrobe. His penis had been pulled off and stuffed into his mouth. It was a message to the 'rats.'

Grider had testified against James Hackett during the Hilltop Murder trial, but Hackett had been found *not guilty*. The word on the street was there was a contract on Grider for testifying against Hackett. The word on the street was extremely accurate. When a contract was rumored to be put out on someone, it was almost always true. Grider's concerns had been real.

The inspectors told me Grider was sent to MCI-Norfolk, a medium security prison, but he was relocated to MCI-Walpole after a fight with another inmate. Shortly after this transfer, he was reportedly stabbed by another inmate. My details on this were sketchy, but those were the basics to the best of my knowledge. Was it just a fight, or was it an attempt on his life? I would guess it was the latter.

Back to the Catch: the transfer was a violation of the 'no Walpole time' agreement Grider had with the Commonwealth of Massachusetts. Even though he was transferred back to MCI-Norfolk, his lawyers filed a lawsuit against the Commonwealth for breaking the plea deal.

The players from the Commonwealth of Massachusetts set up a meeting to discuss state immunity for Grider. We were all dressed in suits for this formal meeting in a then-secret location of the Suffolk County Investigation and Prosecution Project (SCIPP) in Boston, inside a large conference room. The Feds and some of the top prosecutors from the Suffolk County and Middlesex County District Attorney's Offices were in attendance.

All of the crimes Grider had allegedly committed took place in not one, but two counties.

I was seated next to Detective Sgt. Tom White. I was certain this meeting was just a formality and he would be granted state immunity. Besides, we had a backup plan. If the five-year federal statute of limitations ran out, the hijackers could be charged with a state crime. The state statute on armed robbery (banks robberies and my shooting) was ten years, and this would give us more time.

The DAs opened the meeting by refusing to grant Grider immunity. I sat and listened in shock! Grider's lawsuit and the money associated with it were the only topics of conversation. My shooting meant nothing? Was it only all about the cost and the fallout from breaking the plea agreement?

"We are talking here about one of my officers who was almost killed," Detective Sgt. Tom White said in an exasperated tone.

One of the Postal Inspectors added, "Evidently the Commonwealth doesn't seem to understand the gravity of this federal crime and the shooting of one of its own police officers."

The conversation went back and forth as if I wasn't even present. These pompous asses could have cared less I'd been shot. I was furious and could feel my blood pressure rising and my head pounding.

I flashed back to the chase and the shotgun blasts that cracked my skull. Even though I was physically in the meeting, mentally I was back in the chase. I couldn't listen to this crap anymore. I was sweating and I had reached my boiling point. It was time to stand up and tell these so called prosecutors what I thought of them. I shoved my chair back with a loud scraping sound on the polished hardwood floor, like someone running their fingernails on a blackboard. I stood up red faced, shaking with anger.

"Hey!" I shouted, getting everyone's attention.

Detective Sgt. White grabbed me by the arm as if to pull me back down in my seat and said, "Come on, I'll buy you a coffee. Don't lower yourself to their level. You'll waste your breath." Tom White was right.

No matter what I said, it wasn't going to change their minds. The fact a cop had stopped a robbery, had been shot twice in the head and left for dead bleeding in the street, played no role whatsoever in the Commonwealth's decision. They were focused on the money part of the equation.

It was better to take the high road and walk away from an argument we couldn't win. I had to let my feelings go and put on my business face.

*To this day, their attitude still angers me. In fact my blood pressure goes up even now, thinking about it after nearly 40 years.*

Outside the meeting room we held a huddled meeting with the Inspectors.

Bill O'Leary told me, "Don't let them get to you. We can get around this."

"Some prosecution project," I laughed sarcastically.

"We will get a grant of Federal Use Immunity. That way anything Grider says to the federal grand jury or at the federal trial can't be used against him in state court or anywhere else," Bill assured me.

A good friend of mine, who was a former FBI agent, had a saying which fit this absurd situation.

"Dana, you don't understand. It's not the money...it's the money," he would often remind me.

BILL O'LEARY HAD driven me in his unmarked car to the meeting.

Bill said, "Let's call it a day and grab a sandwich and a beer."

He didn't have to twist my arm. The day had been beyond frustrating.

"I know a little dive not far from the office on West Broadway in Southie (South Boston). Not a fancy place, but they have great burgers and steak tips and if you tip the bartender good, every other beer is usually free," he said trying to cheer me up. We pulled into the parking lot and parked, then walked into the Triple O's Lounge, a place I had never heard of back then. On the front door was a big sign:

POSITIVE ID REQUIRED -
DRIVER'S LICENSE – PASSPORT.

The Triple O's Lounge

The crowd was dressed in business suits like Bill and, if I had to guess, was mostly made up of federal cops, lawyers and maybe a few local politicians. Bill was right. The steak tips were great, the bottled beer ice cold, and the third beer was on the house.

Years later, I would read about this infamous bar room in books I read about 'Whitey' Bulger and Kevin Weeks. In the 1970s and 80s, South Boston had benn quite the place.

# CHAPTER TWENTY-FOUR
## *Oxford, Wisconsin*

The U.S. Attorney's Office and the United States Postal Inspector, in charge of the Boston office, granted us permission to interview John Grider in Wisconsin, where he had been transferred for his safety following the incident at MCI Walpole.

He had been interviewed by the FBI, Massachusetts State Police, and the Postal Inspectors several times, but he had been unwilling to name names. We had hoped to get him to testify about the mail hijacking case.

It was early March 1980. The US Postal Inspectors Office held a meeting and decided Inspector Bill O'Leary would conduct the interview. Bill made the case to include me.

"Listen, Dana was the guy shot in this case. He stayed on this and kicked us in the ass, even after we were about to close this file. He was the guy there that night and the only one who will know if Grider is telling the truth. I want him with me," he said.

A street cop is not necessarily a good investigator. I was young, inexperienced and could make an unforced error. Making a mistake now, with only two months left on the statute of limitations, would end our case.

The vote for me to go was unanimous. I know it must have been difficult for them to select me as the second person. At the conclusion of the meeting, Bill pulled me aside.

He said, "Dana, I have great faith in your investigative skills, but there is no room for a slip-up now. You have to act like a pro and stay straight-faced, no matter what Grider might say."

I said with total confidence, "Bill, I give you my word. I can do it."

But I hadn't told Bill about two small glitches: there was no money from the Commonwealth for the trip and I was terrified of flying.

They had to use 'drug money' from the Police Department to buy the plane ticket. This was confiscated cash seized by our drug unit and granted to our agency by the courts. It sounded foolish, but Massachusetts was broke and it was the only way to book a flight ASAP.

So, I drove to Logan Airport in East Boston to purchase my ticket. Armed with $399 in small bills, mostly tens, fives and ones, I showed my badge and ID at the ticket counter so I would not be taken for a drug dealer. I was lucky the lady at the TWA ticket counter seemed to understand my predicament. The ticket cost $298. Bill O'Leary had already booked his flight, using his government credit card.

Hurdle number two was much bigger. I had to actually get on the plane.

Delta Fight 723 crash scene

At 11:08 a.m. on July 31, 1973, seven years earlier, Delta Flight 723 crashed at Logan Airport. It carried 89 passengers. All but two passengers died instantly when it landed short of the runway and slammed into a retaining wall at high speed. One survivor died two hours later. The other, badly burned, died December 1, 1973.

At 4 p.m. the day of the crash, I was sent along with another officer in the Fells 'paddy wagon' to pick up bodies and body parts and take them to the Southern Mortuary in Boston.

We were en route, with other State Police and Boston units, to the airport when a call came over the radio: "All Met units en route to Logan, those packages are now to be delivered to the Twin Skating Rinks on Rte. 1 in Saugus." There were so many bodies they would have to be put on ice at the hockey rink.

"310 (our call sign), 10-4," I responded.

We got in line behind a string of ambulances and police vehicles to do a job none of us wanted to do. The minutes dragged on and I tried to prepare for what I knew would be a horrific scene. I had covered fatal car accidents and seen some gory sites in my years on the police job, but I was not ready for this. The only sound in our unit was the constant chatter on the police radio and the slapping of the windshield wipers, as I watched unit after unit drive onto the runway, blue lights barely cutting through the fog and drizzle.

Then, just as it was nearly our turn to go out onto the runway, a general broadcast called, "All MDC units at Logan Airport are to secure." I turned to the partner I was working with that night, who was the senior man and driver.

"Kelley, we're outta here," I didn't have to say it twice.

I quickly answered Met Control, "10-4…310 securing."

After speaking to the officers who were at the scene of the crash, it had been obvious how many of the cops were deeply affected by the gruesome scene. I was shaken and I had not even seen what the cops, firemen and medical personnel had to endure.

One of the MDC cops at the crash scene had slipped on the foam they use to put out the jet plane fire. He landed face first in a pile of intestines.

Foam on runway at Delta crash scene

ON THE DAY of our flight to interview Grider, one of the Postal Inspectors dropped us off at Logan Airport at Terminal (a lousy word for a place to get on an airplane) 'B.'

We had some time to kill and Bill said, "Let's grab a sandwich and a drink."

"Sounds great to me, Bill," I responded.

I had no idea how I could possibly get on an airplane, with the memories of that Delta crash still in my mind. But I would have to suppress my fear to do my job. It was only fair to tell Bill I was frightened about flying and about the crash of Delta Flight 273.

Bill said, "I understand. I was called to the scene to recover the U.S. mail, which was on board."

He explained that the Postal Inspectors had to take custody of the mail and then aid in the investigation, if a crime had been committed.

After talking with Bill about the plane crash at lunch he asked, "Are you going to be Okay?"

"I don't have a choice, do I?" I said calmly, "I sure as hell can't let this stop me."

With some food and two double Jack Daniels on the rocks in me, I was as ready as I ever would be to travel. I picked up my luggage and tried not to stagger boarding the jet. I had taken my pain and anti-nausea medication for a migraine that had developed and the mix of alcohol had given me a warm buzz.

We headed to Chicago's O'Hare International Airport, where it was snowing. We flew on Piedmont Airlines, the jet with the logo of the flying speed bird on the tail.

"Would you like the window seat, Detective?" Bill asked me to calm my fears.

He knew I never used 'detective', but 'officer' in front of my name. I was a cop on special assignment. Detective was a separate grade in the Police Department, but his knack for saying the right thing at the right time made me laugh.

"Yes, I think I would Inspector," I managed a smile for the first time on the trip.

As my doctor had warned me, the cabin pressure began to bother my old head wound as we climbed in altitude.

Checking on me, Bill asked, "Are you Okay?"

"No, but let's go over things once more, and maybe it will take my mind off this damned flight."

Flying over the socked-in Great Lakes, the pilot announced, "O'Hare is snowed in at present. We will circle for a few minutes until there is a break on radar."

The minutes turned into an hour and I was getting panicky from all the circling and had killer headache.

*I don't know if you ever watched the old Twilight Zone TV shows. In one famous 1963 episode, Nightmare at 20,000 Feet, William Shatner's character saw a gremlin on the wing of the plane.*

*In fact, that episode was so popular it was repeated in 1983, with John Lithgow as the salesman who was recovering from a nervous breakdown. He thought the gremlin prying at the flaps was a hallucination, but in the Twilight Zone, you were never sure if it was real.*

I was sure that *my* monster was going to appear at any minute so I stopped looking out at the wing. I was in my own *Twilight Zone.*

"Ladies and Gentleman, we have a break in the weather. Prepare for landing," the pilot announced over the scratchy public address system.

I had a white knuckle grasp on the arms of my seat, and had to keep reminding myself to breathe. Sitting in the window seat, I watched for the runway, wanting badly to be safe on the ground. As we descended, it had been snowing so hard the runway never appeared until we touched down, the plane bouncing and braking hard, the engines roaring in full reverse thrust. All the business folks and frequent flyers applauded and cheered as we safely landed on the snow covered runway. Well, at least I was not the only one terrified on the flight.

The weather broke and we changed planes to a jet prop, a.k.a. a vomit comet. The sound of the engines were so loud, Bill and I couldn't even chat. The flight to Wisconsin was 'uneventful,' as my friends who flew frequently often responded.

The hotel we booked was called the Porterhouse Motel, tiny yet very clean. It was, not surprisingly, in Portage, Wisconsin, and a twenty minute drive from the federal prison. The cost was $35.36 per room. The area near the Federal prison was rural, to say the least.

We were at dinner in the motel's tiny dining area, and the only other patrons were a party of four. They looked like two retired couples. I doubted they were on vacation in this desolate area.

Watching the only waitress in the restaurant delivering four baked stuffed lobsters to their table, I was thinking how expensive the meals must have been. Lobsters in New England are local and are usually priced reasonably. Lobsters in Wisconsin had to be flown in and were most likely pricey.

The waitress looked like a college girl. I guessed it was her first job. A loud crash startled me and I turned to see the tray of four lobster dinners crash to the floor. The young female server was in tears and any profit for the day was lying in the pile of food and broken china at her feet. I could only hope this was not a bad omen for how our interview was going to go. I ordered a hamburger and a Jack Daniels. Bill had the same meal and his usual bottle of Budweiser beer. After dinner we both dug into our pockets to give the girl a good cash tip.

We talked about nothing but the pending interview. We discussed our roles in detail, and how I would wear a suit and look like a detective, not a street cop. It was my only suit and I saved it for weddings and funerals. Bill felt sure Grider would not know I was the cop shot in the hijacking. My picture had only appeared in a few newspapers and it was of me lying on a gurney in the ER with half of my head shaved. I trusted Bill totally and I had to hope Grider would think I was just another detective, or even a Postal inspector.

Bill assured me even if Grider knew I was the shot cop, it really did not matter. I was trying not to obsess. Bill was the expert here. After several more drinks, enough to help me sleep, I hoped, we turned in for the night.

Bill had been in touch with the prison and they were expecting us. Grider said he was willing to talk, now that he was granted Federal Use Immunity.

The thought lingered in my mind, "Will he recognize me?"

Grider had been incarcerated in the Federal Correctional Institution, Oxford, a medium security federal prison for male offenders situated in Wisconsin. The prison was sixty miles north of Madison, in the middle of nowhere.

I had only seen the inside of two correctional facilities before: the Charles Street Jail in Boston and a medium security jail in New England. Neither had been impressive.

The prison in Oxford had a whole different look. Outside there were rows and rows of high chain-link fences. On the top of the fence were coils of Concertina wire. At the base of each row of fence were multiple long coils of the wire, razor sharp and the rows were about fifteen feet apart. Escape seemed impossible. Armed guards were in the towers surrounding the prison. It seemed the guards could see for at least a mile in any direction. If this was medium security, I could not imagine maximum.

We rang the buzzer on the front door of the brick and concrete building. Above the front door were large white letters F.C.I. OXFORD. When we were asked for identification and our purpose there, we produced our documents and badges. It struck me funny that they gave Bill, a federal agent, a much harder time than me, a cop from the Metropolitan Police in Massachusetts.

After getting patted down and scanned for weapons or any metal objects, we were issued passes. The only things allowed inside the interview room were a tape recorder and our briefcases.

Our escort brought us down long, underground tunnels and through several security doors. The only decorations on the walls were in the lobby. They were pictures of the Presidents of the United States.

We walked at least an eighth of a mile. Each doorway we passed through had an iron door with bars. A guard, seated behind a bullet-proof window at each door, opened the door remotely for us. Finally, the door was opened to the interview room.

We sat down at the long interview table and a guard led Grider in. He was a man I had been chasing for five years. By his own admission, he had participated in at least three bank robberies and the Hilltop Steakhouse robbery-murder. At the time, I had only seen an artist's sketch of Grider. He looked exactly like the sketch of the suspect.

He was about 6' 2" and about 185 pounds. He was in denim prison garb and his face was very pale. I think they call it 'prison pallor.' They obviously did not get outside much in the deep snow and extreme cold.

Grider had become a well seasoned speaker when interviewed by law enforcement and he knew the rules. This would be a high stakes poker game. His demeanor was that of a poker player, holding a winning hand. I had my game face on. We needed his testimony and he knew it.

I was still afraid he knew I was the cop shot in the pursuit. Even if he did know, would it really matter now? I was still obsessing.

The guard left us and said, "When you're done, just buzz," pointing to what looked like a doorbell button.

The room was stark and there was only one tiny window on the door the guard closed. The table was long and made of wood, as were the chairs. There were no distractions for the interviewee to look at.

It was a strange feeling to see him sitting across the table from me and I was uncomfortable. To me, Grider had been the shadowy figure I only read about in reports and interviews by other agencies. Now, I was looking at him, man to man. I had to block out all my emotions and act like a pro.

"I am Inspector Bill O'Leary and this is Dana Owen."

The inmate nodded and we sat down. We did not shake hands but flashed our ID cards at Grider. Bill opened his brief case and handed Grider a copy of the U.S. District Court order granting him immunity.

Grider's opening line was a show stopper.

"I've changed my mind. I'm not talking. I want my lawyer, Ralph Champa, to be here," he announced.

Neither one of us could believe our ears. I had no idea what to say. I hoped Bill and his experience would save the day. O'Leary, like a father figure, calmly told our witness the facts of life.

"This is your last chance, John. Once the statute runs out on the mail robbery, you have nothing to deal," Bill said and sat back, as if he was holding four of a kind.

I just sat there and tried to look as confident as the veteran investigator did, but inside my gut was heaving. The whole thing was going up in flames. I was never much of a poker player, but I would bet Bill was. Maybe the gang member was just trying to flex his muscles one last time. Maybe he truly held the winning hand. I had no idea what to do next.

Inspector O'Leary quickly turned into 'Father' O'Leary. Like several old Irish priests I knew from my childhood, he began to counsel Grider as though he was a parishioner.

I flashed back to when I was a giggling boy at Mass, as young boys do. Father Riley was a tall white haired priest. If he caught you giggling, he would walk you up and down the aisles by the hand during Mass, just to embarrass you. If you were 'walked' by him once, you never misbehaved again. Grider became one of the unruly boys, and Bill, the Irish priest would walk him.

As I was flashing back to childhood, I wondered what the inmate was thinking. I just sat in wonder while Bill explained to Grider we were there to help him. Bill was so sincere he even had me convinced we were there to help the inmate. This was way above any training I had learned in interview techniques. Bill's patience and experience clearly showed.

"I'm not a rat. I want them to get what they deserve for leaving me for dead," Grider emphasized.

"You're not a rat. You are doing the right thing, John. I can understand how you felt when your buddies abandoned you," Bill consoled.

"I told them I wanted to go to my friend's house. Instead, when I passed out they left me for dead in the street," Grider said.

"You have good reason to testify against them, John. Anyone in your shoes would do the same thing," Father O'Leary assured his parishioner.

"I really want my lawyer here," Grider interjected.

"John, there is nothing more he can do for you. He knows you have immunity from anything you tell us or say in court. I just spoke with him a few days ago," Bill said, calmly.

There was a long pause as each of the gamblers examined the cards in his hands. After several minutes of dead silence, Grider said, "Okay...I'll talk."

"You're doing the right thing. Let me turn the tape recorder on," Bill said.

"Hold on a minute. I want to clear some things up first, before you start recording." Grider said.

"Sure, John. Go ahead. It's off."

He went on and on about how he never got a share of the $57,682 from the Hilltop Robbery. He told us how they were supposed to give it to his friend if anything went wrong during the robbery. Maybe, just maybe, he had a premonition, like I had in the police academy, about getting shot.

I had thought about this meeting for weeks, and had lost a lot of sleep over it. I could see myself screwing up the case in the last of the ninth inning. Instead, I found myself having *sympathy* for this guy. I never thought I would have this emotion! But, face to face, it was how I felt. Bill had used compassion and I would, too.

This had been an interview, not an interrogation. We had to make him comfortable or he would never talk. The bantering back and forth went on for at least 10 minutes. The suspense was killing me. He told us how, after one of the bank jobs, he gave his share of the money to their lawyer, for a legal defense fund, just in case. The way a bad guy reasoned things was incredible.

"Ready now, John?" Bill asked.

"Yeah, turn it on."

"This is W. J. O'Leary. The date is March 25, 1980 out at Oxford, Wisconsin. I want to talk to John about the hijacking of a Star Route vehicle in Boston, MA, on June 16, 1975 and the particulars surrounding that hijacking. John, how many people were involved in the actual hijacking?" O'Leary asked his first question.

"Four," John replied.

The interview got going. John went on to name names and gave details on the planning, execution of the hijacking and all the people involved. There had been a total of six. He knew details only a participant could know. For example, he told us what they were each wearing for a disguise, the clothes each wore and what type of gun each used.

We were sure of the roles of all of the other players and conspirators. The only question we really had in our minds was: who was the fourth occupant in the follow-car? Would he name David Toppi, with whom he reportedly robbed the banks, along with Jimmy Hackett? Or would he name Peter Hackett, Jimmy's brother? From day one, we heard these two individuals named by informants. It was a toss-up as to whom Grider would name.

He named Peter Hackett.

Grider went on to say Peter Hackett had filled in for a guy who backed out, the same guy who had backed out of the Hilltop robbery - named David Toppi.

He told us Richie Murnane had driven the getaway car and had been armed with a revolver. Grider was in the front passenger seat 'riding shotgun,' armed with the same Walther PPK pistol he had dropped when he was shot during the Hilltop holdup. Grider told us Peter Hackett was in the back seat, behind the driver, holding a revolver. James Hackett was the one who had jumped in the back seat passenger's side, after running from the hijacked TT. He was also armed with a revolver. After the

Hackett brothers emptied their six shot revolvers at the cop car, James Hackett picked up the sawed off shotgun and blew out the rear window of the brown Ford.

Grider finally admitted to shooting at the cop car, when the car was blocked at Swanton Street. He said he hadn't fired before that time because the .32 caliber gun was not a long distance weapon.

When Grider told us James Hackett shot me with the shotgun, it was anticlimactic. I had worked on this case for so long, I felt only relief. We were finally getting what we had been looking for all these years - a participant's first-hand observations!

It was intriguing to hear the other side of the story. He had an uncanny way of making it sound as if they had done nothing wrong during the mail robbery. He told us they felt an obligation to stop and rescue their 'other guy' in the tractor trailer, Peter's younger brother, James Hackett. He said he yelled at the wheelman Munane, "Get this F***ing buggy moving!" when he saw I was right on their rear bumper on I-93. And he described the near panic and confusion as they got ready to open fire from the follow-car.

He also thought there were at least two, maybe even more MDC cruisers on I-93, pursuing them. My game of cat and mouse had confused them. There had just been one cruiser - ours. I wished there had been more.

Grider went on to say, "Whoever was driving the cruiser knew what he was doing and he pretty much stayed right on top of us. I looked at the speedometer and we were doing over 90 miles per hour."

Bill looked at me and I almost smiled at the backhanded compliment.

"We couldn't shake that cop, so we tried to scare him off," Grider said.

In his mind, they were just doing their job. Fascinating! I should have been angry, but I wasn't. Things were looking up. If there had been a window to the outside of the prison, I was sure the sun had just peeked out of the dark clouds.

As the tape ran out, we had all we needed. The interview lasted sixty minutes.

Grider asked O'Leary, "How is the MDC cop, who got shot, doing?" I must say, he seemed sincere. Bill looked at me then back to the inmate. I kept my poker face.

O'Leary replied, "He's doing Okay."

Grider requested, "When you see him, tell him no hard feelings. We couldn't shake him and he gave us no choice - we had to shoot."

Bill promised him, "I'll be sure to tell him, John."

Grider wanted to talk some more. Talking to us must have been better than being in a cell.

"Did you guys know that same MDC cop broke Jimmy's jaw one night in an alley?"

O'Leary looked at me like an impish leprechaun and said, "No. Tell us all about that."

Grider related the story of how 'the MDC cop' broke Hackett's jaw a few months after the shooting. Because his attacker was the cop he shot, he had to take it and say nothing, said Grider. Great story, but it wasn't me. It was much easier and less embarrassing for Hackett to say it was me, of course.

This was such an amazing opportunity to hear how criminals think. I was soaking it up like a sponge. At the end, we all shook hands, but the conversation seemed to continue.

O'Leary said to our witness, "See you in Boston."

Bill said, "John, I have just a few more questions. Where did you guys get the ideas for the disguises and tape on your nose?"

Grider answered, "From *Baretta.*" It was TV show starring Robert Blake, loosely based on the real life New Jersey police officer David Toma.

He went on to say, "We got most of our ideas for the robberies from cop shows on TV."

We both just shook our heads and smiled. Bill then asked Grider about a statement he had made in prior interviews.

He had said, "Someday, I will tell you something all of law enforcement should learn from the night of the mail hijacking."

Grider finally explained his comment. He said when the Hackett brothers bailed out of the getaway car, they hid behind a set of thick hedges only about 20 yards away from the car. They could see the searchlight from a helicopter pointed towards them. They ducked into the hedges and lay there, as cops arrived and were everywhere. James Hackett told Grider a K-9 cop's dog was barking and sniffing at him through the fog, as he hunkered down in the thick hedges. Hackett said the cop called to his canine partner and then dragged the dog away. Hackett guessed the cop didn't think they would have stayed that close after bailing out of the car. Once the cops were far enough away, the Hackett boys fled in the opposite direction, into the woods.

IT WAS TIME to catch our evening flight. We drove back to the airport to drop off the rental car.

Bill said, "Dana, how about a bite to eat and a 'wee taste' before we board?"

We had plenty of time so we sat down at a table in the airport lounge. Bill had his usual beer and I asked for a Jameson on the rocks.

"Would you like a double for a dollar more?" the waitress asked.

"Sure, sounds good."

I must admit these airport waitresses had a knack for twisting your arm.

Relieved was not an adequate word to describe how I felt after Grider talked with us and we had it all on tape. I asked Bill how he acted so quickly and calmly when Grider refused, at first, to talk. I thought this would be a good time to find out his trade secrets. His years of experience as an investigator had paid off in this situation. Bill laughed.

"I have no idea. I almost shit," he said.

I shook my head and laughed. Another chapter in the five-year case was under our belt.

There would be a ton of paperwork to complete. Bill needed to get the tapes transcribed. The next crucial step was to present the results of our interview to the U.S. Attorney's Office and hope they would deem it sufficient this time, to present to a grand jury.

"What do you think our chances are, Bill?" I asked.

"I would say a hell of a lot better than they were before this trip," he answered with a smile of satisfaction.

# CHAPTER TWENTY-FIVE
## *Surveillance*

We had the names of the people we would seek indictments against, but we needed to find out where all the suspects were, so when the indictments came down we could quickly arrest them. The Hackett brothers were on the top of our list. Peter Hackett was in jail in Florida on a drug charge. The word on the street was James Hackett was in his home turf of Somerville. The gang's headquarters was the logical place to start.

The Ten Hills Café was located on Mystic Avenue in Somerville, Massachusetts, a busy street used by many Boston commuters. There was a small parking lot on the left side of the brick building where the gang and regulars parked. If an outsider parked there or on Mystic Ave., the outsider's vehicle would be noticed at once. There was always a lookout posted, even if he was only a neighborhood kid aspiring to be a desperado someday.

The only real place to 'put a peek' on the Café was from the public parking lot across Mystic Ave., under I-93. There were usually a lot of cars parked in the lot, so we would try to blend in.

I was doing surveillance with Billy Thompson, my friend and a MDC undercover cop. Thompson was a year senior to me on the job and had been assigned to the narcotics division for several years. Billy was without a doubt the best undercover cop the MDC had at the time and he had busted several major drug dealers in the metropolitan Boston area.

We used different undercover vehicles, which were usually rundown and beaten up. Billy looked ratty with a scraggily beard and I tried to blend in, wearing different types of clothes, and hats or caps.

One afternoon, we thought we saw either Massachusetts State Troopers or FBI Agents in the parking lot. The car was a plain-Jane Ford, manned by two well-dressed guys. They had short, military haircuts and looked like cops. When we saw them with a camera and a telescopic lens, we had no doubt they were part of a law enforcement stakeout. I don't think they ever saw us, as Thompson was skilled at the cat and mouse game.

Later, I told my Detective Lt. Tom Keough we felt the Staties (MSP) or Feebies (FBI) had been watching the Café, just as we had. He told me the Bureau would never admit to a stakeout, so he wouldn't bother to ask them. Instead, he would check with Lt. Colonel Jack O'Donovan (MSP). O. D., as he was known, told my Lt. the State Police had no current stakeout of the Café. The next day, the same Ford was there, with the same two guys. We called Detective Lt. Keough again, who told us he would have one of our marked cars stop and ID the guys in the Ford.

"Dana, you and Billy tail them. Then use secure channel 6 and have them stopped by a marked unit, but far from the Café. I don't want to burn them," Keough advised us.

We began to tail them from a safe distance and gave the marked unit our location as we headed down the highway towards Boston. After the marked MDC unit stopped the Ford, they radioed "Troopers" over the private channel.

When we arrived back at our Detective Unit, I heard Detective Lt. Keough on the phone with O. D, who was screaming obscenities at him, wanting to know who the hell Keough thought he was by stopping his guys. Well, so much for cooperation between the MDC and the State Police - and so much for intra-departmental honesty. The next day, the unmarked Ford was missing from the parking lot. For the record, O. D. was known as a great investigator.

A week later I was partnered again, with my TOPS buddy, Paul Halpin, who had grown up in Somerville. I picked up Paul and Billy Thompson at the Wellington Circle Fells Station. A patrolman from the MDC Police Academy (in the same building) asked if he could ride along.

He said, "I've never been on a stakeout and maybe I can use this experience to teach the recruits."

There had not been much activity at the Café. I felt, at the most, he would see how boring stakeouts were, so he came along.

I drove my car with a cold license plate. Thompson rode shotgun in front and Paul and the academy cop rode in the back seat. We parked across the street, under I-93, and I got out my notebook to jot down plate numbers, which was my standard task. Thompson used the binoculars and read off the plate numbers for me to add to my list.

Then, Murphy's Law kicked in. We watched two guys taking handguns from under the rear bumper of Roy's car. He was an alleged wheelman of the crew. This had been the first time I'd seen such illegal gun handling at the Café. Billy wanted to shoot it out right then and there and tried to assert himself as the senior man over me. In fact, I had all I could do to calm him down.

"Billy, it's my case. Let me make the call here," I said trying to reason with him.

After a few tense minutes, he begrudgingly agreed. As we watched, Roy showed the guns to a second guy. Although I was not sure who the second guy was, Halpin thought it was James Hackett. After showing the guns to Hackett, Roy secured them back under the bumper of his Mercury with what looked like duct tape and then drove on to Mystic Ave. The academy instructor in the back seat was getting much more than he bargained for and loved every minute of it. He was a very capable cop and if anything went wrong, there was no doubt in my mind we were in good shape with him aboard. While it was tempting to bust them on gun charges, my main goal was to indict the mail hijackers.

We followed the two gun handlers to an apartment in Everett, a city a few miles away. Thompson, still insisting on busting them on illegal gun charges, radioed Detective Sgt. White for permission to stop the car, while I kept the Mercury in sight. Detective Sgt. White responded, "Do not attempt to stop or arrest them…just keep up the surveillance."

After 'sitting on' the apartment for almost an hour, I felt it was time we got back to our original stakeout. Paul was in the rear seat behind me as I drove my blue Dodge Dart back to the Café. Stopped at a red light on the Fellsway in Somerville, Roy's car stopped next to us on my driver's side.

"Hey…Halpin!" someone in the car yelled to us.

"Hey, how's it going?" Paul yelled back.

After a few minutes when we pulled away from the light, I asked Paul who that was.

"Jimmy Hackett. He recognized me."

I drove back to the Fells to regroup, grabbing a few coffees on the way. I was very concerned we had been made, but Paul felt they would never expect him to be working in plain clothes or investigating people he knew from the old days.

Thompson, who was the pro at undercover work, suggested we send Paul into the Café the next day. The idea was for the bad guys to think Paul just drove through his old Somerville neighborhood. If Halpin stopped in for a beer, hopefully they would believe seeing Paul in my car was just a coincidence. I was not sure it was such a great idea, but Billy was up for anything that involved action and so was Paul.

This was a big decision for me. The last thing I wanted was to see Paul carried out of the Café feet first, which these bad actors were more than capable of doing. I knew what the answer would be if I ran it by the bosses…"No". The good thing about undercover work was the bosses didn't really want to know what you were doing, just that you got it done.

We met the next day at the Fells and switched to a different undercover car, a four door Chevy with New York plates with an 'I love NY' sticker on the rear bumper. We armed up and laid out our plan. I was to drive and Billy would ride shotgun. I put my shotgun and extra box of ammo in the front seat between us. Before heading out, we all checked our weapons in case things went sour. Halpin's .38 caliber Colt snub nose was tucked in his belt while Billy pressed-checked (drew back the slide to make sure a round was chambered) his Beretta 9mm pistol and slid it in the small of his back. Paul said they all knew he was a uniform MDC cop, so it should be like old home week. One thing I had to say about Paul - he had a set of balls like an elephant. He had grown up in the Memorial Road projects and was a former 'project rat', as he said they were known.

As we dropped Paul off, the adrenalin rush was building inside me. I parked on Mystic Ave., just a few yards down from the Café. There were only a few cars in the parking lot in the early afternoon and Roy's Mercury was parked in its usual spot. I hoped there would be only a few patrons in the Café, but it was impossible to tell. This was crunch time so I parked in plain sight in case we had to get out fast. I was basically the getaway driver. I was so focused on our task, I don't remember if there was any traffic going by. Paul walked nonchalantly past the always-present lookout, who seemed unconcerned. The lookout had been talking to another guy, not even looking at us in our Chevy. I was cranked and nervous. Thompson was calm, deadly calm.

After just a few minutes, the lookout went inside and the other guy got into his car and drove away. Suddenly, Paul burst out the front door of the Café, waving for me to pick him up, gun in hand. I gunned the car, screeched to a stop and Billy flung open the right rear door.

Paul jumped in and said, "Let's get out of here! They made me!"

I slammed the gas pedal to the floor and we headed back to the Fells. I checked the rear view mirror but none of the bad guys came out of the Café.

As he caught his breath, Paul said, "No sooner did I sit down, Jimmy Hackett and Roy approached me and started patting me down for a wire. Then they tried to get me in the bathroom or out the back door. I ended up pushing my way out the front door as several patrons ran for the exits, not wanting to get in the line of fire!"

I knew it was the last time I could have Paul help me. We could not afford to screw things up now. The plan had backfired, but with short time until the statute ran out, it just didn't matter. The bottom line was we had to have witness testimony.

I reported the incident to Detective Sgt. Tom White, who was not happy with my decision to let Paul go into the Café.

He told me, "You wanted him to help and he did. Now, it's your job to cut him loose."

"Great. I know," I said, shaking my head.

The next day at the Detective Unit, I told Halpin I needed to talk with him privately. We went into the interview room and he seemed to know what was coming. Judging by the look on his face, this wasn't going to be easy.

"Paul, I am sure you know after the incident I am going to have to take you off the case," I said, trying to assert my role as the lead investigator.

"What's the matter? Don't the bosses have the balls to tell me themselves?" he fired back, his face red with anger, matching his Irish red hair.

"Look, it's up to me and you know it, Paul," I responded.

"I almost get my ass shot off and you're gonna dump me! Nice move, pal."

After a long staring contest, I asked, "If the shoe was on the other foot, would you dump me?"

Paul smirked through his anger and said, "I'm still not fucking happy!"

We both knew it had to be done and luckily we did not lose a friendship over it. It was one of the hardest things I had to do in this case, but the investigation came first.

About a week later, Thompson and I were back at the Ten Hills Café, sitting in a different car. I feared we had been burned and waited to see if we could tell by the activity and the lookouts. To my surprise all seemed normal - or as normal as this place could be.

Billy said, "Only one way to know for sure. I'm going in for a beer."

He was much more experienced at undercover work and I guessed it was the only way to find out. He told me this was his decision and told me to park on the side street and wait in the car. He knew how much time I had spent sitting on the Café and if they did not make him, we were golden. I was a nervous wreck waiting on the side street. Billy was calm and cool, saying he would be out after one beer, in exactly thirty minutes. He left his portable radio and badge in the car and was not wearing a wire. My mind was racing, thinking things could go deadly wrong. But role playing was something Thompson was a master at. In fact, he thrived on it.

The minutes dragged like hours until he finally came walking towards the car at exactly the thirty minute mark. He lit a cigarette and got into the passenger's side. He took a swig from a bottle of Maalox antacid he always carried with him.

Billy told me the place was deserted with maybe a half dozen guys drinking beer. He said he sat at the bar next to Hackett.

"Did he say anything to you or act hinky?" I asked in amazement.

"Nope. He asked, 'How ya doin'?' I said, 'Not too bad. How ya doin'?' He nodded his head and that was it. I nursed my beer, watched some of the game on TV and left without anyone being the wiser."

Thompson assured me we were cool and laughed.

Summarizing, he said, "They ain't that sharp."

I thought about what a dangerous move that was. Knowing the gang members were always looking for cops, it was ironic they just missed one of the best ones sitting at the bar, enjoying a beer in their headquarters.

# CHAPTER TWENTY-SIX
## *The Search for the Suspects*

For the fourth time in as many years the Postal Inspectors met with the United States Attorney's Office to discuss the mail hijacking case. With the additional testimony of John Grider, an actual participant in the hijacking and my shooting, there was finally enough evidence to bring the case before a Federal Grand Jury.

It was early April 1980 and it would be a few weeks before the grand jury would hear the case. If everything went according to plan, we would beat the five year statute of limitations by just days. The Postal Inspectors would have to work long hours and short nights to prepare the mountains of paperwork required for the Assistant United States Attorney to formally present the case. The schedule was so tight the Postal secretaries had one day to transcribe the Grider interview from the sixty-minute audio tape.

If the grand jury indicted the defendants, warrants would be issued and there was little doubt the suspects would flee. Even though the grand jury proceedings were supposed to be kept in strict confidence, friends of the Ten Hills Gang members were on the witness list. Chances were good James Hackett, the leader the Gang and the most dangerous of the crew, had heard he was a suspect in the proceedings. My full time assignment was to keep tabs on him.

Informants were feeding us information about Hackett's activities and current associates, but we needed more current photos of him and the other suspects. I asked for and was assigned a MDC Police photographer. I wanted to try a new location to put a peek on the Ten Hills Café. I parked our MDC undercover van, high above the Café on the I-93 overpass, and in the breakdown lane. Even though the lookouts always looked *around* for cops, they never looked *up*. It was the perfect spot to watch the action with binoculars and a camera with a long range lens.

Informants told us James Hackett was in the company of a man named Mulligan (a pseudonym), a new player on the scene. One afternoon, while looking down on the parking lot from our perch, I observed two men, resembling Mulligan and Hackett, talking with each other. I told my photographer to start shooting pictures. Two handguns were removed from the trunk of a regular's car. Through the binoculars, I watched as the one I thought was Hackett put a handgun in his ankle holster and the other guy tucked a gun into his waistband. My police photographer confirmed he took some great close-up photos of the gun transaction, which he watched through his 35mm camera's view finder.

*Unlike today's digital cameras, he would need to get the film developed.*

Two days later, the photographer told me he ran out of film developing solution at the MDC lab in South Boston, so he dropped the film off at a nearby drug store for processing.

"You're not going to believe this," the photographer said.

"Believe what?" I asked.

"The clerk at the drug store told me they send out the film to be developed." He paused. "The company that does the processing ...lost our film," he said nervously.

"No shit? You dropped them off in South Boston? Nice move!" I was royally pissed off and he knew it.

It had been a stupid move on his part. At the time, Southie was under the control of mobster James 'Whitey' Bulger and there was no way a South Boston drug store clerk would want to get involved in delivering photos of a gun deal - to cops. Having worked at a drug store when I was in high school, I knew the clerk's job. It was to review the envelopes when they came back from the company that does the developing, and make sure the pictures belonged to the name on the envelope. I figured he saw our photos, got nervous and destroyed them.

"Drive to the drug store. I want to see this place," I demanded.

As he pulled up in front of the drug store, he tried to triple park beside the other cars that were double parked, a standard practice on the narrow South Boston streets. As he did, he scraped the side of a parked car with our van. No one saw the minor accident.

"Take off!" I yelled.

"What do you mean?"

"Take off! Before they make our van!"

I leaned over and pressed my left foot onto the accelerator, forcing him to flee the scene. I had no intention of giving up the identity of our undercover van. Although bonded by the MDC, our van had untraceable MA plates and no registration or insurance certificate. Having to exchange papers would blow our cover. I didn't like it, but five years of work was not going down the drain over a scratched car!

Back at the Detective Unit, I explained what had happened to my Detective Sgt. White. Although he wasn't thrilled, he didn't reprimand me.

Within a few days, my stakeouts became unproductive. I sat on all of the Hackett's known haunts, from the Ten Hills Café, Pal Joey's (the backroom) and the Paddock on Winter Hill. Even the snitches said he had become impossible to find. There was no sign of James Hackett.

Then on May 1, 1980, I was at the MDC Detective Unit when I got a call from Bill O'Leary. He told me James Hackett had shot and wounded a guy at a Somerville VFW Post the night before. The shooting victim, Robert Martini, was said to be an associate of Howie Winter, the noted boss of the Winter Hill gang. The word from an informant was Hackett and Mulligan had been juiced up at the VFW Pointer Post, where Martini worked and 'held court,' as the manager and bouncer.

When Hackett and Martini got into a heated argument, Martini's son, a former boxer (who years later joined the MDC Police and became a friend of mine), stepped in and punched out Hackett. According to the informant, Mulligan revived the unconscious, embarrassed and angry Hackett. They went to the Ten Hills Café, got a handgun and a sawed-off Stevens double barreled shotgun they had hidden in the men's restroom, and then went back for revenge.

*These guns were most likely from the same stash of guns used in the mail hijacking and the Hilltop robbery and the murder.*

Hackett returned to the Pointer Post gun in hand and, bursting through the front door, found Martini. Hackett fired the pistol, just as Martini reached out to grab the gun away from him. The bullet went through Martini's hand and into his stomach. The pistol jammed and Hackett fled with Mulligan, who turned and fired the shotgun at the door as it was slammed shut.

Later, when the cops interviewed the wounded Martini in the hospital, he told them he had been shot while jogging. It seemed the 'Hill' would take care of this, themselves. Almost immediately, word hit the street a contract had been put out on Jimmy Hackett for shooting the unarmed Martini.

Just a short time after Bill's call about the shooting, our Detective Clerk told me I had a phone call waiting. The caller refused to identify himself to me. There was no caller ID in those days and I was sure he had called from a pay phone.

The unidentified caller said, "Listen, pal. We're lookin' for the same guy. We can help each other out. Me and you - maybe meet some place safe and we can swap info. We both wanna see this bum caught."

He said he would call back in an hour and hung up.

The caller sounded like a character from The Sopranos television show. I pictured him in a black shirt and white necktie, a 'dese, dems and dose' character. He wouldn't have been calling me if he really had good information and I had a gut feeling he was looking for my help to catch Hackett. Something just didn't feel right. How did the caller know I was looking for Hackett? And what would I tell him when he called back?

I ran it by my boss, the Detective Sgt., who answered my question with a question, "What do *you* think?"

"I'll tell him...no...because...," I replied, pausing for just a moment. Then it came to me, "If they whack him, I would be considered an accessory to murder."

Tom White smiled knowingly, "You're learning."

When the anonymous caller phoned back, I didn't take the call.

# CHAPTER TWENTY-SEVEN
## *The Hunt Continues*

Before the Martini shooting, Hackett was reported to be drinking heavily, using drugs and acting like a caged, desperate animal. It had become so intense that I started wearing my bullet proof vest under my denim shirt and kept my trusty police-issued 12-gauge shotgun nearby. Partnered up with a Postal Inspector for safety, I increased my surveillance activity, putting in many more hours and switching cars more often.

The 48 hours after the Martini shooting, that first week in May, were like a whirlwind. News had traveled fast to the bad guys in Somerville - lightning fast. In those days, they had a better and faster info pipeline than law enforcement had. Now, there were two groups searching for Hackett. The first was the gang he angered by shooting Robert Martini, Senior. The second was the law enforcement community he enraged when he shot me.

We didn't know who issued the contract to kill Hackett, or who would execute it. Informants told us there were four men, cruising around in a car, hunting for him. And they almost got him. They pulled up beside a car Hackett was in, with the younger brother of a gang member who was 'mentally challenged.' But the shooters did not want to take the chance of missing Hackett and accidently killing the innocent kid. They drove off without taking the shot.

I admit I hoped the bad guys would find Hackett first and end his reign of murder and mayhem. It would be poetic justice if they caught him and it would save us a lot of time and money.

Without the Postal Inspectors help and briefings, there was no way we could have kept up with Hackett's movements. At the end of that week, they told me James Hackett and his cohort, Shawn Mulligan, had flown to Ft. Lauderdale. To pay for their tickets, they used a credit card issued to a man from Medford, MA, known to frequent the Ten Hills Café. They rented a maroon 1980 Ford LTD at the airport. Hackett liked the Ford LTDs, not just for getaway cars. Unfortunately, despite additional resources, our guys were always a day or two behind them.

> *Tracking bad guys was so much more difficult back then. Today, we can get immediate data about credit card usage and GPS coordinates based on cell phone activity.*

They were closing in, but the suspects stayed just out of our reach.

The handwritten notes of the Postal Inspectors read:

> *"They stayed at Castaways in Miami Beach."*
> *"May 6, at 4:50 in the morning, James Hackett was stopped for speeding in Ft. Lauderdale."*

Hackett had been cited and released. This shouldn't have happened! There had been a federal warrant on the mail hijacking out for this guy. The cop either didn't run his name for warrants, or the computerized NCIC (National Crime Information Center) system was down, which often happened in 1980.

The inspector's notes went on to say,

> *"He produced a counterfeit Massachusetts driver's license."*

Sources told us Hackett's license had been revoked but he managed to obtain the counterfeit license for $250 from a connection at the Massachusetts Registry of Motor Vehicles in his own name. Always planning ahead, he must have known he would need the counterfeit one to rent cars and produce for cops in case he got stopped. It worked!

When he was interviewed by the Florida Postal Inspectors, the cop who pulled our suspect over said Hackett was with an unidentified white male, probably Mulligan. I was thankful the cop was not shot by Hackett, who was probably armed and certainly dangerous.

Back in Massachusetts, the Medford man had been questioned about his credit cards. He said they had been stolen from his car, but he had not reported the theft. What a surprise! Fred Ricker and I started tailing him, hoping he would lead us to Hackett. He didn't.

# CHAPTER TWENTY-EIGHT
## *The Folder*

On May 9, 1980, the federal statute of limitations on the bank robberies ran out. A day or two later, I heard a knock on my front door. It was 9 p.m. and I was sitting with my wife watching television in our den. Our house was on a cul-de-sac and I could always hear a car pull up. I got up and looked out the window, but there was no car. I had no idea who it could have been at that hour. I grabbed my revolver, stuck it in the waistband of my jeans and cautiously walked to the front door.

Standing on my tiptoes to peer out of the small glass windows at the top of the door, I saw a man I met during the investigation. He was with federal law enforcement. I relaxed. As I opened the door slowly, he was holding a large, expandable folder in his hand.

He spoke first.

"You are going to need this," he said, putting the folder into my hand.

Before I could say anything, he slipped back into the darkness.

My wife asked, "Who was that, at this time on night?"

"Just one of the investigators," I replied.

I took the folder into the dining room and started browsing through the papers. Report after report was filled with information from the state, local and federal investigation into the bank robberies, mail hijacking, and the Hilltop Steak House robbery and the murder.

There were pages and pages of valuable interviews with members of the Ten Hill Gang I had never seen. I really could have used these in our investigation. The first report I read was about one of the bank robberies, which included a witness description of a switch car used in one of the holdups. The car was a green Plymouth Duster with a pink flamingo toy in the rear window of the car. Attached to the report was a certified copy from the Registry of Motor Vehicles of an identical car registered to one James Hackett.

At first, I could not figure out why this person handed the files to me. Then I remembered the date. The statute of limitations had run on the bank robberies and the reports were useless to that branch of investigators. But why had this info been hidden from our primary investigation team?

I called over to my wife, "I just need to look these over. I'll be in to watch TV with you in a few minutes."

She was always a very understanding woman. The minutes turned into hours. In fact, I made myself some coffee and stayed up half the night. I sorted the reports by the type of crime and by the date of the report. There were so many reports, they covered my dining room table.

The Postal Inspectors, federal and state Agencies and I had worked on this case, supposedly together, for five long, hard years. Why were these reports not shared before? Cops and law enforcement agencies had been so incredibly cooperative and helpful in the search for the suspects the night I was shot. How the hell could they have sat on such vital information? After I was shot, I felt bad enough, physically and mentally. This was worse...I felt betrayed. Why the hell had I even bothered to work my ass off on this case? Maybe this was how the Boston cops, who came to see me in the hospital days after I was shot, felt when they said they were treated poorly after their shooting incidents. I had to let the bad feeling go and move on.

Early on, the Postal Inspectors and my MDC detective bosses warned me not to trust the other agencies. At the time, I found that strange. Weren't we all on the same team? Now I understood why.

The state police detectives did not trust the MDC detectives and vice versa. Nobody trusted the Boston FBI back in 1980, because of the FBI Agent John 'Zip' Connolly/James 'Whitey' Bulger connection. Unfortunately, this was an age old problem in law enforcement. It was obvious from the reports - the FBI was only interested in taking down the Ten Hills Gang themselves. And all the other agencies only really cared about getting credit for catching the felons and the arrests.

> *The mistrust between agencies hindered the investigation at every point. The lack of cooperation and all the jealousies between law enforcement agencies continues to this day.*
>
> *The Boston Marathon bombing is a prime example. Accusations the FBI did not notify the Boston Police of vital information regarding the bombing suspects and the potential for terror threats were tossed back and forth in the press reports. To me, it is downright sad and I doubt it will ever change.*

While all of these thoughts and questions swirled around in my head, I continued to scan through the mountain of reports. While reading over each report, I noticed the same problems kept cropping up in their investigations, too. The green Plymouth Duster, registered to Hackett, looked like a great lead, at first. But the witness who saw the switch from the stolen Ford getaway car to the Plymouth was unable to identify any of the occupants. Still, it corroborated what we had known about Hackett.

Fingerprints lifted in the four bank robberies did not match any of the Ten Hills Gang. However, this was to be expected as they always wore surgical gloves during a robbery. The federal and state agencies all had the same names we did. Reading over the interviews of the prime suspects, they were all uncooperative. In fact, in the interviews of James Hackett, investigators noted he had been smug and cocky, even laughing at the interviewer's questions.

In each crime, the participants wore gloves and disguises: fake moustaches, beards, and tape on their noses, so a witness would focus on the tape, not on any facial features. Hats and sunglasses were always worn. These guys were well organized, armed and prepared for each robbery.

After reading through all of the documents, there had been only one really good piece of evidence. The only one interviewed who admitted involvement in the bank robberies had been John Grider. But, just as in our investigation, Grider would not talk specifics without immunity and none of the reports suggested any agency was willing to offer him that protection.

The next morning I went into the Postal Inspector's office, showed them the folder and told them where I got it. They could see I was visibly upset and discouraged.

Fred Ricker told me, "Welcome to our world, buddy."

He went on to tell me a story to help me put things in perspective. He said when he reached out for help on a prior mail case, which involved thousands of dollars in stolen postage stamps, he contacted a special agent in the Boston FBI. Fred went to see this agent, who showed him 'all' of the files pertaining to the post office break-in. As Fred was looking at the paperwork, a secretary came in wheeling a small cart with tall stacks of papers.

She innocently asked the agent, "Did you want the rest of the files to show Inspector Ricker?"

Fred gave me some advice, "Don't take it personally. It's just how things are, buddy."

Fred was not upset at all, and in his unique and calm manner, he explained the facts of life in the law enforcement world. He told me he relied on certain cops he could trust. If I wanted to become a detective, he told me I would need to develop my own connections with people I trusted and I would have to be circumspect with the others.

"Thanks, Fred," I said shaking my head, realizing it was just the way things were and still are.

I knew how lucky I was to have guys like Fred Ricker and Bill O'Leary on my case. After Fred's explanation, I felt somehow refreshed and we got back down to business. There was no time for anger or self-pity.

# CHAPTER TWENTY-NINE
## *James Hackett*

We believed James Hackett shot me; we believed he shot and killed the Wells Fargo Guard at the Hilltop Steakhouse, but he beat the rap when the gang threatened all the witnesses and the prosecutor made a procedural mistake; and we believed he shot Bobby Martini, Sr. Hackett was the most deadly of the Ten Hills Gang and we had to get him off the streets before he killed again.

*While doing research for the book, I found Hackett's grandfather had been named Jesse James Hackett - how appropriate.*

We received fresh information about Hackett and Mulligan's activity during the month of May. Within ten days of each other, Mulligan and Hackett each obtained fraudulent passports in Miami, Florida. Mulligan got one under the alias of Joseph Anthony Frederico, and Hackett called himself William George Burns. The trail became muddled after Miami. Their whereabouts were based only on sketchy info from snitches. A rumor had them traveling to Washington, D.C. or to New York City, but we couldn't find them in either place.

Then, there was a sighting on Memorial Day weekend. Hackett and Mulligan had somehow slipped back into the Boston area, evading the contract killers and us. An informant had seen them on May 30 at 3:00 a.m. in Somerville. But, again, the trail ended there.

I could not have been more frustrated. It looked as if we would never catch James Hackett. He seemed to lead a charmed life, always dancing just out of our reach.

IN EARLY JUNE, I knew something was up when I arrived at at the South Boston Postal Annex. Bill O'Leary had more than the usual smirk on his face before our morning status update. We went into the conference room where the poster boards were covered with handwritten notes and teletype items, along with surveillance photos and mug shots of our suspects.

Bill looked like 'the cat that just ate the canary.' I thought he was going to tell us Hackett's body had been found - maybe the hit men got him first.

Inspector O'Leary began the briefing, "I just got a call from the State Department. Hackett is under arrest."

"Great, Bill. Where is he?" I blurted out.

"Kuwait," Bill smirked.

"Kuwait? Where the hell is Kuwait?" I said in shock. (This was long before the Gulf Wars.)

Bill went on to tell the story. "He was involved with Mulligan in an attempted robbery of a leading jewelry store in the town of Fahaheel in Kuwait."

The Arab Times-Kuwait reported they were part of a six member gang, including several Jordanians, formed in the US to carry out a series of robberies in Kuwait.

"How the hell did he get to Kuwait?" I asked.

"We don't know, but now we know why they got those fake passports. And their accomplice was a Kuwaiti, who turned out to be a police informant. At 6:00 p.m. yesterday, they were placed under arrest."

This took a while to sink in. Kuwait! Bill told us they would be tried in about two weeks in Kuwait and would face six years in a Kuwaiti Jail. There was no extradition treaty between the USA and Kuwait so they would remain in the custody of the

Kuwaiti authorities. Bill said he would petition the State Department to fly over and interview Hackett.

The request had been denied because the U.S. State Department deemed Kuwait 'too politically unstable.' Bill's contact at the State Department told him if Hackett was convicted and went to jail in Kuwait, he would serve the time in the desert. The Kuwaitis, according to what we had heard, were not known for kindness or comfort in their prison system. Rumors of torture were routine. It would be hard, hard time.

The trial took place in two weeks, unlike the months or years it takes in the states. They were both convicted and sentenced to six years at hard labor. I thought this would be the last we would hear of Hackett, but, I knew in this case, anything could happen.

# CHAPTER THIRTY
## *The Grand Jury*

We believed we had done everything we could to identify and keep tabs on the six suspects. Grider, and the Hackett brothers were in jail, in different parts of the world. Capone and his uncle Bimber were accounted for in Medford at their respective homes. Only Murnane was missing.

In June of 1980, five long years after I was shot, the statute of limitations was closing in on us. It seemed, as if suddenly, there was just one week to get the indictments, and we would be crushed if we hadn't caught these guys just because we ran out of time. I had to get Captain Desk Jockey's words out of my head.

Members of a federal grand jury had been impaneled and would finally begin hearing our evidence.

> *A federal grand jury decides whether or not to indict a person for a serious crime. The U.S. Attorney, in this case Paul Healy, presented the evidence we gathered to the jurors, who would decide whether there was probable cause to prosecute someone for the crime. The jurors operate in secrecy.*

259 WEEKS AFTER THE crimes had been committed, it would all come down to the opinion of these men and women. If they returned a 'true bill,' we could take the next step and prepare to put them on trial. Otherwise, if the grand jury returned a 'no

bill,' it was all over. Five years of suffering - by me and my family, five years of lying awake with my .38 caliber gun nearby as I listened for strange sounds in the night, and those months and months spent trying to fit the pieces of this puzzle together - would all for be naught.

I was about to make my first appearance before a grand jury and I was nervous wreck. I had testified in state court many times, but this was different…this was personal. I wondered whether Grider's account as the participant and my testimony as the victim would convince the panel. I worried I would choke on the stand or even worse, be overcome by emotion while reliving that horrible night when I almost died.

Just before my grand jury testimony, a meeting had been set up to go over the case at the United States Attorney's office in downtown Boston. I parked my car at the South Postal Annex (parking in Boston was nonexistent or very expensive), and Inspectors O'Leary and Ricker, and I walked the few blocks to the old federal building in Post Office Square for the 10 a.m. meeting. I was trying hard not to look like a kid in a candy store, but I looked around at my surroundings, in awe of the buildings - some historic and some new - in this section of Boston.

We were greeted by the Assistant United States Attorney Paul Healy and I was introduced to his boss, Edward F. Harrington, the U.S. Attorney, at the time.

To me, Paul was what an Assistant United States Attorney should look like. I think this is the best way to describe him: if you 'googled' U.S. Attorney, an image of Paul would pop up. He was tall, bespectacled and wore a conservative suit. He simply looked the part.

The desk he sat behind was massive and unlike anything I had seen in the state courthouses. Paul ran the meeting in a soft spoken and business-like manner. We decided which surveillance photos would be shown to the jurors and reviewed the transcript of the Grider audio tapes. We had worked on this case for five years and there was no room for a last minute fumble. Fred reviewed his list of potential witnesses with us, while Bill made jokes every chance he could get. I envied his sense of humor and it helped to ease our edgy emotions.

At the lunch break, I asked Paul how I should dress for my grand jury appearance. For the meeting, I had worn my new detective's clothes: brown corduroy sport coat, blue oxford cloth shirt and necktie and, of course, my cowboy boots.

Paul said, "What you're wearing today is perfect, but lose the cowboy boots."

"Yes, Sir," I said. But I smirked, and thought, "So much for my trademark."

ON JUNE 4 AND 9, 1980, evidence on the mail hijacking was presented to the Federal Grand Jury. When my name was called to give testimony, I straightened my necktie and buttoned my sport coat and entered the courtroom. Expecting a very formal procedure, I found the opposite. There were about twenty people and most were dressed casually. At least two had their heads on the table napping. The grand jurors continued reading or doing whatever they were doing when I entered. I was a little surprised. I didn't know grand jury proceedings were so much more relaxed than a regular trial.

After I took the stand, Assistant United States Attorney Healy asked my name and title, and then said, "Officer Owen, please tell the jurors where you were on the evening of June 16, 1975, and what your duties were that evening."

As I started to tell my story, the jurors began to perk up. Newspapers were put down and a few jurors even started taking notes. My voice was filled with emotion - it would crack, unexpectedly, now and then - as I related the events of the night I was shot. I made eye contact with each of the jurors, trying to make a connection with these strangers. After a few minutes, I could see the jury members were hanging on my every word.

While I was on the stand, I thought back to the scene from the movie *Flash Dance* when Jennifer Beals tried to get into an exclusive dance school, performing her 'flash dance' before a panel of stuffy dance judges. Her judges seemed bored to tears.

> *If you've seen the movie, it's a good visual of my testimony. Her dance routine started off slowly; in fact, she took a fall and had to start over.*

And then, suddenly, she found her rhythm and won them over. In an analogous way, by the time I finished testifying, the grand jurors seemed mesmerized.

"You may step down, Officer," Paul said. I walked out with my spirits high hoping they would return an indictment. If the gang was indicted the clock would be set back to zero. The statue of limitations would no longer apply.

There were two days of testimony with a long list of witnesses to be questioned. On the second day, O'Leary and I were called into the prosecutor's office. Paul said, "We have a small problem."

My heart sank as I waited to hear what had gone wrong at this late stage. Every time there was a high in this case there was an immediate low. This rollercoaster ride was exhausting and I was sure it showed on my face.

Paul said, "Dana, relax. It isn't that bad." He went on tell us one of the jurors had a question and wanted to speak in private.

The juror said, "I think the guy who provided the guns and disguises is my Uncle."

Paul inquired, "What is your Uncle's name?"

The juror replied, "Joe Capone."

Paul dismissed the juror from the jury, but not before he explained the proceedings were to be kept secret under penalties of law. He warned the juror the punishment for telling his uncle anything about what he had heard during testimony, would include time in a federal prison.

After the juror left the office, I shook my head in disbelief. "You have to be kidding me! What are the odds of this happening?" I asked the Assistant U.S. Attorney.

Mr. Healy answered calmly, "About a million to one."

I asked Paul if he felt the juror would tip off his uncle.

Paul said, "In a close Italian family, what do you think?"

"We'll keep our toothbrushes packed, Paul," Bill said, in his always jovial manner.

Fred smirked, "Hey, buddy. Are you surprised by anything in this case?"

I didn't answer, but thought, "Would this ever end?"

We went back to the South Postal Annex and tried to keep busy while waiting for the decision. Nervous does not adequately describe my emotion. I kept thinking: Had we put together a coherent picture for the grand jury? Did we implicate each of the gang members in the robbery and the shooting? Or had we left something out, forgotten a crucial detail, or left a gap in the chain of evidence?

Finally, we would get the answers to these questions. We were all together in the Postal Inspector's office when the phone rang. Collectively, our hearts skipped a beat.

Bill picked up the phone and said, "Inspection Service, O'Leary." He listened to the caller. Then, he looked straight at me and gave thumbs up.

When he hung up, he said, "They returned a true bill."

Thank God. There were handshakes and congratulations all around, but it was time now to prepare for the arrests and trial. Things were looking up at long last.

# CHAPTER THIRTY-ONE
## *The Reporters and the Arrests*

On June 9, 1980, the secret indictments had been returned by the Federal Grand Jury and the arrest warrants had been issued. Only two of the five criminals indicted, had not fled the jurisdiction. The plan was to arrest them as soon as possible. The grand juror who had been excused by the judge probably tipped off the gang.

The next morning Detective Lt. Keough, Detective Sgt. Thomas White, Postal Inspectors O'Leary and Ricker, and I met with a newspaper reporter, at MDC Headquarters. Our Public Relations Officer Frank Muolo had scheduled an interview with Timothy Dwyer from *The Boston Globe*. I was told my story would hit the street in that newspaper the following morning, if the arrests were made. I was very guarded talking to the reporter, because I honestly felt the media attention was a little premature.

Frank Muolo told me, "Dana, I have total faith in this guy. Just relax and answer his questions."

Dwyer was a young reporter and very friendly. I am sure he sensed my distrust, but he worked around it like a pro. Both Detective Lt. Keough and the Postal Inspectors had given me more credit in the investigation than I felt I deserved; so much so, they had embarrassed me.

Keough told Dwyer, "Dana had the tenacity of a bulldog."

I had to admit it was great to hear such accolades from fellow cops and that line had an especially good ring to it. I was thrilled when Dwyer used this phrase for the headline of his story.

Much to my surprise, the interview went relatively smoothly. I was able to relax and answer all of the reporter's questions.

Dwyer asked, "Were you unconscious after you were wounded and on the way to the hospital?"

Trying to respond accurately, I answered, "No, I was semi-conscious."

"And he's been that way ever since," Postal Inspector Ricker added, without missing a beat.

> *Tim Dwyer used this line in his article on the front page of the Boston Globe the next day. "Everyone had a good laugh over that - even Owen. It's easy to laugh when the story - and investigation - has a happy ending," he wrote.*

Sleep eluded me that night before the arrests. I kept going over the scenario, a hundred times, in my head. We had planned to arrest the inside man who had worked at the South Postal Annex and the person who supplied the guns, disguises and clothing, and the stolen car. Joseph Bimber, the inside man, had retired from the post office and was Capone's uncle. The 'supplier,' Joe Capone was married, and came from a close-knit family. We did not expect any resistance from either of them, but we always had to plan for unexpected events. Over the years, too many cops had been killed during the arrest of 'harmless' suspects.

The arrest teams, including Postal Inspectors and MDC cops, arrived at the MDC Fells Police Station at Wellington Circle in Medford on June 11, 1980, at 4:30 a.m. At 5:15 a.m., the teams rolled out for the pre-dawn arrests, dressed in plain clothes and wearing bullet proof vests. I went with Inspector O'Leary and my investigation Team members, including Inspector Roger Hunt to arrest Capone.

Bill asked, "Do you want to put the cuffs on him yourself?"

"No thanks, Bill. It's your arrest. I will cover the back of the house with Roger."

I took up my position in the back yard, crouching on one knee. My eyes were locked on the back door, knowing Roger had taken cover to my right. I strained to listen to any noise - especially for the sound of someone trying to flee down the back stairs. We waited for what seemed like an eternity, but in reality it had only been about twenty minutes.

My shotgun rested on my bent knee, at the low ready position, the entire time. This Remington short-barreled police 12-gauge pump shotgun was issued by my department. I had loaded it with 5 rounds of 00 buck, ironically the same type of round I had been shot with. I put one in the chamber and pushed the safety on and off several times, to make sure it was ready to go. I had carried this weapon since I started the investigation. I was not going to find myself on the short end of another gun battle.

Suddenly, the inspector's portable radio squelched: "Package #1 has been delivered!" Number one was Bimber. I was still watching the back door of Capone's house. Then, about five minutes later, it was all over: "Package # 2 has been delivered! All units secure!" Five long years of work had finally paid off. I felt a huge sense of relief, but knew the next chapter was about to begin. This story was still far from over.

Bill asked if I wanted to do the customary 'perp walk,' the traditional police parade of the suspect in handcuffs before the waiting TV cameras. The selection of the cops who walked with the arrestee was always political.

12 THE BOSTON GLOBE WEDNESDAY, JUNE 11, 1980

## 2 nabbed in hijack

■ HIJACK
Continued from Page 1

"We saw a truck with two men in it," Owen said in a recent interview. "It was unusual for two men to be in a truck because there had been a lot of layoffs at the time. We thought it might be the truck because of that, and when I looked at the man in the passenger side, he put his head down and tried to shield his face."

The two policemen followed the truck for a short distance and checked the registration. When they were convinced it was the right truck, they pulled it over.

"We were behind the doors of the cruiser and using the P.A. (public address system) to tell them to get out of the truck. We knew they were armed," he said.

Before they could take the men into custody, a car came along and picked up the man from the passenger side of the truck. The truck driver screamed to the two policemen that they had hijacked his truck.

The chase was on. It reached speeds of 100 mph and the two policemen had more than a dozen shots fired at them. It ended in Winchester when the getaway car was involved in an accident after passing five or six cars. Owen, who was driving the cruiser, passed the same five or six cars and ended up with a bullet in the face.

"When we passed the last car we were right on top of them and everyone started shooting. The only thing I could do was duck," Owen said.

Owen is a shy man who has worked hard on the case, along with US Postal Inspectors F.A. Ricker and W.J. O'Leary. He downplays his role in the investigation, but over the last five years, he has gradually picked up more and more information,

and always kept in touch with Ricker and O'Leary, who never forgot the case.

The case went well for the first few months but then died. Once in a while there would be information picked up, but the investigation was getting nowhere. The federal statute of limitations runs out on June 16. For a time, it looked like whoever shot Owen and tried to hold up the truck would walk away.

Then about a year ago, Owen began to develop information from a man now serving time in a federal prison, according to sources familiar with the investigation.

The case began to pick up steam and Owen, who normally works in uniform, was put on special assignment with the MDC Detective Bureau.

"I just gave him free rein the last three months," said Lt. Detective Theodore Keough, head of the bureau. "He has gone out and interviewed (persons involved) with the case) and continued to give evidence to the postal inspectors.

"It's been in his craw for five years. He vowed that he was going to solve it and he did," said Keough.

If you talk to Owen, it seems like it was all in the line of duty. That night five years ago, he was shot once while he was driving and the bullet grazed the top of his head. He kept driving.

"He got hit once and kept going. He got hit twice and kept going until he collapsed," said Keough. "He is one tough SOB."

The federal grand jury handed down the secret indictments last week. This week, Owen looked relaxed. As he told the story of the shooting, he got some good-na-

**JOSEPH J. BIMBER, 69**
Retired postal worker

**JOSEPH G. CAPONE**
Offered no resistance

tured kidding from the men who worked with him the last five years. He was asked if he was conscious on the ride to the hospital after he was wounded.

"I was semiconscious," he said.

"And he has been like that ever since," said one of the postal inspectors.

Everyone had a good laugh over that — even Owen. It's easy to laugh when the story — and investigation — has a happy ending.

The first two arrests

"No, thanks. I'll grab the coffees on the way in."

I believed the arrest belonged to the Postal Inspectors. I was more than happy to stay in the background. I also needed some time alone to calm down and savor this long awaited victory.

ON THE MORNING of the arrests, I felt very much a part of the team. Over the years, I had been able to contribute a great deal to the investigation. I was most proud of my ability to act as a coach and cheerleader. When the investigation dragged on, or seemed to be at a dead end, I would call the Postal Inspectors.

"Let's meet for lunch or coffee," I would say.

They never refused.

"Okay. Where do we go from here?" was my standard line. "I have a couple of ideas."

They always listened. I knew as our friendship grew they wanted to solve this as much as I did.

Feeling like the coach, I wanted *my guys* to get the credit they deserved. After all, this had been like winning a state football championship.

Back at the Fells Station, reporters from the three major TV news channels in Boston, and from the local newspapers had gathered. I went into the station, through the back door, and delivered the coffees. Maybe Tim Dwyer was right: "Owen - a shy man…," he had written.

It was already too hot inside the station and, as usual, it had that musty smell. I needed to catch a breath of fresh air, and went back outside. The bustle of the rush hour morning traffic filled the air. The sun was shining and the day was heating up quickly.

As I took off my corduroy sport coat, I could feel the sweat had soaked though the back of my blue oxford dress shirt. I was even tempted to loosen my tie. My brown leather shoulder holster, holding my service revolver, was starting to become uncomfortable under my arm. The gun was a .38 Police Special; it was stainless steel and, with oversized wooden grips, had the appearance of a much larger caliber gun.

My Public Relations Officer told me I was to do several on camera interviews for the Boston networks. I could see some of the reporters in front of the station, drinking coffee or preparing their stories. I had been amazed at how many of them were covering my story and the two arrests. I recognized Ron Gollobin from Channel 5 in Boston, who had interviewed me from my hospital bed, the day after I was shot. I liked his reporting and often watched the Channel 5 news anchors of that era - Chet Curtis and Natalie Jacobson.

I chatted with Ron about how it had been five years since we last spoke. His cameraman and other reporters were gathered around, setting up cameras and lights.

Ron asked me, "Dana, what kind of gun is that?"

Feeling pretty cocky, I paraphrased a line from the *Dirty Harry* Clint Eastwood movie.

"It's a .44 magnum. The most powerful handgun in the world," I said.

Everyone laughed, except for Ron. He had never seen the movie. The other reporters explained the joke.

"He got you good, Ron," one guy laughed.

As he prepared me for my first TV interview, Ron gave me last minute instructions.

"Remember, just look at me, and not the camera or microphone. Just talk directly to me," he said.

I started to get nervous and could feel my heart pounding. The last thing I wanted to do was to come off as some dumb cop, stumbling over his answers.

I put my jacket back on, combed my hair to cover my old scar, and was as ready as I would ever be.

> *If you think you get scared knowing your interview will be on the noon and 6 o'clock news, you're absolutely right.*

The cameraman stood behind Ron, who held the remote microphone in front of me.

"So, Officer. The last time I saw you, you were in a hospital bed, and now, five years later, you have arrested two of the men that allegedly were involved in the crime." Ron said.

"How does that feel, **Dirty Dana?**" he asked.

I stood with my mouth opened, totally blank.

Ron said, with his southern drawl, "Got ya back!"

"Was the camera on?" I stammered.

"Of course not," Ron chuckled.

Everyone laughed, including me. I thought, "This is what I get for messing with a pro." Ron succeeded in getting me to relax and I finished the interview.

The next interview was with Charles Austin from Channel 4, one of the first African American television news reporters in the Boston market. I was to retrace the route of the chase in a cruiser much like the one I had been shot in. The only difference was this one was the newest and cleanest cars in the fleet. Public Relations had insisted. Mr. Austin, holding his microphone, sat in the front seat where my partner used to sit, and the cameraman was in the back seat.

I set up where we first spotted the truck that night on I-93 and off we went. While I drove, I recapped the events of that night, still crystal clear in my mind. From the corner of my eye, I could tell Mr. Austin was looking at me, then looking out the windshield, and looking at me again, completely absorbed in my story.

When we reached Spot Pond in Stoneham, I parked the cruiser where the mail truck had pulled over. I described how the guys in the follow-car picked up the hijacker, which caused me to initiate the pursuit of their car.

The cameraman got out and set up his equipment. Then, he told me to drive off just the way I did in the pursuit, with tires screeching, blue lights flashing and the siren wailing. I would do the 'camera take' several times and wondered if the passing motorists thought we were making a movie. I drove back, picked up the news crew and we continued to retrace the exact pursuit route, while I commented along the way.

As we passed over the railroad tracks on Washington Street, I pointed and said, "This is where they started shooting at us."

Up until then, I had been completely in control of my emotions. Then something happened…I started to get anxious. I tried to shake it off.

"Right about here is when the shotgun was fired the first time," I continued, trying hard to seem calm, but, in my mind, I was flashing back to the chase.

"What did it feel like when you were shot the first time?" I was asked.

I don't remember what I said. The more questions Charley asked, the more I sweated. My heart was racing and I was sure he could hear how I felt by the tone in my voice. I struggled just to get my voice to work and to answer the questions. I continued to drive while all this was happening.

It was easy to remember the chase route, but I felt as if I was in the chase all over again. Even the sights, sounds and smells of the chase had come back to me.

It seemed liked I blinked, and suddenly we had pulled up in front of the White Hen Pantry on Swanton Street. This would be the last camera shot for the newsman's report. We got out of the cruiser and I pointed to the spot where I had slid my cruiser to a stop. I could hear Charley Austin narrating - he sounded so far away - as the cameraman zoomed in, on the gutter where I ended up lying in the street.

This was my first time back to the scene since the night I had been shot. I thought of what I must have looked like: my body hanging out of the cruiser, head first, as my blood pooled in the street. My blood stains had long since washed away, but the memories had not. It was all too real for me. I didn't think Charley or his cameraman suspected I had been experiencing horrendous flashbacks. Again, I heard Charley's voice, but it sounded garbled as I stood staring at the gutter, wrestling with my brain to bring myself back to reality. I was visibly shaking and it became impossible to conceal.

As Mr. Austin finished the segment and the camera was turned off, he put his hand on my shoulder and asked, "Are you Okay?"

"Yes, thanks. I'll be fine," and I pulled myself together.

The thing I remembered most about this interview was that Mr. Austin was a soft spoken gentleman. He had been laid back and understanding. My opinion of reporters changed as a result of these interviews. These reporters were real people, the cream of the crop, and were doing a difficult job. In fact, in many ways they were very much like us cops.

I became much more comfortable as we drove back to the Fells Station in Medford. I parked in front and spoke with some other newspaper reporters and had my picture taken a few times. It seemed weird. I was getting all the attention and the Postal Inspectors stayed out of sight.

I even asked my Public Relations Officer Frank Muolo, "Why am I getting all the credit?"

"You have got to be kidding. This is a great human interest story: *The cop shot five years ago now makes the arrests,*" he said. Finally, it all seemed to sink in.

While the Postal Inspectors were finishing their reports, I drove over to Mr. Donuts to get more coffee. There, in the newspaper vending machine, was the late edition of *The Boston Globe*.

On the cover, the headline read:

**Tenacity pays in arrests for officer shot 5 years ago**

Next to the headline was my photo taken that morning. The caption under it read:

"PATROLMAN DANA OWEN knew he'd catch them"

The Boston Globe's front page story on me

I was smiling from ear to ear. Still looking down at the headline, I handed the donut clerk a few one dollar bills and asked for some quarters, for the machine. I bought every single copy. I handed the first one to Mrs. Foley, who worked in the donut shop. She had been the lady who sent me the card in the hospital and told me I went back to work too soon.

All I could think of was the day I was transferred to my special secret assignment and the TOPS clerk's premonition: "I better see you on the front page of *The Boston Globe*."

> *I do remember being in 5th grade, Mr. Leary's class, when it was days before the statue of limitations would run out and they caught the bad guys. I either brought the newspaper article to school with your picture, or it had been cut out there. [Daughter Heather's Memories]*

When I got back to the station, the Postal Inspectors said, "We want to take you to dinner." It was time to celebrate. They had decided on a place over on Revere Beach, called the Driftwood.

I rode with the inspectors and the arrest team and left my car back at the Fells Station. The restaurant was well known for its great seafood and great views, and we could see the ocean from our table.

"Order what you want. This is on us," Bill said with a smile.

"Thanks, Bill. I will," I said.

I thought back to the night in Wisconsin and the 'dropped' dinners.

"I'll have the baked stuffed lobster," I ordered.

The waitress asked, "The one and a quarter pound or the two pound? And what will you have to drink?"

Not difficult questions for a New Englander. "I'll have the two pound and a Jameson on the rocks."

The meal was delicious and the dinner conversation celebratory. Knowing I did not have to drive, I enjoyed a few more glasses of Irish whiskey. I was feeling relaxed for the first time in quite a while.

*If you have not dined overlooking an ocean, you don't know what you're missing.*

I listened to the sound of the waves crashing and the squawking of the seagulls as they searched for food. The smell of the salt air and the late afternoon sun made the scene seem so tranquil.

After lunch, a few of the inspectors left but I stayed a little longer. It was almost 4:30 p.m. when my pager went off, displaying the number of MDC Police Headquarters. I couldn't imagine why I was being paged. Maybe it was someone who just wanted to congratulate me.

I made the call to Headquarters from a pay phone in the lobby. To my surprise, the Captain told me to get myself back to Somerville and meet with Ron Sanders from Channel 7 for a live interview…for the 6 o'clock news! What??? The interview was to be held at the on-ramp to I-93, where we had first spotted the hijacked truck. I couldn't find the words to respond. I was alert enough to realize I was on my fourth Irish whiskey, and I tried to quickly come up with an excuse as to why I couldn't make it to the interview.

But before I could think of one, the Captain barked, "And don't be late," and hung up.

As I tried to walk in a straight line back to our table, Bill asked, "Is everything Okay?"

I told them about my situation, and they all laughed. I quickly ordered a coffee. I was sure my speech was slurred and I was certain I would make a complete fool of myself on a major Boston news channel - live and in color.

After two more cups of strong black coffee and one more for the road, we headed to my final interview of the day. The Postal guys, who drove me back, were having a great time at my expense. I was the recipient of an endless stream of jokes. But that was Okay. These men had become my friends and I could take a joke as well as dish one out.

One asked me, "Did you enjoy your last supper?" I just sipped my coffee and tried to sober up.

Another Inspector quipped, "Hey, relax. You won't be the first drunk cop to be on television."

We pulled up to the on-ramp to see the remote news van, and the cameras and lights all set up. A huge boom from a Channel 7 news van had been extended up in the air, reaching high over the rush hour traffic. I met Ron Sanders, another familiar face from television news. He reviewed the questions he wanted to ask me and explained this was going to be a live shot, and not tape. I hoped my head would stop spinning and tried hard to focus only on him, just as Ron Gollobin had instructed me, earlier that day.

He asked questions - I answered. I have no memory of what he asked me. I was more worried about how I looked and sounded. Maybe my red face looked like I had sunburn, I thought. I hoped not. Was my speech slurred? I really don't know, because I never saw the interview.

The last question he asked was, "So, Officer. After a five year investigation, finally making the arrests and all the notoriety, what do you think it will be like when you go back on duty tomorrow?"

The question was very sobering to me. I don't know where the words came from, but I answered, "I think... things will go back to routine."

I received many calls from friends, family and fellow cops telling me *that* interview was by far my best.

The next day one of my fellow MDC cops called.

He said, "Did you hear Paul Harvey on the news this morning?"

*At its peak, Mr. Harvey's listening audience was estimated at 24 million people a week.*

"No, I didn't. Why?" I asked.

During his broadcast segment called, *The Rest of the Story*, Paul Harvey, with his distinctive voice, related how a cop, shot in the face and left for dead five years ago, had just arrested two of the guys allegedly involved in the shooting and how justice had prevailed. I never heard it, but the fact my story made national news simply amazed me.

# CHAPTER THIRTY-TWO
## *The Hunt for the Wheelman*

Back at the Fells Station, the Postal Inspectors and I were finishing our Incident Reports on the arrests of the two men from Medford and were already talking about our next move. Getting back out there to round up as many of the indicted hijackers as quickly as possible would be our next step. We decided to turn our attention to Richard Murnane, who was the suspected wheelman in the case.

Murnane had been a mysterious figure throughout our investigation. It was hard for the informants to keep tabs on him and I had not spotted him at the Ten Hills Café during my surveillances. He could have been driving the car I followed to the Hilltop Steakhouse on the timed run, but I never could identify any of the occupants in the car that night.

Here's a little background on this character. In 1979, almost four years after the warrant was issued for his role in the Hilltop Steak House incident, Murnane reappeared in Arizona on August 13, coincidentally my birthday. He was stopped on a North Phoenix side street for driving under the influence and several other offenses. This time the cop was able to check NCIC for warrants. The Phoenix cop's patrol car had been equipped with a new and innovative computer terminal. When the cop typed in Murnane's social security number and date of birth, he got a hit. Even though Murnane gave his name as Ronald Bonney, the new computer system ended his four years on the run. The felony warrants from Massachusetts were displayed on the screen and he was arrested.

*The terminal was the size of a shoe box, the forerunner of in-car laptops. Although we didn't get this technology until 1988, the MDC was the first Police Department in New England to install in-car computers.*

During his booking at Phoenix P. D., he listed his occupation as cab driver. It had been rumored he had formally driven a cab in Somerville, MA. With experience as a cabbie in a large city, he would be well suited for the job of 'wheelman.' Most of the Ten Hills Gang listed occupations when they were arrested, but were really bank robbers and hijackers.

The alleged wheelman in my case had used the aliases of Michael Morrissey and James Dowling in prior arrests, before technology caught up to him. He was brought back to Massachusetts and held on $25,000 bail. For reasons I never understood, he was not prosecuted, charges against him were dropped and he was set free...and once again, he fled to parts unknown. The Postal Inspectors and I had been totally shocked.

WHILE WE WAITED for the news conference to begin. Bill O'Leary asked me if there was any way the MDC could pay for me to fly to Arizona with Postal Inspector Roger Hunt. Roger was one of the younger guys on the task force, but experienced. He had been a Captain in the Marine Corps and a helicopter pilot in Vietnam.

Bill had asked his higher-ups if they would pay my way, but budgets were tight and there was no guarantee Murnane would be found on the first try. I ran it by my boss, but the answer was no - the MDC could not afford to pay for this trip.

Five years of my life had been committed to catching these guys, keeping the promise I made to myself when I was shot. The thought of arresting the wheelman and transporting him back to Boston along with a federal cop in an airplane was pretty damned cool for a street cop like me. I was torn, but realized my ego and not common sense was driving my need to go along. I told the Post Inspectors I wouldn't be able to make the trip. In reality, they really did not need me to arrest Murnane, but Bill had been nice enough to try to include me.

*Days before, I'd talked with my wife about the possibility of using our own money but we would be out about $1,000 we really could not afford. Telling me I definitely made the right decision, Roger said, "If you ever decide to be a full time detective, never use your own money on a case."*

Roger Hunt told me he would keep me advised of the progress in Arizona. A few days later he called from Arizona to say they were close, but not able to pick up the wheelman.

*"Information was received from street sources that Richard Murnane was in Arizona. It is known that Murnane has an associate and friend named Ronald Bonney who recently purchased a bar in Benson, Arizona. Inspector Hunt was dispatched to Benson, AZ on June 11, 1980 with the expectation of arresting Murnane before he received the news of his indictment and fled to parts unknown. Information about Murnane has been developed indicating that he may be a 'weak link' in this gang and it was planned to grill him with the hope of having him testify against the others. Ronald Bonney was questioned by Inspectors Hunt, Alan Kiel and Peter Hickock of the Tucson, AZ Domicile on June 12, 1980 and stated that Murnane was in Benson but left about two (2) weeks previous. He said that Murnane was probably still in Arizona but he didn't know where. Bonney was advised of the consequences of*

*harboring, aiding and abetting a fugitive. He said he expects to hear from Murnane soon and agreed to talk to him about cooperating with us. The phone number of the Tucson Domicile Inspectors was left with Bonney." (Bonney was one of the aliases Murnane went by). [Report of W.J. O'Leary]*

Inspector Hunt phoned me to say, "It's impossible to blend in in this small local cowboy bar, especially with my Boston accent. Our local Inspector wears cowboy boots and jeans, but I stick out like a sore thumb. It's 118 degrees here today, Dana, but it's a dry heat."

"I should have lent you my cowboy boots, Roger. So you're telling me I am not missing much." I laughed, knowing he was just trying to make me feel better about my decision to pass on the trip.

"You got that right. See you back in Boston. I'll buy you a cold beer," Roger replied.

Roger felt certain the getaway driver had been tipped. With the hope local Postal Inspectors and local cops would locate Murnane, Roger returned to Boston.

WHILE ROGER HUNT was in Arizona, I spent time in South Boston at the office of the Postal Inspectors. I wanted to review all of the reports on the case to see if there was anything we were missing. So I sat at Roger's desk, coffee in hand and started poring over the reports.

At the end of one of Bill O'Leary's reports written in late 1979, he noted the investigation was at a standstill. The U.S. Attorney's Office had declined to present the evidence they had gathered to a grand jury, for the **THIRD** time. In fact, Bill noted the case might have to be marked closed. The Postal Inspectors had a heavy case load and many new investigations were waiting to be handled. However, after my meeting with the Inspectors in

February of 1980, the Postal Inspection Service not only asked me to join the team but redoubled its efforts on my behalf.

This put things in a whole new perspective for me and I sat thinking how fortunate I was to have these men assigned to the case. My boss, MDC Detective Lt. Thomas Keough, had given me free rein and assigned Detective Sgt. Thomas White and Detective Leo Papile to replace the detectives originally assigned. And we got all of our really useful informant leads from MSP Detective Lt. Jack Dwyer, the former Somerville cop. The task force Bill O'Leary organized was made up of an amazing group of investigators.

UPON ROGER'S RETURN, we decided to step up the search for Murnane. Bill advised me he would apply to his Washington, D.C. headquarters for a wanted poster for Richard W. Murnane. We had no surveillance photos of him and had only managed to obtain a couple of small color photos of Murnane, from Detective Lt. Jack Dwyer, which were not good enough for a wanted poster.

O'Leary said, "We need to get his booking photo from 1010 Commonwealth Avenue in Boston."

The address was the location of Photo ID section of the Massachusetts State Police in 1980, an old building which had seen better days; in fact, it was run down. Bill had been there many times and knew his way around. It was my first visit, so I just watched him work the system. He signed out the jacket on Murnane. We went into a viewing booth to see if the mug shot would work for the wanted poster. What we saw was a mug shot of a dark haired male, who looked like he might be Italian.

Bill said, "Wait a minute. This isn't Murnane!"

Bill looked at the back of the photo to see if we had the right folder. The name 'Richard W. Murnane' was stamped with his aliases and other information.

Bill said, "I'll be right back."

He returned a few minutes later and said, "This is a photo of Sal Michael Caruana, a big time drug dealer from the north shore of Massachusetts."

Caruana                    Murnane

"How did that photo get in there, Bill?" I was puzzled.

"I think I know what is going on. The FBI signed out his folder last week and they must have 'mixed up' the photos," he said sarcastically.

This only added to our suspicion that Murnane had been an FBI informant.

"Don't worry about it. I know where I can get his real mug shot. No sense of even asking the Bureau," Bill said.

I asked, "Bill, have you ever had this happen on a case before?"

He smiled and just said, "Who knows? Maybe he's a snitch. Come on. We have a lot of paperwork to do."

Bill was able to get his real mug shot from the Saugus Police, the town in which the Hilltop Steakhouse was located.

The wanted poster for Murnane was dated (again my birth date) August 13, 1980 and posted in every post office in the United States.

Case No. 72-26328-MD R (1)
NCIC No. W 233896356
August 13, 1980

# WANTED BY
## POSTAL INSPECTION SERVICE
### FOR HIJACKING OF A POSTAL VEHICLE
#### RICHARD W. MURNANE

**ALIASES:**
Michael Morrissey, James Dowling, Ronald Bonney

**DESCRIPTION:**
AGE: 40, born 9-22-40
HEIGHT: 5 Ft. 8 In.
WEIGHT: 145
EYES: Brown
HAIR: Brown
RACE: Caucasian
SSN: 038-30-3754

**VIOLATION:**
Conspiracy, armed robbery, and possession of an unregistered firearm. Arrest Warrant No. 80-00190-S, issued 6/10/80 at Boston, MA for violation of Title 18, USC, Section 2, 371, and 2114; Title 26, USC, Section 5861 (d); U.S. Marshal, Boston, MA holds warrant.

Signature of Person Fingerprinted

If located, please cause his immediate arrest and notify the undersigned or nearest Postal Inspector, COLLECT, by telephone, telegraph, or teletype. Postal Inspector in Charge, Boston MA 02107, telephone (617) 223-2223 TWX 710 321-6445

Wanted poster for Murname

Once again, the search was on for the slippery wheelman. It had become an absurd game of catch and release, but I had no intention of giving up.

# CHAPTER THIRTY-THREE
## *The Trial*

The members of the Ten Hills Café gang from Somerville had robbed banks, shot a cop (me) during the commission of a federal crime, murdered a Wells Fargo Guard, and dabbled in international jewelry theft. Even though this bunch was not part of the powerful Winter Hill Gang from Somerville, they felt they were the up-and-coming next generation.

It was June 11, 1981, a year and a day after the pre-dawn arrests of the indicted suspects, and the first day of the trial of Capone and Murnane. I often doubted the trial of the bad guys involved in my shooting would ever take place. I was surprised at how calm I was when we filed into the Courthouse. I felt a great deal of satisfaction on that day. We had done our job: stopped the hijacking of the truck and caught the perpetrators.

It had slipped my mind the six year anniversary of the hijacking was only days away and my youngest daughter would turn fifteen. It would be a great present to her if we could convict the guys who almost took her Dad's life on her fourth birthday!

The John W. McCormack Federal Building was located in the heart of Boston's Financial District, known as Post Office Square. In 1874, it had been named for the Post Office located in the front of the building. The courthouse itself was built in the early 1930s in the Art Deco style. It was twenty-two stories high, which was unique for a building of that design. (A new Federal

Courthouse, the John J. Moakley U.S. Courthouse, was built in 1999, overlooking Boston Harbor.)

Five men from Somerville and Medford, Massachusetts had been indicted:

1. Peter Hackett had been a career criminal with a long record. He had been serving time in a Florida prison for a drug violation at the time of the indictment. Upon his release, he was arrested in Boston on August 25, 1980 on our federal warrant. And (I'll bet you figured it out)...he made bail, and then skipped town. Peter Hackett had become a federal fugitive.

> *I believe in our system of justice, where the defendant is presumed innocent until proven guilty. But the ability to make, and then jump bail is extremely frustrating. To me, it seems foolish to let guys, who had a long criminal record, out on bail.*

2. James Hackett, who had been the leader of the crew we called the Ten Hills Gang, had been imprisoned in the Sheikdom of Kuwait, for a jewelry store heist. At least, he wasn't going anywhere.

3. Joseph Bimber, who was Joseph Capone's uncle, had been the 'inside man' at the South Postal Annex. He worked at the South Postal Annex. When we interviewed Grider in Wisconsin, he told us about his meetings with 'Uncle Joe' at the Ten Hills Café. He claimed Bimber told the gang about the 'star route' (the leased truck) in detail. Uncle Joe figured out a large cash payroll was being loaded onto a tractor trailer when armed guards were present at the Annex. The gang had planned the robbery for over a month, during which time they had made several dry runs. At seventy-one, Bimber had been deemed incompetent to stand trial 'because of his age and mental deterioration.'

> *David Toppi had been a suspect early in this case and alleged to have been involved in several*

*of the bank jobs with Grider. He died locally, in Malden, MA on May 5, 1981, a month before this trial. He reportedly took his own life, supposedly over a dispute with a girlfriend. I was told he shot himself in the head with a .357 caliber Derringer, a nasty little high powered handgun.*

We were at the Courthouse that day to try these two felons:

4. Richard Murnane, the accused wheelman, had been arrested on December 17, 1980, on the hijacking warrant in Phoenix, Arizona. This time he *was held* without bail.

5. Joseph Capone had given James Hackett and his crew the details of the mail truck containing the money. He reportedly supplied the guns, disguises, and the stolen car, which was used as the follow/getaway car.

The defense attorney for Capone was a well-known trial lawyer. I had seen him in action once or twice before in state Superior Court. I didn't think he had ever lost a major case. He was well known for his antics in the courtroom and was a master at cross-examining witnesses. It was the way he put the questions to each witness and not necessarily the answers themselves, which seemed challenging enough to leave doubt in the mind of the jurors. I once saw him really anger a cop testifying on the stand, causing the cop to discredit himself. The defense attorney was 'a big gun' and the last person I wanted to see on the other side of the aisle. On the other hand, had I been the one on trial, I might have wanted him as my lawyer. I was sure he didn't come cheaply, and wondered where Capone got the money to hire this guy. After all, Murnane had been deemed indigent and was assigned a public defender.

The federal judge in the case, Judge Walter Jay Skinner, was well-known and a no nonsense jurist.

*He became best known for presiding over the Woburn, MA water contamination case, which was about high levels of chemical contamination found in City wells. The contaminated water had been blamed for the suddenly higher rate of child leukemia, described in the book and movie* A Civil Action.

During pretrial briefings, I listened as the Judge explained the rules to both the defense and prosecution teams.

In a stern and commanding tone, Judge Skinner said, "This is United States District Court and my courtroom. There will be no theatrics, by either side. If there are, I will admonish you only once. The second time you will be found in contempt. Is that perfectly clear?"

Both sides replied, "Yes, Your Honor."

I had testified in state courts many times, but this was major league. This was like the Red Sox played the New York Yankees, at Fenway Park…in the World Series. I wanted so much to sit in and watch the proceedings. But U.S. Attorney Paul Healy explained to me only Inspector O'Leary, the lead investigator would sit with the prosecutors. He knew I wanted to be there, but I as a witness I would not be allowed to listen to the testimony of the others witnesses. This time around I was not the cop, but a witness and, even worse, a victim of the crime. I would wait in a conference room, which was ours to use during the trial. From time to time, Paul Healy would call in to say he had a question for me. In between drinking too much coffee, I would stick my head out into the corridor to see what was going on.

The first day of the trial in the old Federal Courthouse, several of the Ten Hills gang crew were in the hallway of the courtroom. I recognized some of the same guys who had hung around at the Hilltop trial, years ago. Over years of observing the action at the Ten Hills Café, I had collected information on about twenty guys. I could tell you what cars they drove, where they hung out and at what time of day, where they lived and what was on their criminal record. During my surveillances of the gang, I had learned some interesting facts, one of which I kept as my ace in the hole. There had been outstanding warrants for two of the gang associates. They were misdemeanor warrants, but nevertheless I figured they might come in handy someday.

> *Technically, if a cop is aware of a warrant he should arrest that person immediately. However, if I had arrested that person during the investigation, it could have tipped our hand. It was better to bend the rules this one time.*

I would play my ace. I had a plan to restrict the behavior the gang members displayed during the Hilltop trial. I was sure the presence of the gang during the state trial had been a huge factor in that outcome. They were there to support their buddies and to frighten the witnesses. They looked like leg breakers and all were big guys. Either way, they had no respect for the judicial system and intimidated the witnesses who were called to the courtroom. I was told this was not something that would be tolerated in federal court, but I wanted to be sure.

They had been laughing and horsing around in the corridor outside the courtroom, much as they had done in state court. I recognized one guy, who I was pretty sure had an outstanding warrant, and I pointed him out to one of the U.S. Marshals. He made a phone call to make sure the warrant was still in effect.

There *was* an active warrant! The bad guy looked completely shocked when he was placed under arrest. Squirming in his handcuffs, he seemed to look around trying to figure out who fingered him as he was led away. It was fun to watch the other gang members, who seemed a little dazed and confused, as they tried to figure out what to do next. Then, they just walked out of the courthouse. I had put one over on the gang! I never saw them again during the trial.

A little while later, I was called to take the stand. I had gone over this moment in my mind many, many times. I entered the courtroom, standing as tall and confident as I could. The room was huge, but felt like a sauna with no air conditioning on the hot day. There were several fans that moved the air around, but not enough to cool down the old courtroom. I took the stand and when I was given the oath, I said, in the loudest and clearest voice I could muster, "I do, so help me God!"

I had testified many times during my eleven years on the MDC. I understood the importance of demeanor while on the stand. Testifying was not new to me, but in District Court there usually was only a judge, and no jury. When there was a jury, there were six jurors, usually for OUI cases. This was my first time before a twelve-person jury. I had waited for this moment for six years and I tried to look confident, but it still felt like the first time I testified on the witness stand. I was nervous, but totally focused on the task at hand. Recounting the shooting without any emotion would have been impossible. It was probably good for the jurors to see I had been emotionally wounded too, but I was afraid I would be so nervous I might break down.

After being sworn in, I sat down in the witness box. The members of the jury sat in two rows, behind a waist-high wooden railing.

Paul Healy said, "Please tell us your name and occupation."

"Dana Owen. I am a Metropolitan District Commission Police Officer," I proudly responded.

"On the night of June 16, 1975, were you on duty …?" Paul went on.

I recounted the facts of that night in detail. I tried to control by voice but it would crack from time to time. No matter how many times I told the story, I became emotional. It was difficult to focus on the prosecutor as he asked his questions. My words seemed distant to me. The evidence table in front of me was distracting. I was drawn to two items lying on the table: the sawed-off shotgun and two of the handguns used in the shooting.

I had only seen them before in photos. I tried not to stare at them, but it was impossible not to.

When I looked up from the table, I saw the defendants. This was the first time I had seen the wheelman, Murnane. He was ruddy faced and appeared to be drunk. The word that he was a heavy drinker seemed accurate. The other defendant sat calmly and confidently but never so much as glanced at me. It was hard to grasp - I never thought this day would come and now I was just a few feet away from the suspects. It was very satisfying.

As I finished telling my story, my thoughts shifted to what cross examination would be like. I was already dreading it.

I was daydreaming, when I was startled by Paul's voice, "Thank you, Officer. Your witness…"

I was sure the defense counsel would try to tear my testimony apart or at least make me say I could not positively identify any of the defendants.

Capone's lawyer looked up at the judge from his chair, simply said, "No questions, Your Honor."

Judge Skinner responded, looking at me, "Thank you, Officer. You may step down."

I nodded to the judge and tried not to appear stunned.

I walked toward the exit and though - what just happened? There would be no cross examination? I didn't take me long to realize what a good move it had been on the part of the defense. The defense attorney probably thought the jury would have sympathy for me - the 'shooting victim' - on cross examination and he didn't want to risk questioning me. I took a deep breath and left the courtroom, confident I had told the truth and hoped for the best.

Now, it was John Grider's turn. Grider pled *guilty* to the Hilltop incident, and was serving jail time for that robbery and the murder. He had been transported back to Boston by the U.S. Marshals from his prison in Wisconsin, to testify for the prosecution. Our 'star' witness had been a participant in the crime, my shooting and the hijacking. We had a strong circumstantial case, but we needed Grider's eyewitness identification. A different jury found James Hackett *not guilty* of the murder of the Wells Fargo Guard, even after Grider testified against him.

He was really the only one they needed to discredit. It would boil down to whether the jury would believe a man convicted of murder. There was nothing more I could do. It was all up to the U.S. Attorney and the defense now.

THE TOPIC OF the guns in the barn was bound to come up, but Paul Healy had a plan. It would be hard for the defense to get around the issue of the guns. The informant, T-1, had viewed the guns and disguises in the barn a month before my shooting. All the guns recovered the night I was shot had been in that barn and had matched the make, model and serial numbers on the list T-1 had given to the North Reading Police detectives.

The U.S. Attorney's Office had discovered the error that may have let Hackett off the hook during the Hilltop robbery and the murder trial. When the informant, T-1, testified at the trial, he was had been by the state prosecutor, if he had seen a stash of guns at a certain address. The prosecutor somehow asked the wrong address number. T-1 was able to answer without committing perjury and without correcting the prosecutor. However, this put reasonable doubt in the mind of the jurors. The prosecution presented the evidence of Grider's gun, which he had dropped a gun after he had been shot, and the fact that the gun was on T-1's stash list. Incredibly, this information, played no role in that trial.

I was there when T-1 and the owner of the barn, where the guns were found, were called into Paul Healy's office. Paul informed them they would be required to testify and this time he would ask the correct street number. He told them if they did not answer correctly, he would have them charged with perjury. T-1 said if he went along with the plan, it would ruin things for him with his in-laws.

But T-1 refused. He said he would invoke his Fifth Amendment right, against self-incrimination.

*I had no sympathy for him. He had made the move to become an informant and now he would have to pay the price.*

Paul simply said, "I'll have immunity granted for you both. If you refuse to testify, I'll have you brought before a judge and you will be held in contempt and jailed until you decide to testify. The punishment for such contempt will be indefinite. After thirty days, I will have you taken back to court. If you keep refusing you will be sent back to jail and returned to court every 30 days until you testify."

Paul explained all of this in a calm, but chilling tone. T-1 finally decided he didn't want to go to jail, so this is how T-1 was compelled to testify and tell the truth. The owner of the barn, also a family member, decided she would also have to testify.

I was really very impressed, although it doesn't adequately describe how I felt. The federal prosecutors had picked up the error in the Hilltop trial and found a way to correct for it in this trial.

AFTER GRIDER'S TESTIMONY, a short recess was called. I was waiting in the lobby outside the courtroom, dying to know the Inspectors out how the proceedings had gone. However, I couldn't ask until the trial was over because I had been a witness, and could be recalled to testify.

The large door to the courtroom opened and Judge Skinner walked out and through the metal detector, accompanied by his clerk, no doubt heading to his chambers.

The Judge in his black robes, hunched over from what I was told was scoliosis, looked at me and said in a quiet voice so no one else could hear, "I don't like your witness, Officer."

He was referring to Grider. My heart sank into my stomach. I was speechless. It felt like the case might have just slipped away. And yet, I could not believe this Federal Judge had just spoken to me. I was not sure if his dislike for our witness would affect the case at all. Why would he have said that to me? I was extremely concerned. I didn't tell the inspectors what he said, but I am sure I looked stunned.

I wondered what Grider had said during his testimony. I would have given anything to have heard it.

> *Later, during my research, I was told by Paul Healy that Grider was combative under cross examination and at one point he told the defense counsel to "get out of my face or I'll break your jaw!" Of course, he was reprimanded by the judge, but the Feds said the jury appeared to have sided with our star witness, even as the lawyer tried to tear him apart.*

> *In a recent conversation with retired U.S. Postal Inspector Kevin McDonough, who was present during Grider's testimony, Kevin repeated what he remembered: "I was at the trial and one of the defendants who turned [Grider], testified that they [the gang] didn't hijack the tractor at South Postal because of the presence of the Postal Police. So, they decided to take it about 100 yards away on the highway ramp. The same guy testified that he was trying to kill the police officer in order to get away. The truck was carrying a large cash payroll destined for Vermont. This was during the FBI turmoil of the late 1970s and 80s. Of course, the FBI withheld important information."*

After the fifteen minute break, the Judge made his way back to the courtroom. I was waiting near the metal detector when he walked by me again.

He stopped, turned to me and said in a low voice, "But I like you. You've got a set of balls."

I tried hard not to smirk. Later, Bill asked me what the judge said.

"Not much, Bill. He just complimented me on my professional testimony."

I never told anyone what he said until now. It had obviously been meant for my ears only.

When the testimony ended for the day, a recess was called before the closing arguments. Bill and I took the elevator up to the U.S. Marshals' office, were he had to fill out some paperwork. When the doors opened, there, with his wrists cuffed in front, was John Grider. His testimony was over, and he was being taken back to some undisclosed prison and into the witness protection program. Bill asked the U.S. Marshals if we could talk to Grider, privately. The Marshals obliged and Bill thanked Grider for his testimony and wished him luck.

In his usual impish manner and distinctive voice (I always thought he had the demeanor of Jack Webb in the old *Dragnet* TV show), Bill said, "John, you asked how the MDC cop you guys shot was doing."

Grider responded, "Yeah, how is he?"

"Why don't you ask him yourself? He's standing right here," Bill said, and turned his head to look at me. Grider had never been told I was the cop shot in the hijacking.

The look on Grider's face was priceless. I can still see it to this day. At first, he was speechless. He just stared at me.

Then, he said, "Hey, man. It was strictly business…nothing personal. We couldn't shake you off our ass."

Trying to come up with an appropriate response, I replied, "I understand, John. If I had the chance, I would have shot back at you guys."

Not my best line, but that's what I said.

Grider was a kid from the projects of Somerville - a former U.S. Marine who had fought in Vietnam. According to him, and his friends we interviewed, he came back from the war 'screwed up.' He was shot during the Hilltop robbery, and dumped on the streets of Somerville to die. And he never got a nickel of the $57,000 loot from the robbery.

It may sound foolish, but instead of hating him, I tried to understand where he was coming from. Too bad he had taken a different path after the war and become an armed robber.

I was going to ask Bill if he planned this all along. It would have been a rhetorical question, judging by the grin on his face. Some things in life you never forget. This moment was one of them.

# CHAPTER THIRTY-FOUR
## *The Closing Arguments*

By the time we finished talking with Grider and drank more coffee (I thought I would explode from drinking courthouse coffee for six days), it was time for closing arguments by both the prosecution and defense. I had been allowed to sit in for the closing arguments, and walked into the old courtroom, which was stifling in the hot humid June weather in the city of Boston. Most of my cases had been Judge-only (without a jury), but it seemed, from television courtroom dramas I had watched, many cases were won or lost on closing arguments.

Paul Healy instructed me to sit behind the defendants and *not* with the Postal Inspectors.

Paul said, "No matter what happens, just sit there like an altar boy."

I had no idea why he wanted me to sit there, but I felt the case hinged on his closing remarks, so I sat a few rows behind the defense table, hands folded on my lap.

The prosecutor always goes first on closing arguments, so Assistant U.S. Attorney Paul Healy addressed the jurors first. His demeanor was calm as he methodically laid out the government's case. I thought of how much he sounded like Mr. Spock, the Vulcan in the *Star Trek* TV show. His delivery was directed to each juror in a deliberate, personal and logical manner.

*I can still remember some of what he told the jury. Paraphrasing what he said, "I would rather have had a priest or rabbi as my star witness, not a man convicted of armed robbery and murder. However, it was not a priest or rabbi who participated in the hijacking. It was John Grider."*

The defense was next. I tried to put myself in the place of a juror listening to the arguments. I watched the jurors, trying to read the faces of each of the twelve men and women as the defense argument was presented.

The defense attorney responded with a more passionate and emotional appeal. Grider should not be believed, he argued. He explained his reasoning: his client, Capone, had nothing to do with the hijacking and had no knowledge of the crime. He tried to convince the jury Grider was only testifying to get an early parole for the Hilltop Murder. Defense counsel, in my mind, may have swayed some of the jurors to his way of thinking. It was like watching a tennis match as the ball went back and forth - conviction or acquittal? I had the advantage of knowing the truth. If only they knew what I knew.

Then the prosecution presented the final argument, called rebuttal. Morning turned into afternoon and the temperature in the courtroom was near 85 degrees, and muggy. Everyone was perspiring and the heat only made the tension worse.

Paul Healy summarized the government's case, presenting each point, each piece of evidence. Then he rebutted the contention by the defense that the government had coached Grider on what to say when he had been interviewed in Wisconsin.

Suddenly, he turned away from the jurors and faced me. He raised his arm and pointed his finger at me. The jurors, following the length of his outstretched arm, twisted their heads, and looked in my direction, as he pointed me out. Just as they looked at me, I had figured out why Healy told me to sit there. Healy was a genius! In order for the jurors to see me, they had to look through the defendants seated directly in front of me.

Healy addressed the jury:

> "...They failed to point out to you that when they went out [to Wisconsin], Officer Owen, seated in the courtroom, was there. The same man, that six years ago today, lay on the ground wounded. He's the man who went out there and he talked to Grider and they (the defense) suggested his testimony had been shaped by the government."

A few minutes later in closing his remarks, pointing at me again, the prosecutor said:

> "(T)he government would submit to you that it has proven its case beyond any reasonable doubt, all reasonable doubt, that six years ago today Officer Owen lay there in the street wounded and he sits before you today awaiting the truth, awaiting your verdict." [Quoting from a transcript]

It was a show stopper! A *Perry Mason*-like move. Defense counsel for both of the defendants jumped to their feet, slammed the table, and yelled, **"Objection!!!"**

The jurors had to be removed from the courtroom, while the lawyers approached the bench to discuss the objection from the defense. A very heated bench conference took place. I think the defense saw this as the final nail in the coffin.

Again, quoting from a public document:

> "Appellants' counsel immediately moved for a mistrial on the grounds that these remarks were an inflammatory appeal to the jury's passions.
>
> The trial judge denied the (mistrial) motion, but instructed the jury to disregard the remarks. Appellants' claim that it was error to deny the motion for mistrial, that the judge's instructions could not cure the harm done by the prosecutor...

...the trial judge gave a strong, explicit, cautionary instruction. He told the jury: I am going to vary the usual order of instructions, because I do wish to deal with a matter raised in the last seconds of (the) rebuttal argument; that is, concerning Officer Owen, who is clearly from the testimony that we have a very brave and lucky officer, but his interest is not served and it is not your duty to serve his interest, if it were served, by anything other than a truthful verdict as you see it. The suggestion that one verdict as opposed to another is something that he is waiting for is something that you should disregard. I assume that neither he nor anyone else would want a verdict that reflected anything other than the truth as you see it given the burden of proof which the Constitution and laws of the country put upon the government in criminal cases."

As far as I was concerned, the fatal wound had been delivered. Paul Healy managed to put things in very human terms. Finally, it was in the hands of the twelve men and women on the jury.

# CHAPTER THIRTY-FIVE
## *The Verdicts*

We had not eaten since we had coffee and a bagel that morning.

Paul said, "Let's grab some food."

Not far away was Purcell's, a local hangout for cops and prosecutors. We walked a few blocks through the downtown streets, in the late afternoon heat. It reminded me of the weather the night I was shot. Looking up at the skyscrapers I felt like a child again, shopping in Boston with my grandmother.

The four of us - the two inspectors, the prosecutor and I - went into the pub. It was a nice quite place to sit and await verdicts and was only a few blocks from the courthouse. We were seated at a table for four and pictures of many local politicians adorned the wall.

I ordered a turkey club sandwich with french-fries, and the young waitress asked me, "Anything to drink?"

What a leading question, I thought in this Boston watering hole.

"I'll have an iced tea, unsweetened," I answered.

Not what I wanted of course, but discretion…you know the rest.

"Lemon?" she asked.

"Sure," I said.

Paul Healy was quiet and pensive. My mind was racing out of control. All I could think about was what verdict the jurors would return. It was an eternity before the silence was broken.

Bill asked, "What do you think, Paul?"

He just shrugged his shoulders, looked down at the sandwich between his hands, and took a bite. Words did not come easily... we knew it was all on the line. We sat in silence as we ate our meals. The prosecutor and the inspectors had been through this many times, but this was my first time waiting for a verdict on the most important case of my career. Thinking back on other felony arrests I had made in my eleven years on the job, this was the only one I had become personally involved in, or even really cared about. In state Superior Court, the cop just went home after testifying.

After we finished eating, Fred started a conversation about the Red Sox. I think Bill said, "Wait until next year", the standard line about the Boston team which had not won a World Series since 1918. It was obvious we could think of nothing else, just the pending verdict.

The minutes dragged on into two hours. Paul would call his office from time to time. The waiting was brutal for us and for the defendants, I imagined.

Paul said, "They are still at it. They may go home for the night...not sure yet."

Not more than fifteen long minutes later, the waitress told Paul there was a phone call from his office. Our guess was they would adjourn for the night. It was about 8:00 p.m. and the date, by coincidence, was June 16, 1981, exactly six years to the night I was shot. In fact, it was almost to the hour.

Paul came back to the table very calmly.

Amazingly, he announced, "Let's go. They're coming in with a verdict. Don't get your hopes up... they really didn't take all that long."

Bill picked up the check. I was sure Uncle Sam paid. My stomach was killing me. Usually a quick verdict meant *not guilty*, but not always. What if they had found them *not guilty*? I was preparing myself for the worst.

My pulse was racing as we briskly walked the few blocks. The city at dusk, with all the tall buildings lit up, looked so clean and bright. Traffic was sparse as we arrived at the courthouse in Post Office Square. The air seemed so calm compared to the chaos I assumed we were about to walk into.

After a pit stop in the men's room, we sat and waited for the jury. Fred and Bill were in the row behind me. The judge and his clerk came in first. Judge Skinner warned outbursts would not be tolerated by either side, no matter what the verdict was. The suspense was killing me and I squirmed in my seat. All I could think of was if we lost the case against these two, we would probably lose the case against the others, as well. I thought of praying for a conviction, but I had broken most of the deals I made with God the night I was shot. So I just sat and waited.

The family of the 'supplier' Capone was there, as they had been for the last six days. The family seemed to be close-knit and supportive.

My wife was at home with our kids. I thought of how hard the waiting must have been for her. She had been totally supportive but I knew she wanted this all to end, too.

When I looked over at the defense team, they seemed smug and confident. I could picture them gloating if their clients were found *not guilty*.

"All rise!" was announced as the jurors were led in. They never even glanced at the defendants. They just looked straight ahead. Each juror seemed very somber, even exhausted.

I felt a tug on my shoulder. Fred, after seeing the jurors had not looked at the defendants, whispered in my ear, "We got 'em!"

The defendants and defense lawyers stood. Then, the Judge asked the jury foreman if they had reached a verdict.

"We have, Your Honor."

"Mr. Foreman, please hand the envelope to the clerk."

The clerk opened the envelope. Even though I understood what Fred said, I looked down. I could not bear to see all these years go down the tubes. I had a feeling of doom.

All I really heard was the first...***"Guilty!!!"***

Both of the inspectors shook my shoulders as the verdict came down on each count. The jury foreman read *guilty*, again and again. Then, I thought I heard one *not guilty* against Capone, for the possession of a sawed off shotgun. The judge had instructed the jurors about the role of conspiracy in the defendants' behavior.

He had said, "It was like a snowball rolling downhill - the conspirators could be found *guilty* on anything it [the snowball] picked up along the way."

Despite what the judge had said, the jurors found him *not guilty* of the one charge, knowing it would tack on fifteen years to a mandatory ten year sentence. It did not matter - they had been found *guilty* on all major counts.

A woman seated with Capone screamed and fainted.

The judge calmly said, "Will the court officer take her out to get some fresh air? It is really hot in here."

He seemed to be used to this kind of drama in his courtroom.

The jury was polled to make sure each agreed with the verdicts. They all did. A date was set for sentencing and the judge and jury left the courtroom. I was smiling from ear to ear - so relieved all of our hard work had paid off, and amazed at the prosecutor's skill. Justice at long last!

It was over.

Well...not exactly.

I saw Capone take off his large gold neck chain, thinking he was about to be led away, and hand it to who I thought was a family member. I guessed he had not heard the Judge say he was free on the same bail, until sentencing. Murnane would remain in custody.

I was sitting in my row, alone with my thoughts. I was scanning the old courtroom, thinking about the last moments of the trial. Incredibly, Capone began to walk back to my row. At first, his lawyer did not see him coming toward me, as he was busily putting away some papers. The Postal Inspectors were at the prosecution table congratulating Paul Healy. I noticed the court officers walking toward Capone as he entered my row, looking crazed. I thought he was going to come over to punch me. He sure as hell wasn't coming over to shake my hand. I quickly decided I would take a dive better than any crooked boxer had ever done.

He stopped a few feet away from me. Standing in my row he smirked, "Your witness, Grider, was the one who shot you. I hope you're happy."

I didn't know what to say, or if I should even respond.

I simply said, "I know he shot *at* me...," knowing this was highly unusual and, and thinking like a cop, the less said the better.

His lawyer grabbed him by the arm and angrily told him, "Keep your mouth shut!"

The defense attorney's stance throughout the trial was his client didn't even know Grider. Not a smart move on his part.

I walked over and shook hands with the Postal Inspectors and the Assistant Unites States Attorney.

Paul asked me, "What did he say to you?"

I told him what he said.

Paul, in his usual business-like manner, said, "Dana, let's go to my office. We have a lot to go over and I want you to write down exactly what he said to you. I can use it against him in the sentencing phase."

I should have been elated I guess, but I simply could not rest until we brought them all to justice. I had to stay focused on capturing the others. It was time to get back to work.

# CHAPTER THIRTY-SIX
## *The Sentencing*

The two convicted men, Capone and Murnane, were back in federal court on July 13, 1981, for the sentencing hearing. Each side would have an opportunity to plead their case. The prosecution would ask for the maximum prison term, and the defense would counter with a request for leniency.

We were back at the old Federal Courthouse. It was even hotter and more humid in July than the last time we were there in June. The courtroom was deserted, no spectators and no reporters.

There was a different look about the defense team. They said Capone's lawyer, who I felt would have played a big role in the sentencing, was on vacation, so a second stringer showed up to represent Capone. Paul Healy's closing argument had been a winner in the trial, and he would do a first-rate job this time, too.

Paul called me to the stand to testify about what Capone had said to me after the conviction.

The defense team strongly objected and said, "Your Honor, we can't think of anything our client had to say to Officer Owen that would be of interest to this court."

I sat quietly and waited for the judge's ruling.

With what I would call a smirk, Judge Skinner replied, "Oh, I could not disagree with you more. This court is very interested to hear what he said to Officer Owen."

I went on to recount the conversation. I thought the fact that Capone admitted to knowing Grider, and the role Grider played in the hijacking could hurt him at this sentencing phase.

After listening to both sides, the judge handed down the sentences. Capone was given the required mandatory minimum, which was 10 years in federal prison for armed robbery and five years for conspiracy, to be served concurrently. Had he been convicted of the sawed off shotgun charge, he would have faced twenty-five years. It was apparent to me the jury did not want to see Capone, whose family was present throughout the trial, get the additional time, despite the fact the shotgun was in the stash of guns proven to be under his control. I felt the conviction and ten year sentence was still a huge victory.

The Judge imposed a twenty-five year sentence on Murnane: twenty-five years for armed robbery and assaulting a federal employee, five years for possession of a sawed off shotgun and five years for conspiracy, all to be served concurrently. I thought it was only fair. He seemed to have beaten the system, until now.

He had never been charged or prosecuted for his role as wheelman in any of the bank robberies, and he had not been tried for his part in the Hilltop robbery and the murder. Justice had finally won over Murnane.

I marveled at the reasoning of the jurors. They found the guy who had the sawed off shotgun under his control *not guilty* on that one charge, even though it had been proven by the list of guns and serial numbers provided by T-1. Instead, the wheelman Murnane was found *guilty* of the sawed-off shotgun charge, even though he was never in possession of the weapon. I never talked to any of jurors, but would love to have known their reasoning.

*Almost a year later, the convictions were appealed to the United States Court of Appeals, First Circuit. The appeal 693 F.2d 582 (which is public record) was argued on April 6, 1982 and decided on July 22, 1982. The convictions were*

*affirmed (upheld). Justice Breyer, who now sits on
the Supreme Court, was on the appeals panel.*

When I read the entire appeal, during my research, I laughed
when I got to the part that Murnane's court appointed attorney
tried another avenue, probably out of desperation. He implied the
empty shell casings, from the Walther PPK pistol Grider used in
the mail robbery and dropped at the Hilltop robbery and the
murder, were planted in a search of Murnane's apartment in the
Somerville Projects. A Massachusetts State Trooper named
Ronald Guilmette, whom I know, was said to have planted the
shell casings, in order to link Murnane to the Hilltop murder.

Ron retired as a Lieutenant Colonel from the Massachusetts
State Police. I showed him the appeal.

He shook his head and sarcastically said, "Well, Dana, looks
like you and I were the bad guys. It just shows you that they had
nothing to go on for the appeal."

Included in the appeal was a statement of a 'jail house snitch.'
The snitch claimed Grider made up the whole story for revenge.
Then, there was the statement of a New Hampshire police
detective, who explained the snitch was only trying to get out of
jail himself and had tried this on several other occasions. The
appeal was baseless and justice prevailed this time.

I felt so relieved that all of those years of hard work had paid
off and that I never gave up. I hated to even think of how I would
have felt if we had lost, or if this conviction had not been upheld.

To me, it was fate. Justice had prevailed - plain and simple -
at long last. I felt refreshed and renewed, mentally and
physically, and it was time to go after the remaining bad guys.
The chase was not quite over, even after seven long years.

ABOUT EVERY TWO years, I would receive a phone call
from the Federal Parole Board regarding this pair's incarceration.
Each time, the caller, who had been assigned just to review the
status of the case, was a different person. And each time, the

caller asked the same question: Did I feel Capone or Murnane, or both of them, should be paroled?

My opening line was always the same, "You mean the guys involved in shooting me twice in the head, and almost killing me?"

There would usually be a long pause, followed by, "Then your answer is you don't feel they should be paroled?"

I guess the good thing was I did not have to attend the parole board hearing. I knew the victims and the families of victims had to show up at these difficult and disturbing meetings, year after year.

I don't know if they were ever paroled. A cop's job is over once the convicted defendants go to jail and I had done my job.

## CHAPTER THIRTY-SEVEN
### *Undercover Narcotics*

After the arrests and convictions, there wasn't enough work on my case to keep me busy full-time. I was told I would have to justify my time in the MDC Detective Unit, if I wanted to remain on special assignment. When I was not working on my case, I had been partnered with another detective to work on active felony cases committed on MDC jurisdiction. This even included the murder of an Assistant District Attorney.

Detective Sgt. Tom White told me the only way I could stay on special assignment was to work with the detectives in the Narcotics Unit. I agreed and was sent to a two week school offered by the Drug Enforcement Agency (DEA). The course was attended by cops from many surrounding agencies, including Boston P. D. It was informative and I learned about another side of police work. Robert Stutman, the head of DEA in NYC was one of my instructors at Babson College, where the training was held.

I completed the course and was certified as a Narcotics Investigator. What irony…I had never used drugs in my life, had been in uniform for eleven years and knew nothing about the drug culture.

I was supposed to be a 'coordinator' for the undercover 'narcs.' The deal was I would not have to make any drug buys or be an undercover narc. This was much like promising me 'the check is in the mail,' and I knew it.

I was given a new identity, Dana O'Neil, and had a driver's license to prove it. I also grew my hair longer, and sported a Fu Manchu type mustache. I was supposed to act like a mid-level Irish cocaine dealer. My undercover car was a two-door 1976 Cadillac Deville…baby blue. It had been confiscated during a drug bust during which I was the uniformed back-up cop. After the bullet holes were repaired, it became the first confiscated vehicle to be used in an undercover drug bust by the MDC. In fact, it was the first in the Commonwealth of Massachusetts.

I wore my Irish Scally cap, tried to act like a dealer and hoped I would be believable in this role. This was not who I was and I was selling my soul, but it meant I could stay on my case.

I had broken the second promise I had made to my wife and myself when I came on the job. No motorcycles and no narcotics undercover was the pact. Both were dangerous duties and I knew several undercover cops who got messed up with the role-playing aspect. They basically lost their own identity and started acting like the role was real life.

My wife had already received the call that night in 1975, the call all cops' spouses fear. She saw me after I had been shot and then again injured badly in the police motorcycle accident. I knew I had made a stupid decision by joining the narcotics unit and had betrayed her trust. My only defense was, I have to catch the guys who shot me. I had to do this, but the more I thought about what I was doing, the more I knew it was time to step back and be honest with myself. *But*, if I did not keep the investigation into my shooting going, who would?

In late November, there was a shortage of personnel and I was assigned to go undercover and make some drug buys. The war against drugs was underway and we were often loaned to another Police Department in the region. My assignment was to work in a town on the south shore of Boston, called Braintree, MA.

An informant was to introduce me as a cocaine buyer at a popular lounge in that city. The informant was a young man who had been busted for drugs and was 'flipping' to cut a deal on his sentence. The only way to work our way up the ladder of dealers was with an introduction from someone they 'trusted.'

"Just tell the dealer I want to buy in ounces and don't overdo the introduction," I told the junkie.

He was so high he made me nervous. I could only hope he wouldn't blow the whole deal. I talked to him for maybe fifteen minutes before we arrived at the lounge. I was as keyed up as he was, but without the drugs.

I was super uncomfortable. I knew everyone in the bar would assume I was an undercover cop. I imagined they would see me wearing my uniform instead of my civvies. It was my job to convince them I was not. What a sick game.

I sat down and ordered an Irish whiskey, but I just couldn't shake the feeling. The lounge was dimly lit and mobbed, mostly with people in their early twenties.

*Back then, people could smoke in a lounge and*
*as a non-smoker my entire life...I was miserable.*

I wanted to have several drinks to relax, but that would have been a stupid and dangerous idea. This was not a game and it could have turned deadly at any moment. My snub nose was in my boot - a great place to conceal a gun, but a lousy place to try to get to it in a hurry.

The dealer, who was in his twenties, looked at me suspiciously, but my age of 34 seemed to help sell my cover.

"This is my buddy, Dana. He wants to buy some coke, and I told him you got the best stuff," the snitch said, his voice shaking.

Trying to sound in control, I said, "Your buddy tells me you can deal in ounces."

"He ain't my buddy and how do I know you're not a cop?" the target replied.

As I was trained to do, I got up and said, "You want to play games? I'm outta here."

"Sit down, man. I had to ask. It's cool," he threw back at me.

The dealer said, "I can only sell you a gram tonight. If I you like the stuff and I trust you, I can do ounces."

He got up and said he had to make a phone call. He was a small time drug dealer, but he was also suspected of stealing from the department store he worked at. So, he was my primary target.

In the few minutes he was gone, another dealer came over to me to say, "Hey! I got better stuff. He's small time." The word had spread like wild fire - I was there to buy.

No sooner had he left, when a third dealer came to my table with this sales pitch: better cocaine, larger quantities. My head was spinning. Drugs were everywhere. I was getting an education of how prevalent drugs were. I could not believe they had not made me as a cop. There were lots of dealers but I needed to focus on the subject I was assigned to bust. Let's call him Jim Johnson. I bought a small amount of coke off him that night, in the parking lot of the lounge. We sat in his brown VW bug and I told him I needed to buy in ounces for my people.

"Here, try some. It's good stuff," he said.

I knew he was testing me to see if I would.

"I just buy and sell. I don't use," I shot back.

That might have worked with this low level dealer, but never with a big fish. I was not willing to break the law - or my own rules - to prove I was not a cop. I hated this assignment already and it would only get worse. I started to think my wife was right: undercover was a stupid, dangerous idea.

I headed home for the night, after booking the evidence into our drug locker. We could work any hours we wanted or needed to and I could see why some of my fellow cops liked this assignment. There was a ton of freedom, unlike uniform duties.

In fact, too much freedom and some of the narcs I knew stepped over that fine line to make a pinch, at any cost.

I called Jim the next day from an untraceable phone in our Drug Unit.

"Hey, the stuff was Okay. Let's meet and we can do some more business."

He was late for the next meeting, but I bought another few grams of cocaine. Each time he arrived in a brown Volkswagen bug, each time alone and always late. His modus operandi (MO) was to circle our meeting spot three times - to look for cops. It became like a comedy to me, but I could not let my guard down for a minute. Most of the low level dealers were users selling to support their habit. They were unpredictable, dangerous people.

On the third meeting, in December, I bought about three grams of coke.

"I need to buy ounces. My people want bigger quantities and they are not happy with me, Jim. Shit or get off the pot," I said with total confidence. "If you can't handle it, we can't do business anymore."

I was taking advantage of this small time dealer/user. He was interfering in my family life. My oldest daughter had been in a play at her Catholic school. But, I had missed the play to buy drugs from Jim. The agency I was working for was thrilled, my wife was bullshit, and my daughter was upset I didn't attend her play. I was getting depressed. The only other time I missed an activity that my kids were in was the ballet recital for my youngest two weeks after I was shot, when I was still just too paranoid to be in a crowd.

The suspect told me he could do ounces and wanted to meet on December 24.

"What?...Are you crazy?...That's Christmas Eve," I said.

It was obvious he only thought about drugs and money. This was spiraling downhill. My bosses wanted me to give him another chance. It seemed the town cops wanted this guy badly.

So, I spent that Christmas Eve waiting to buy a few more grams of coke in the parking lot of a hotel on Union Street in Braintree, instead of being home with my family. Jim never showed up.

Cops miss many holidays with their families because they have to work, but to miss a holiday to buy drugs? The drug world was a depressing dark place and I hated being a part of it.

Finally, the big deal was set for set for January 5, 1981. I would buy a half ounce of cocaine for $1,500. I was sure this was the most Jim had ever attempted to sell, but with a larger quantity, the Braintree P. D. would have a better case against him.

The Braintree Captain handed me the cash for the drug buy. He said, "Remember, the money is the most important thing, because we did not have time to mark the bills."

I handed him the cash back and said, "You're wrong. I am." After a heated debate, I prevailed. I was the most important thing…or was I?

This buy was to be a 'buy and bust.' As soon as I had the coke, I was to signal to my backup units and they would come in and make the arrest. This is one of the most dangerous parts of undercover narcotics. The bad guy might try and rip off the 'buyer,' or may feel he is going to be ripped off. All too often they end up in a shootout. A lot of cops had been shot, or had to shoot a suspect during this type of a deal. The Cadillac I was driving had been seized after a buy and bust, which turned into a shooting. I just didn't have a good feeling about this night and was ready to call it off. The trouble was I knew I had to go through with it.

The deal was set in the parking lot of a donut shop in Braintree. The 'donut maker' was my undercover partner Ron. Ron was my first African American partner. He was, at one time, the New England area full-contact-karate champion and had been a sparring partner for Marvin Hagler, who was the undisputed World Middleweight Champion from 1980 to 1987. Ron was a great undercover cop, fluent in Spanish and a good guy to watch your back. He could see the parking lot clearly from the store window. I sat in the Caddy (the car reeked of cigarette smoke from my fellow undercover partners) sipping my fourth coffee of the night. My partner 'made the donuts' in an apron and chef's hat.

I had backed into a parking space a few spots from the store front. Across the street were my other backups in a van. My heart was racing as I looked for the brown VW, but as usual, Jim was late. Dope dealers were just lousy businessmen - never on time or never showed at all.

After I had finished the deal, I was to exit the car and take off my Scally cap. This was the signal for my backups to move in. Like many undercover operations, this one started to go bad. A large delivery van parked between my car and the doughnut shop, and my partner's view was totally blocked. I was not wearing a 'kelset' (a transmitter) so the backups could monitor me...but it seldom worked anyway.

*In fact at the time, McDonald's had better radio equipment at the drive through window than law enforcement did.*

At least the cops in the van across the street could see me, so I was still in good shape. I introduced myself to them earlier in the night so they would not mistake me for a bad guy, if things went sour...or at least I hoped they wouldn't.

I was really cranked and watched a Pontiac Grand Prix with two white males drive by me, three times. This was Jim's style - he would always circle three times looking for cops - but he always came in the VW. It was too dark for me to see if he was in this Pontiac. Another truck parked a few spots down on my right. Great! Now, none of the backup units could see me. I had a really bad feeling in my gut.

The Grand Prix pulled in next to me on my right. Sure enough, Jim was in the passenger's seat with another guy driving. I sensed it was going to be a 'rip off.' Of course, my service revolver and my issued shotgun were in the trunk of the Caddy, along with the $1,500 in cash. I was in deep trouble. Like an idiot, I did not have my snub nose in my boot that night and I don't remember why. That was a huge mistake on my part. I had obviously been too complacent about this drug dealer.

Jim opened the passenger door and got into my car. I decided to go on the offensive.

"You guys are cops!" I yelled at him.

"No way. My VW is in the shop, he is a friend and gave me a ride. Here's the coke."

He handed me a large clear baggy with the half ounce of cocaine. I had to stall for time because none of my backups could see me. They had been told the target would be in a brown VW, not a Pontiac. The only thing I could think of was to break one of the rules we were taught in DEA School. I took out my pocket knife, cut into the taped up bag and rubbed a tiny bit of the white powder inside my lower lip. I had seen someone do it in a movie. I had no idea how to tell if it was 'good stuff,' but when my lip became numb instantly, I guessed it was.

I knew I had screwed up. My guns and the money were in the trunk and I was protecting the cash even though I promised myself I wouldn't. It was time to regain control of this nickel and dime dealer, before I got my ass shot up!

"Stay here while I get the cash, and tell your buddy to stay in his car," I ordered.

I got out of the Caddy and took off my hat. I was waiting for the cavalry to arrive with bugles blaring…but nothing happened. My backup could not see me because of the trucks. Walking back to the trunk, I was madly waving my hat in the air, not caring how foolish I looked. Still…nothing. I opened the trunk and looked at the cash and guns. I picked up my heavy barreled stainless steel service revolver and hid it by my side, while the cash stayed in the trunk. My issued shotgun was in the trunk, but I decided to stay with the police revolver, so I would look like a cop, not a bad guy to my backup units. I was shaking from all the coffee and was so angry with myself.

I walked back and opened the driver's door with my left hand as if to get back in, trying to catch Jim off guard. Positioning myself between the seat and the car door, I took a crouched shooting stance, and pointed the gun at Jim's chest - center mass, as we had been trained. I don't think I had ever seen fear in anyone's eyes like his.

"Please don't shoot me, take the coke it's yours!" he begged. My mind was racing, and I realized I had not identified myself. I quickly said, "Police! Don't move!"

He raised his hands and with a sigh of relief blurted out, "Thank God!"

The backup units raced into the parking lot and blocked the Grand Prix. Cops, with guns drawn, were everywhere. I had been blinded by all the brilliant blue lights and prayed some excited uniform cop wouldn't mistake me for a bad guy, so I quickly lowered my service revolver to my side, and pointed it to the ground.

My partner, Ron, came running out in his chef's apron, badge in one hand, gun in the other and said, "Nice job, partner."

He was covered with white flour from his attempt to make donuts. The sight of him made me laugh.

The uniform cops had removed Jim and his buddy from the vehicles and had them lying face down on the pavement and handcuffed behind their backs. Marked units kept pouring into the parking lot, with blue lights flashing and tires squealing to a stop. The lights reflected off the large windows of the donut shop, bathing the parking lot in a shade of flashing blue. I guess I should have been happy as the cops patted me on the back congratulating me, but I was just numb. I stood there dumfounded. I honestly felt like I was in shock. Jim thought I was a bad guy and that I was going to rip him off or kill him. This was getting way too bizarre. The scene was something out of a TV cop show, but this was real life.

They took both suspects away in marked cruisers to be booked. The guy who drove the car for Jim was to be booked for conspiracy. Ron radioed our other narcotics unit the arrest had gone down. Armed with a search warrant, another team of cops hit Jim's house and recovered a huge stash of stolen goods taken from the department store where he worked, along with various quantities of drugs.

Finally, it was time to go the local Police Department to make out reports. Ron asked, "How do you want your coffee?"

"I'll take a large black...with about three shots of Irish whiskey."

Ron laughed and said, "You got it, partner."

This was my first and **last** undercover buy!

# CHAPTER THIRTY-EIGHT
## *Peter Hackett*

The trial and conviction of Capone and Murnane was over. It was a huge victory, but we were not done. It was time to go after the Hackett brothers. James was still in prison in Kuwait. Bill O'Leary gave me a clipping he found in the the Arab Times - from Kuwait, dated July 8, 1980. There, on page one, was James Hackett and Paul Mulligan with their accomplice, Abdul Hadi. Hackett was holding the toy gun he used in the robbery. I was told years would go by before Hackett was ever returned to the states, if he survived the hard prison time in the desert. We would turn our attention to his brother Peter.

We had been trying to pick up Hackett in the Framingham, MA area and I was involved in several stakeouts with the goal of taking him into custody. Hackett was well known to Framingham P. D. and had been seen driving a late model Ford Mustang in late January 1981. The car had been rented from Framingham Auto Sales, Inc. On Monday, February 4, 1981, I went to Framingham Auto to speak with the rental manager. He told me when he arrived at work that morning, the Ford Mustang was parked in the lot with the keys in the ignition. The remainder of the bill, $500, had not been paid. I asked to see the number of the credit card used to rent the car, but he told me Hackett paid the deposit in cash.

According to Framingham Police, Hackett had been seen several times at a local hotel and at a lounge in Framingham called Duca's. Officer Bill Vinci, from our narcotics unit, and I went to Duca's the next night, and nursed a beer. We observed two males, one with a beard and the other one, who fit Hackett's description, was clean shaven. We had several photos of him. He had been clean shaven in some and bearded in others. But, even with the photos, we not able to make a positive ID of either subject. We made no attempt to make an arrest in the crowded lounge because we were not positive it was Hackett and, if it had been him, he was always armed.

Shortly after that, Peter Hackett fled to Florida, just as his brother James had done. The trail had grown cold. There seemed to be a connection between the criminals from Somerville and Florida. The older Hackett kept his movements to himself; the informants had no idea as to his whereabouts. As the months passed, it was obvious we would need a break to capture him.

Case No. 501-26328-ECR(1)
NCIC No. W255731134
August 21, 1981

# WANTED BY
## POSTAL INSPECTION SERVICE
### ARMED ROBBERY OF POSTAL VEHICLE
PETER E. HACKETT

Fingerprint Classification
14 I 29 W 100 15 Ref 29
I 28 W MOI 20

**DESCRIPTION**
Age: 40, born 4-2-41 at Peabody, MA
Height: 6 feet
Weight: 205 lbs.
Eyes: Blue
Hair: Brown
Race: Caucasian
Occupation: truck driver, carpenter
SSN: 029-30-3238
FBI NO.: 649 774 J5

SHOULD BE CONSIDERED ARMED AND DANGEROUS

**VIOLATION:**
U.S. Marshal at Boston, MA holds warrant for arrest of PETER E. HACKETT, for violation of 18, USC 317, 18, USC 2114, and 26, USC 5861(d).

Signature of Person Fingerprinted

If located, please cause his immediate arrest and notify the undersigned or nearest Postal Inspector COLLECT, by telephone, telegraph, or teletype, Postal Inspector in Charge, Boston, MA 02107. Telephone: (617) 223-2223, FTS 223-2223, TWX 710-321-6445, USPS-ISAT

Wanted poster for Hackett

On August 21, 1981, the Postal Inspection Service issued a wanted poster for Peter E. Hackett. It was to be hung in Post Offices all over the United States. The only difference between the Murnane wanted poster was this one said, 'SHOULD BE CONSIDERED ARMED AND DANGEROUS.' When we were putting together the info and picture for the wanted poster, Bill O'Leary filled me in on Peter Hackett's criminal past. He showed me the following report.

> *"Peter Hackett is incarcerated in the Zephyrhills, Florida State Correctional Institution serving a term for a drug violation conviction on March 14, 1979 in St. Petersburg, FL. He is eligible for parole on this conviction on July 8, 1980 but he also has an 18 month sentence hanging over him for a Middlesex County, New Jersey drug violation conviction when he is released. He is also facing charges in Suffolk County, MA for firearm violations dating back to his arrest in Revere, MA on September 13, 1971. The U.S. Marshals' Service has filed a detainer at the Zephyrhills Institution relative to the indictment returned against him by the Federal Grand Jury at Boston, MA on June 9, 1980."*
> *[Report of W. J. O'Leary June 18, 1980]*

However, after he was transported back to Boston on our warrant by the United States Marshals, he was arraigned, made bail and just as quickly, disappeared. By the end of the year, we had no idea where he was hiding out.

"HAPPY NEW YEAR!" the voice said as I answered my home phone.

I recognized it as Bill O'Leary right away.

"Happy New Year, Bill. What's up?" I asked.

"Not much…except Peter Hackett has been shot in Florida and is in custody."

I could see the impish grin on his face in my mind.

"You're kidding? Great!" I responded.

Bill went on to tell me Hackett was involved in what was thought to be a botched hit on Christmas Eve, December 24, 1981.

"We are not sure if the hit was on him, or the hit was on the guy he shot. Either way, he's in the hospital and expected to survive. They have him in custody on our warrant," he said.

There was an article in the *Boston Globe* on Saturday January 2, 1982, by Richard Connolly that gave a lot of details about the shooting. It explained how Peter was wanted in my shooting and recapped the events of June 16, 1975. I thought the last paragraph was the best:

> *"One puzzling aspect of the case was disclosed by a Massachusetts investigator who said he heard details of Hackett's shooting from 'street sources' in Somerville, before Hackett's identity was disclosed publicly in Florida."*

Another interesting detail was:

> *"While police were questioning him in the Pinellas Park shooting of 44-yr-old Joseph Francis Nelson, reported to be a former resident of the Boston area, he was quoted as saying, "I'm Peter Hackett...call the FBI."*

This came out of nowhere. We never figured out exactly what he meant.

Had he been an informant?

Nelson was shot with a .410 caliber shotgun about 6 a.m. (which sounded like a hit) and he fired three shots at his assailant with a 9mm pistol. Robbery was ruled out when police found $4,000 in Nelson's pocket and $13,000 in a briefcase in his home. The other shooter was reportedly shot in the ass as he fled. This matched Hackett's wound.

Nelson survived and Hackett checked himself into the hospital, where he was taken into custody.

On January 19, 1982, Inspectors W. J. O'Leary and F.A. Ricker interviewed Peter Hackett in the prison ward of Tampa General Hospital. The following is from the report of the interview:

> "Hackett said he wanted to take a polygraph because John Grider put him in the getaway car instead of his [Grider's] friend David Toppi. Toppi had died on May 5, 1981 in Malden, MA, in what was ruled an apparent suicide.

The Postal Inspectors had the warrant for his arrest. They interviewed him to see if he would incriminate himself further in the mail hijacking.

The following was taken from the Postal Inspector's written notes of the interview of Peter Hackett:

> The inspectors gave Hackett three possible versions of his shooting:
>
> 1.   He was robbing a victim
> 2.   He was whacking out the victim
> 3.   He spotted the contract and shot him first
>
> Hackett said he was shot running out of a bar 30 miles away from [where] the actual shooting [took place]. It was a beef in the bar. He refused to say who - why - when - where – [and] laughed at the 3 versions. He says that there were no State charges [Florida] against him for the shooting. His prison hospitalization was due to our Federal fugitive charges.
>
> Peter Hackett wants to take several polygraph tests, wants John Grider to take same tests.
>
> Hackett wanted to talk to us because he claimed he is innocent. [He said he] wasn't there [at the mail hijacking] and the person who played out his

*the role [he was being accused of] is now dead, by suicide - David Toppi. Toppi is the best friend of John Grider. Grider wouldn't put Toppi into the case [didn't want to rat on Toppi] but because of his bitter feud with the Hacketts, Jimmy and Peter, and Jimmy was there [he was part of the hijacking], he put Peter into Toppi's spot [said Peter was there when it was really Toppi].*

*John Grider hates Peter Hackett, because Grider thinks that the money from the Hilltop Steak House robbery/murder was given to Peter Hackett for safe keeping. Grider alleges that Peter refused to give Grider his split and used the money for Brother Jimmy's defense. Peter arranged for Harvey Brower to defend Jimmy. Grider alleges that Peter Hackett used the Hilltop (robbery) money for his own support and even gave a big party for Jimmy after his acquittal, using the Hilltop money.*

*Peter Hackett [says he] was approached to participate in the mail truck hijack, but after listening to the plans, wanted no part of it. He said all the participants were at the meeting. They wanted him because he was a truck driver by trade and they wanted him to drive the mail truck. Asked if Capone was at the meeting, he didn't want to say. Of course, he wouldn't have mentioned Jimmy as being there. [He] said Toppi and Grider were there.*

*The reason for declining, Hackett said, was that the plan was ridiculous and his share of $100,000 would be only $20,000. In June 1975, Peter was "booking and collecting" [shylocking (lending money at exorbitant interest rates]). He was* *making a lot of money, and, in a way, which [it] was easier and cleaner than robbery. Peter Hackett was shown the photo of James Nelson, the other man involved in the shooting; he said he didn't know him.*

*Peter Hackett and Howie Winter are bitter enemies and Howie wants Peter dead. Hackett stole, or bilked Winter out of a lot of money. When Howie wanted 50% of Hackett's collections, Hackett refused and went to Boston (Jerry Anguilo) and got permission to work Boston. Winters wanted Hackett dead; Hackett went to Providence and (Ray Patriaca) sent word to Howie to "lay off." Howie Winter was livid; they had a bad, loud argument and threatened each other's lives.*

*Hackett said Winter wants him dead, would kill him in Boston, but wouldn't send a "hit man" to Florida looking for him. Peter Hackett is also concerned with a New Jersey connection. Early in the conversation Hackett mentioned that during his fugitive period he spent time in New Jersey.*

*Diane, Peter's wife, called and told Hackett that she had received a telephone call from a criminal associate in New Jersey who wanted to get together with Diane. Diane is scared. Peter figures he knows a lot about the New Jersey operation and the New Jersey group wants to be sure Peter didn't turn on them. Hackett is concerned for Diane's safety. Hackett mentioned he spent most of his fugitive time in the Boston area. He threw out, during the conversation, [he was staying at] the Colonnade and the Sheraton – Boston. He did spend time in New Jersey and, lately, in Florida. When asked what he was doing for a living, he said "nothing" and "the usual."*

*He was asked where he adopted the name Peter Phillips, "the name used when he was first hospitalized for the gunshot wound", also where he got his identification. He said he just pulled the name "Phillips" out of the air at the hospital. He did not have any identification in the Phillips" name. Hackett had a full beard and long hair. He had gained a lot weight and appeared to be fat, even though he has been hospitalized [had surgery during his stay] for a stomach operation [colonectomy]. He doesn't resemble his photograph on the wanted circular, where his hair was short and he had no beard.*

For someone who claimed he was not involved in the mail robbery, Peter knew way too much about the crime. From the beginning, the only dilemma in the investigation had been whether Peter Hackett was the fourth robber in the getaway car, or David Toppi was there that night. I believed Grider's story during the interview in Wisconsin. If he had 'interchanged a player or perjured himself,' Grider would have lost the deal he had made with the Feds. He simply had too much to lose. Hackett, however, had the most to gain by claiming it was Toppi, and not him, in the getaway car.

The investigation reports never included Peter Hackett as a prime suspect in the bank robberies. The FBI reports said they interviewed witnesses on March 5, 1975, regarding the holdup of The State Street Bank and Trust Company, were there were three robbers.

One of the witnesses said a robber yelled, "What do you think we're doing here, looking for a job?"

He also heard the third individual ask, "You about ready, brother?"

All the robbers were white males and this was the second time the term 'brother' was used in one of the bank robberies. This made me feel that Peter Hackett had been involved in the bank robberies as well. After the interview of Kevin Trainor, I was convinced the fourth player was Peter.

Peter Hackett was tried in U.S. District Court on April 19, 1982. After a three-day trial, the jury began deliberating. On the third day of deliberations, they told the judge they were deadlocked and could not reach a verdict. The judge dismissed the jury.

The Postal Inspectors spoke to several of the jurors after the mistrial. They were told the jury was hung eleven to one to convict. On the first vote the single juror said, *"Not guilty* and I don't want to talk about it and won't change my vote."* That juror was reported to have been from Somerville. Had the gang gotten to him? We never found out, but it would not have surprised me at all.

On June 7, 1982, the second trial of Peter Hackett commenced. Thinking back to these trials, I hardly remember testifying. I know my written testimony was read by someone else and placed into evidence in the retrial. I was mentally exhausted by that time, and I just have no memory of his trial. I doubt my written testimony, read aloud by the prosecutor, would have the same effect on the second jury.

After another three-day trial, he was found *not* guilty of the charges relating to the hijacking. I think the defense must have been able 'to leave doubt' in the mind of the jurors because I did not testify in person.

On June 14, 1982, coincidentally almost seven years to the date of my shooting, Peter Hackett pled *guilty* to jumping bail and received a sentence of one year in the custody of the Attorney General of the United States.

I felt this had been less of a defeat than the Postal Inspectors or the prosecutor had. From the beginning, I was never 100%

sure of Peter Hackett's involvement as a suspect in the hijacking. But after the interview in Wisconsin, I believed Grider. He stated Peter Hackett was the fourth guy in the car that night. To me, Grider had too much to lose if he had lied.

I felt we were already way ahead of the bad guys. I took the outcome of this trial in stride.

The only one left was Peter Hackett's brother, James, who was jailed in Kuwait.

# CHAPTER THIRTY-NINE
## *The Wrap-Up*

I had been transferred from my special assignment back to the Motorcycle Unit, and then to the MDC Police Mounted Unit. Riding a horse instead of a motorcycle was a way for me to experience a different side of policing. The duties were actually fun and something I did as a family hobby at the time. Getting paid to ride my police horse on the Esplanade in Boston and on the MDC beaches at night, often on overtime, was not a bad deal.

On a night in late February 1986 my phone rang at home. I had learned to hate the phone ringing in the evening. It was usually some kind of bad news.

This time the caller was Postal Inspector Bill O'Leary.

We had not really spoken much since the *not guilty* verdict of Peter Hackett back in June of 1982. The only person left to bring to justice was Jimmy Hackett and he was doing six years in prison in the Sheikdom of Kuwait.

From time to time, Bill had petitioned the U.S. State Department to allow us to fly to Kuwait to interview 'the last man standing' in the case, but the State Department had not approved the trip. We had been told the area was too politically unstable; in addition, there was no extradition treaty with Kuwait. We would just have to wait until we could get our hands on Hackett and take him to court for the 1975 Mail Hijacking.

"Dana, you won't believe *this*!" Bill said in an excited tone.

"Bill, I don't think there's anything I won't believe, after all these years," I responded casually.

Bill said, "The Kuwait authorities have sent Jimmy Hackett back to the U.S., after he served his term for the jewel heist. The U.S. Marshals arrested him on our warrant as he stepped off the plane at JKF Airport in New York City. I will be in touch...we'll need you to testify, again."

I thanked Bill for letting me know and I hung up. I really couldn't believe the guy, who had been the leader of the gang and the one who had shot me, would finally be brought to trial in my case! And yet, I could not help but wonder how on earth we would convict him after eleven years.

Hackett was arraigned on March 3, 1986 at U.S. District Court in Boston, MA and held without bail at the Salem, MA House of Correction, while awaiting his trial. I did not attend the proceeding, but Bill kept me in the loop by phone.

On June 16, 1986, exactly eleven years to the day after I was shot, I was served with a subpoena.

> *The coincidences in this case could not have been made up. The shooting incident-related things that occurred on my daughter's birth date of June 16, and on my birth date of August 13 had been amazing. It seems as though someone had a master plan for me.*

The subpoena read:

United States of America V. James Hackett
TO: Dana Owen, MDC Police
PLACE: John W. McCormack Post Office & Courthouse
Devonshire Street
Boston, Massachusetts 01109
Courtroom No. 2 - 12th Floor
June 24, 1986 At 10:00 am
DATED: June 16, 1986

Yes, I still have the original subpoena. The eight days, between the time I received the subpoena and the arraignment were long and drawn out. I was just plain mentally exhausted. All the emotion and memories of the chase and lengthy investigation flooded into my mind. This was the person I wanted most to face justice. He was a cowardly murder and had beaten the judicial system. I secretly hoped he would never make it back from Kuwait.

It had taken me a long time to get my mind straight. Now, over a decade later, I did not want have to rehash my shooting and go through the roller coaster ride of testifying to the details all over again. I had moved on with my family life and police career, but I knew this was the last step in this long ordeal and hoped justice would be served. I became obsessed with the court process and getting a conviction. Would we replay the Hilltop trial and end up with a verdict of *not guilty*? All of these doubts raced through my mind. I really just wanted it to be over. Besides, this was very old and forgotten news. Even though there had been an article in the newspaper about Hackett's capture and return, they got his first name wrong, calling him Peter - the brother who had been found *not guilty* on his retrial.

Paul Healy called me at home a few days before the trial. He told me he wanted to offer a plea bargain to James Hackett. If found *guilty* in a jury trial, Hackett would face twenty-five years in federal prison. On the other hand, if he took a plea, they would recommend five years.

Paul discussed the offer he wanted to make to Hackett with me. He explained the pros and cons of going to trial with a case that was over a decade old. I understood all of the variables and the difficulty in rounding up the witnesses. Hackett told Paul he would not rat on anyone. Paul said he laughed and told Hackett that he had been away too long because there was no one left for him to testify against.

Paul said, "Dana, if you don't want to go along with the plea bargain, I will go to trial."

I was pleasantly both surprised and honored. He did not have to ask me - it was his decision. The respect and consideration shown to me by him, and by all of the Postal Inspectors, had been awesome.

"Paul, let's go with the five years. And, thank you - very much."

I felt without a doubt this was the best way to handle the case.

ON THE DAY of the trial, I wore the same sport coat, shirt and tie I had worn at the trial in 1981, for old times' sake. I guess I felt like a baseball player, wearing his lucky uniform - this was my lucky outfit. Sliding my service revolver into my shoulder holster, I looked into the mirror. I attached my badge to the holder, and guided the clasp over my belt. Reaching behind me, I tucked my handcuffs over my belt near the small of my back, where they hung freely. I looked in the mirror, one last time, and was ready to head into Boston.

Once again, I made the drive to the South Postal Annex, through the heavy Boston rush hour traffic. When I arrived at the lot, my mind wandered back in time, as I looked at the tractor trailers being loaded on the loading docks. This is where it all began. It was where the 'Star Route' truck had been loaded with over $100,000 in cash, on that fateful night back in 1975. And it was where I would work on special assignment for six months, under the pressure of a deadline - the expiring statute. Thinking back, I had fond memories of days with the Postal Inspectors, despite the ups and downs of the investigation.

I was daydreaming when the uniformed United States Postal Police Officer at the security booth questioned me as to my business at the Annex. I was no longer a regular and this U.S. Postal cop looked so young. I was thirty-nine years old and this kid had to be in his early twenties. He was all business and called me Sir when I showed my badge and ID.

"Sir, please put your vehicle in the visitor parking lot and I will notify the front desk you are on the way." My reserved parking spot was long gone and 'the kid,' the nickname the inspectors had given me, no longer fit.

After signing in, I was issued a pass to go up to the Inspectors' office. There were a lot of new and younger faces, but everyone there seemed to know who I was. I guess I had become somewhat of a legend in the Boston office.

Fred Ricker smiled and said, "Are you ready for another trial buddy?"

"As ready as I will ever be, Fred."

It was really good to see these guys again, but it was time to head to the arraignment. I secured my gun and handcuffs in their office gun locker, they put on their suit coats, grabbed their briefcases and, once again, we walked to the Federal Courthouse. Dodging the Boston drivers who paid no attention to the pedestrian lights, we talked mostly about how our families were doing. We knew this was the final chapter in what was the longest investigation the Postal Inspectors had ever been involved in. No matter how the trial turned out, we had all done ours jobs.

The courtroom was empty, except for the prosecution and the defense. No spectators and no reporters. It was an eerie scene. I felt lonely in the massive courtroom.

I never thought Hackett would come back alive from Kuwait with all the rumors about his treatment there, but there he was. Before the formal proceedings, I had a staring contest with James Hackett. His eyes were cold, almost as if in a time warp. He may or may not have known who I was, but he obviously hated anyone seated on the side of the prosecution.

He was dressed in denim prison garb, much like Grider in the 1980 interview. Before he fled to Kuwait, I had seen him often outside the Ten Hills Café. At the time he had about 200 pounds on his 6' 2" frame. Appearing gaunt, now he was more like 160. He looked like I did, after I had been shot and lost a lot of weight. Hackett was definitely not the threatening figure he had once been. The word was one of his fingers had been cut off and one of his eyes had been gouged out in the Kuwait prison, but he appeared pretty intact to me.

I was looking into the eyes of the man who we all believed to be a cold blooded killer. He had been, without a doubt, the leader of what we had labeled The Ten Hills Gang, so defiant he gave the Feds the finger when he spotted the surveillance they were conducting. He wielded the sawed off shotgun I had been hit with - twice. We all believed he shot the Wells Fargo Guard in the back in cold blood, for no reason, at the Hilltop robbery. Even Grider called him 'the one and only' when we showed him Hackett's photo in the federal pen in Wisconsin.

I think I fantasized about his demise once, when I saw him arming up with his pals in the parking lot of the Ten Hills Café. I ran the scenario through my mind, as I watched from our surveillance van. I was the one who was armed with the 12-guage shotgun then. He would not surrender, but try and shoot it out. The tables would be turned and he would be the one outgunned this time. Justice would be served.

Then, I realized I could not sink to his level. I had to play by the rules. What if I killed an innocent bystander? What if the media called it a revenge shooting? This was not who I was or wanted to be. The smug bastard probably knew it. I always felt at a disadvantage and it sucked.

We had hunted him after the indictments in 1980 and after he shot Bobby Martini's Dad. In his book *Citizen Somerville,* Bobby wrote:

> *"Jimmy (Hackett) was dangerous as a kid. He and a local guy had robbed the Hilltop Steak House in Saugus and murdered a security guard*

*for no reason. Hackett also had the attempted murder of a police officer under his belt."*

The police officer was me. When Bobby Martini, Jr. joined the MDC Police, we became friends and still are to this day. Because of James Hackett, we have a common bond.

I had seen transcripts of Hackett's interviews with various law enforcement agencies during his crime spree in the mid-1970s. He knew he was dealing from a strong hand, back then, denying everything the authorities threw at him, even laughing at them. He had no cards to play now. Harvey Brower, the lawyer who got him off on the Hilltop murder, was in jail. This defense lawyer was a public defender.

James Hackett appeared before Judge Joseph L. Tauro and pled *guilty* to the conspiracy count against him. Counts two and three of the indictment had been dropped in the plea bargaining agreement. His case was continued for sentencing to August 4, 1986, and he was returned jail. It looked as if the final chapter was closed and he would spend the next five years in prison.

This was cause for a celebration and once more I went out to dinner with the Postal Inspectors. They had worked tirelessly on this case and it was time to savor the finale.

We decided to go to the Hilltop Steak House in Saugus. This was the same place I had tailed the car from the Ten Hills Café, just a few days before Hackett shot and killed the Wells Fargo Guard in the daylight robbery on October 3, 1975.

The Hilltop was one of the largest steakhouses in the United States. It had an eighty foot high green cactus sign out front, said to have cost $68,000 in 1964. As you entered the building, there were plastic life size cattle standing at the entrance.

The Hilltop Steak House's famous sign

When we got inside, amongst the western décor, the hostess asked us if we were celebrating a special occasion.

"Yes, Ma'am. We just won the World Series," I quipped.

She laughed and sat us in a booth overlooking busy Route 1. Sitting there, I started to think about how the families had suffered - the families of both the good guys and the bad guys. I never talked about the investigation with my kids; in fact, I seldom talked to them about my job. Several of the bad guys had families. I wondered what it had been like for them. The family members seemed to have been the victims, too.

I daydreamed about how my four year old saw me on television in my hospital bed amid the news reports of my shooting.

*I remember sitting in the den watching the TV*
*and I tried to talk to you while you were on the*

*news. You were lying in a hospital bed. I was really upset because I couldn't figure out why you wouldn't talk to me, too. Mom tried to explain it to me, but I still couldn't make sense of why you were inside the TV. I'm pretty sure she told me you were in the hospital and that I could talk to you there. [Daughter Kendra's Memories]*

She told my wife she needed to know if her Daddy was alive. Trying to talk to me through the TV screen, she had asked, "Why doesn't Daddy answer me, Mommy?" My older daughter, at age six, tried to explain to her younger sister that I could not answer. But my younger daughter could not grasp the concept she was watching me on TV, during my interview with Ron Gollobin from my hospital bed. I remembered my kids had to come to the hospital to see me in person, to know I was alive.

*I remember going to the hospital and seeing you in a wheelchair. I was in my ballet costume, the 'rainbow' one. Your hair had been 'cut' and you had the 'Sun' on your forehead so you looked different...I think I wanted to touch it to see what it felt like. I also seem to remember that I wanted you to pick me up....not sure if I asked you to or just thought it to myself.*

*I remember you were talking slowly and sat funny, and I'm pretty sure I danced for you, but I knew something wasn't right. I also think I was confused that you weren't coming home with us...that you were staying at the hospital. [Daughter Kendra's Memories]*

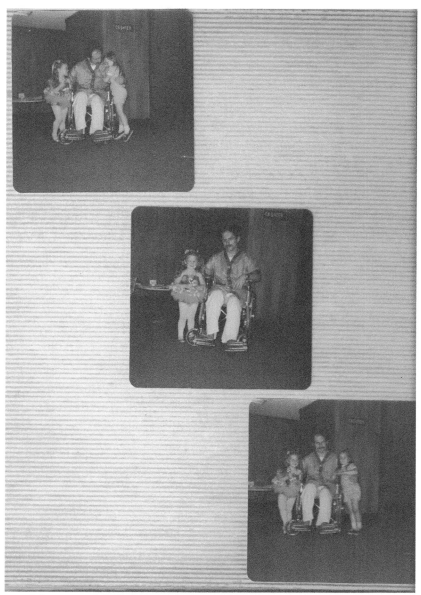

My young daughters visiting me at Winchester Hospital

*I remember you being in bed or being in a wheelchair, and your head was shaved. 2 big bandages, above your forehead, and one on top of your head. I do remember you showing us your bandages "where the bad guys shot you". I don't think our visits lasted long. You were probably too tired and groggy for visitors. I remember one day we waited for you in a lobby-like area and they brought you down to us in a wheel chair. I believe that was the day Kendra was in her recital costume. [Daughter Heather's Memories]*

THE WAITRESS HAD BEEN WAITING to take our order. Bill O'Leary ordered a bottle of Budweiser beer and I had my Jameson Irish Whiskey on the rocks. Fred had his usual tonic water, with a lime. We all ordered a large sirloin steak, for which the Hilltop was famous. It came with freshly cut french fries and a huge salad. I ordered my steak medium rare, and it was cooked to perfection - pink in the middle and charcoaled on the outside. For some reason, the Jameson was one of the best I ever had. It was also the only one I had, as I was driving my own car that night.

I thought to myself, "Nothing can go wrong tonight."

As we reminisced, we first toasted Louis Silva, the Wells Fargo Guard. He had lost his life at this very restaurant, trying to stop the guys we had now brought to justice. It was the most fitting place we could dine and celebrate, without question. I think we toasted everyone who had worked on the case. The stories went on for hours. It was without a doubt one of the best meals I ever had, not to mention the company.

What it boiled down to was this: three men who had never given up had become good friends. Fate seemed to be the only explanation. I doubt anyone else would have put up with me all those years, except my wife, of course. Without her support, I would never have returned to work back in 1975, and I never would have celebrated this victory with the two Postal Inspectors.

I took great pride as the driving force in this case, pushing the investigation forward for so many years. It had been my job to make sure no one would give up. Maybe I had been a small cog in a big wheel, but a vital one.

I'd done my job well. Had I not been tenacious, there would have been no arrests or convictions. On the other hand, without the skill of the investigators and prosecutor, there would have been no case. The good guys prevailed.

Bill and Fred talked about how relieved they were it had ended like this, and that they would both be retiring soon. We talked about justice and how the system managed to have worked this time. It had been an unbelievable eleven years.

I think we went over every aspect of the case - the crooked or lazy MDC detectives who hindered the case at first, the lack of cooperation, and the jealousy and mistrust between agencies. In addition to the wins and losses during the many battles, there were many ironic twists and turns. Now, it had all came to fruition.

As we walked out into the night air, much like that night back in 1975, we shook hands knowing this would be our last meeting on 'the case.'

Fred said, "Hey, buddy. You ought to write a book about this."

I laughed. "Me? Who struggled through English in college? Sure, Fred."

"Hey, when I retire I'll even help you," he replied.

I smiled, but never answered him.

James Hackett had been a survivor, much like I had been. I could not get that thought out of my mind. He had survived a shootout at the Hilltop Robbery. He was found *not guilty*, even though everyone in the law enforcement felt he was *guilty*. It had always bothered us that the mistakes in the trial were inexcusable.

He had survived several attempts on his life, according to sources. We were told there was a contract out on him for the Martini shooting in Somerville, but now he would go away for five more years. I felt satisfied the sentence was as good as we could get. I should have known the roller coaster ride would continue.

ON JUNE 29, 1986, only thirteen days after the arraignment, Bill O'Leary called me at home, again. "Are you sitting down?" he asked.

"I am now," I said, slumping into my recliner and taking a deep breath. "Don't tell me, Bill. He escaped?"

Bill, in a tone hard to describe, said, "No...he's dead."

I don't think I answered for a few minutes.

Then, I said, "You're kidding," my usual stupid response to shocking news.

Obviously, he wasn't. Hackett had died the night before. The cause was listed as 'natural causes-asphyxia.' He was forty-two years old. Someone said he died from conditions he suffered in the desert of Kuwait. The word on the street was he was whacked on the contract put out before he fled to Kuwait. Either way, his life of crime had finally caught up to him. After taking a life for no reason, he had lost his. 'He who lives by the sword...'

The North Reading Transcript ran an article dated July 3, 1986, mentioning my shooting and the killing of the other North Reading resident, Louis Silva, at the Hilltop. When writing about the sentence Hackett was facing, the reporter, Robert Turosz, said it best:

> *"However, Death exacted a stiffer penalty, probably as a result of the hardships he suffered as a guest of the Kuwait penal system."*

It was now over. I had kept my word.

**"If it was the last thing I ever did, I would catch these guys."**

There were so many peaks and valleys, so many sleepless nights. What drove me the most was justice and not revenge. Had

I let my emotions come in to play, I felt I would fail. This was business...my duty...and it had to be this way.

The words closure and healing are used so often today. They just don't seem to express the way I felt. It had been the end of a long pursuit and I had caught them, as I vowed I would.

I had survived the gunshots and the police motorcycle accident. There had to be a reason why I was still alive. Maybe, just maybe, I was a warrior like my father was in the D-Day Invasion. I had never given up, even when the odds seemed overwhelming, just as they were on the assault on Omaha Beach. Then again, maybe I was just an iron head, as many of my friends kept telling me. Either way, the Captain on the commendation board could no longer say, *"They didn't even catch them."*

FOR AN AVERAGE cop from a small town, this part of my life had past. But, the friendships I made during the investigation would last a lifetime. My family life had suffered enough from, what at times, seemed to have been an unreachable goal, even to me.

A few years later, Inspector Bill O'Leary's coworkers and friends honored him at his retirement party. As Bill thanked his friends and coworkers, he pointed to me, called me by name, and asked me to stand. Most of the guests knew of the mail hijacking and investigation. Bill told them he would never have felt whole, if we had not solved this case. I felt honored by his gesture - an honor few ever get in a lifetime. We exchanged smiles of satisfaction. Smiling at Bill, with my Irish whiskey in hand, I raised my glass to him.

In August of 2009, U.S. Postal Inspector Fred A. Ricker passed away at age 80. He had been a true friend and a legend at the Boston office. We kept in touch over the years and I had spoken with him a few times on the phone, just weeks before he passed. I asked him if he could help me write this book, reminding him he volunteered after our victory dinner in 1986.

"Hey buddy, I would love to. Give me a few days," he said in a very weak voice.

At his wake, I knelt at his open casket to pray for his soul. He was as stately in death as in life. There were many family photos of Fred, and of his days in the Marine Corps. I spoke with his widow, who I had met, many times. We often had coffee at his house before the drive into Boston.

She confided in me, "Fred really wanted to help you with your book."

With tears in my eyes, I said, "He is."

# *Epilogue*

I wrote this book from my memory of what happened during the high speed pursuit and the eleven year investigation that followed, and from notes I took after re-reading the many police reports and newspaper clippings. As I read my own story, it seemed to read more like a novel than real life. It is what struck me most. I've tried to be as accurate as possible, researching and interviewing as many of the 'good guys' and 'bad guys' as I could contact.

Bob Power, my partner the night I was shot, remained in the motorcycle unit. While I was working plain clothes, I got a distressing call from the TOPS Unit clerk on the night of April 2, 1980.

"Dana, your former partner, Power, has been in a bad accident on his motorcycle. He is in the hospital in Stoneham," he said.

"How bad is he hurt?" I asked.

"It is not life threatening, but they are not sure they can save his leg."

"Thanks. I'll go see him in the morning."

At the hospital, I saw Bob. His leg had been pinned and stitched up, and he was in a lot of pain. I thought how lucky I was for escaping damage to my legs in my two motorcycle accidents. He had not been so lucky. He told me what happened.

"I was hit by a little old Irish lady who blew a stop sign," he said. "Figures. She is the mother of a Connecticut State Trooper and has an Irish brogue you can cut with a knife."

"How's the leg?" I asked.

"The doctor did an unbelievable job. He said I may even get back on the bike in a year or so."

Bob sounded so much like I felt, when I had been hit by the drunken sailor. I guess most of us cops are just stubborn.

"You aren't going to believe what she said when they asked her what happened," Bob continued with his story.

"Try me," I replied.

"I'm lying on the street waiting for the ambulance, one foot facing up, and the other one down. One of our MDC cops asks, 'Ma'am, what happened?' In her thick brogue, she answers, 'I saw the motorcycle, but didn't know he was a policeman, so I hit him.'"

I tried hard not to laugh, but failed.

Bob was out of work for the next two years on injured leave, while his fractured leg healed, followed by a long stint of physical therapy. He would be forced off the job eventually on disability.

United States Postal Inspector Fred Ricker and North Reading Police Chief Henry (Hank) Purnell passed away during the years I was writing my book. Both of them knew I was working on it and I am sorry they never got to read the finished product. May they rest in peace.

I lost track of United States Postal Inspector Bill O'Leary after his retirement party in 1986. Bill handed me copies of many of the reports, photos and notes on the case when he retired.

I remember him saying, "Dana, someday you may want these."

I didn't realize it at the time but somehow he knew they would become valuable to me.

Not one to give up, I located Bill in early June of 2012. On August 13, 2013, my 66th birthday, four retired guys, who had done pretty well in their careers, reunited at Jake's Seaside Restaurant on Nantasket Beach in Hull, MA. Former Assistant United States Attorney Paul Healy, retired United States Postal Inspectors W. J. (Bill) O'Leary, W. R. (Roger) Hunt, and I sat together, once again overlooking the ocean.

Paul Healy, Bill O'Leary, Roger Hunt, Dana Owen

During our luncheon conversation, Roger told me I had been given a nickname by the inspectors. It was 'the kid.'

Roger said, "It was mostly because you looked so young. It was certainly not for your lack of experience and courage."

I also found out Bill O'Leary's nickname had been 'Monsignor O'Leary.' I had to laugh because 'Father O'Leary' is how I referred to Bill in the book. It seems the good guys and bad guys all had nicknames back in that era.

Paul had just retired as Chief Justice of the Framingham, MA District Court. We shared some great stories over lunch about the trial and appeal. Paul showed me the transcripts of the appeal of

Capone and Murnane (683 F. 2d 582 - United States v. Capone) and let me borrow them for my research.

North Reading Police Detective Ed Hayes has retired and is now a practicing attorney. When we met for coffee, I kiddingly told him he had gone over to the dark side. Only last year, Ed told me the story about how the lazy, scared or corrupt MDC Detective 'Blue' hung up on him. Without the list of guns from the North Reading P. D.'s informant, T-1, and Ed's persistence, the investigation would not have been successful. I think if, at the beginning of the investigation, I knew everything I know now, I would have been so discouraged I may not have stayed with it all those years.

No member of the Ten Hills Gang was ever arrested or prosecuted, by the FBI or the Commonwealth of Massachusetts for the string of bank robberies leading up to the mail hijacking. No one was charged by the Commonwealth of Massachusetts for the assault and battery with intent to murder my partner and me with guns, the bullets of which came within millimeters of taking my life. Despite considerable evidence and ample opportunity to do so, they did not pursue it. It was easy to see how cops could get soured by the job.

Of the four hijackers we chased in the follow/getaway car, only John Grider is still alive. I tried to contact him, but at first, was unable to connect with him. He moved frequently, I assume to keep a low profile, and, it seemed, to avoid whatever demons were chasing him, real or imagined.

Perhaps due to my tenacity, I was finally able to contact someone close to him in April of 2013. I informed this person I was writing a book and that I would discuss his role in the hijacking and my shooting. I had hoped to ask him a few questions, but it was not meant to be. He would not talk with me about the incident. At least, I tried. Seems the demons won out.

As for me, it was a very long eleven years.

I had been told about two MDC detectives who were either corrupt or too afraid to get involved in my case. I tried to find out if the Ten Hills Gang was involved with, or part of the Winter Hill Gang. So, I went to the source. Howie told me they weren't.

I saw the jealousies between police agencies and politics get in the way of what should have been a productive joint investigation. I hope things will change in law enforcement, but I sincerely doubt it. It seems its part of being human - temptations, competition, fears and frailties all come with the job.

It would take me years to get the post-traumatic headaches half-way under control. After the case was finally closed, I thought about taking a disability pension when I had a bout of double vision. After a series of tests at a major Boston hospital, I was told I might have a brain tumor. Weeks later, they told me they misread my X-rays! I was informed the diagnosis was a based on a *shadow* from my old gunshot wound and depressed skull fracture. They scared me, and my family, to death and then told me it was post-traumatic stress causing the double vision.

I had started the process of applying for retirement and then changed my mind, when my family doctor told me I was suffering from the 'what-do-I-do-now?' syndrome, as he called it. In time, I would receive counseling from a Police Psychologist for PTSD.

I wisely decided not to take the disability and I am glad I completed a twenty-seven year career. I met some great people along the way and made some friendships that will last a lifetime. Taking two bullets to the head wasn't fun, but in a strange way, surviving it made me a stronger person and a better cop.

After the plain clothes assignment, I went back into uniform on the motorcycle. But I knew I was daring the grim reaper, after a second motorcycle accident. During a stolen car pursuit, my police Harley was struck by an onlooker's vehicle. Once again I was extremely lucky to come out of it with just a concussion and sprained ankle.

My next adventure was with the MDC Mounted Unit. I was a decent equestrian and had four good years there, but something was missing - I couldn't quite put my finger on it.

My interest in officer survival in the face of enemy fire and my abilities with firearms led me to become an instructor at the Metro (the post-1986 name for the MDC) Police Firearms Training Unit. It was a perfect fit for me and I eventually became the Armorer and Firearms Coordinator for the 650-member force. I was also a part of the team that trained our Special Operations Unit (SWAT team) in firearms and tactics. Ironically, I always played the bad guy in scenarios, which entailed getting shot with paint balls and 'simunitions' (paint filled cartridge), and thrown to the ground, handcuffed and arrested.

The Special Operations Unit team members surprised me one day and voted me into their unit. I participated in a SWAT raid on a notorious crack house in Mattapan, on the day of the perfect storm - October 30, 1991. I learned it was much easier to teach the proper use of firearms and tactics, when you have 'walked the walk and talked the talk.' Credibility had not been an issue.

Many police academy directors invited me speak to their cadets about my shooting. I discussed the chase with these young men and women, who were just beginning an exciting but difficult career. I tried to explain what being shot does to a person - it made me live each day as if it were my last. But after a few years, I sent the thoughts of my mortality to the back of my mind. The one thing that never changed was how I treasure each and every day with my family.

Long after the academy talks, I met some of those who had attended my lectures. They could retell the parts of my story, verbatim, which affected them most, as they began their own careers.

I met one last year, a uniformed officer in a coffee shop who recognized me. He related exactly what I told the nurse before surgery way back in 1975, down to the strawberry shortcake with vanilla ice-cream I had for dessert. I had been humbled and honored he remembered my story.

Another speaking event that stands out in my mind was when I talked with students at the Massachusetts Criminal Justice Training Council, along with Special Agent Gordon (Gordie) McNeil of the Federal Bureau of Investigation. Gordie was shot three times in the infamous Miami Dade FBI shooting on April 11, 1986, during which two agents were killed and five were wounded. Both suspects were shot and killed in the gun battle. The shooting changed the way cops were trained. It also spurred the move to arm the FBI and Police Departments nationwide with semi-automatic pistols with high capacity magazines. Most of the FBI agents, armed with either 5 or 6 shot revolvers, ran out of ammunition during that gunfight.

After the presentation, my wife and I took Agent McNeil out to dinner. We talked about our families, and the conversation was one I will never forget. I told Gordie that I did not feel my shooting was in the same league as his, in addition to the two FBI agents who were killed.

He responded, "You have to be kidding! You almost died, which puts us both in an exclusive club neither of us applied for."

I also became a member of the MDC Police Shooting Response team. I would speak with cops who had been shot or had been involved in a line of duty shooting, much like the Boston cops who had visited me in the hospital, back in 1975.

On January 30, 1988, as part of this team, I was called to visit MDC Detective Joe McCain, who had been shot the night before, and like me, survived. We had a private and intense conversation and afterwards, I felt I helped Joe a great deal. Joe McCain's shooting was documented in Jay Atkinson's book *Legends of Winter Hill: Cops, Con Men and Joe McCain, The Last Real Detective.*

Both Gordie and Joe have sadly passed away. Cancer took Agent McNeil; Joe died from complications from his gunshot wound, many years after his shooting.

In 1992, the Metropolitan District Commission Police, Registry of Motor Vehicles Police and Capitol Police merged with the Massachusetts State Police, creating a single 2,400 person agency. Because of my background, I was selected to participate as a member of the Orientation Staff.

As a Massachusetts State Trooper, I was assigned to the Armorer's Office as the assistant armorer and promoted to Sergeant in 1995. When the Armorer, who was my Lieutenant, retired in 1996, I was promoted to the Armorer, in charge of all the weapons for the newly consolidated agency.

In 1997, I retired from public service and went to work for Glock, Inc., a major gun manufacturer. I worked as a district manager and sold semiautomatic pistols to Police Departments in New England.

In 2001, I went to work for another major gun manufacturer, Sig Sauer, and sold guns to police agencies in both New England and to law enforcement and the military in Canada.

Finally in 2008, it was time to stop being a road warrior and I went into, what I like to call, semi-retirement.

In the spring of 2009, on a lark, I emailed Ron Gollobin, the reporter who interviewed me twice, when I was shot in 1975 and then again in 1980, when we made the first arrests in my case.

On a beautiful day, over coffee in Winchester at an outside café, I reminded Ron about my shooting and told him a few other war stories. I told him I had been thinking of telling my story in book form, but had never written a thing and didn't know if I could get it down on paper. Ron had been non-committal, but reassuring.

He said, "Put something on paper and email it to me. I'll take a look and give you my honest opinion."

His email response after reading my first chapter was "Wow!!!"

The rest is history; he has been my mentor throughout. He helped guide me to what you are reading now - always honest when something I wrote was good and just as honest when it 'sucked' (his word).

In the fall of 2013, I reconnected with Athena Z. Yerganian, on LinkedIn, after almost twenty-years. We'd worked together during the police merger, on the consolidation Orientation Training Program Team. A few years later, when I became the Massachusetts State Police Armorer, she assisted me in developing a computerized weapons database. We needed an up-to-date and complete inventory of the new Department of State Police weapons, and the system she built improved our capabilities.

Athena seemed pretty interested in my book. Although we had worked together, I never told her the whole story of how I got shot and worked on catching the bad guys. I sent her a few chapters to read, and she suggested a few 'adjustments.' I asked her to help edit the book and she made sure the chronology was accurate, translated cop-shop talk, and added the final touches.

All and all it has been an amazing five years. My hope is that some young cops just starting out and cops, who have been shot and survived, will read my book and gain something from my story. I have tried to tell it as accurately as it happened.

## *Acknowledgements*

There are a number of people I want to thank: those who read my chapters, listened to me, edited and proof read my work and took an interest in the project, and those who allowed me to quote them in *Shotgunned.*

First and foremost, I want to thank my wife, Sandy. Without her support from the moment I was shot, I would never have returned to work, much less chased the bad guys for eleven years. She put up with the many pre-dawn hours I spent at the computer writing and rewriting my story, or as she called it, 'lost in space.'

I want to thank both of my daughters Heather and Kendra, who recently shared their memories of when I was wounded - private thoughts I had never heard or even asked for over all these years.

Next, I want to thank to Ron Gollobin, who I reached out to five years ago. He was the reporter I always trusted the most. I asked Ron to co-write the book with me, but he felt it was something I needed to do myself and tell it in my own style. Ron has been my mentor in the project and came up with the idea of asking my wife to write a chapter on what it was like for her when she got 'the phone call, all cops wives fear.' It was the first time anyone had ever asked her how *she* felt. When I read her chapter, it brought tears to my eyes. I sadly realized even I had never asked her how she felt.

I truly believe Ron had as much fun as I did and was as frustrated as I was, when things got bogged down. It also gave me a chance to talk with friends with whom I had lost contact, retired cops and reporters, many good guys and a few bad guys. Ron was able to accompany me on several occasions to conduct interviews and meet with retired Postal Inspectors Bill O'Leary and Roger Hunt. I can't find the words to express what those luncheon meetings were like.

My thanks to Athena Yerganian whose computer and editing skills were invaluable. I have given Athena the nickname 'the closer.'

Thanks to the many newspapers who gave me permission to use the articles about the 1975 mail hijacking and the aftermath: The Boston Globe, Boston Herald, Daily Times Chronicle, and the North Reading Transcript, just to name a few. Also, I extend my appreciation to the many news photographers, most of whom are now retired.

U.S. Postal Inspectors W. J. 'Bill' O'Leary (ret.) and F. A. 'Fred' Ricker (deceased) were not only the leaders in the task force, but became great friends. U.S. Postal Inspector W. R. 'Roger' Hunt (ret.) was one of the younger members of the investigative unit back then. Roger became a lifelong friend, just like so many of the Postal Inspectors. I also found another U.S. Postal Inspector Dennis Kelliher (ret) on Linkedin. He not only hooked me back up with Roger and Bill, who I had lost track of, but called me on the day of the Boston Marathon bombings, to say he could not help thinking of me on that sad day.

I want to acknowledge several others: MDC Police Officers Paul Halpin (ret.) and Frank Muolo (ret.), MDC Police Detective Eugene A. Kee, Jr. (ret.), FBI Special Agent Jim Pledger (ret.), ATF Special Agent John Gibson (ret.), Massachusetts State Police Lieutenant Colonel Ron Guilmette (ret.), North Reading P. D. Detective Ed Hayes (ret.), Massachusetts Port Authority Police Captain Albert J. DeRosa (ret.), New York State Police Sergeant Frank DiNuzzo (ret.), former Assistant United States Attorney and Framingham District Court Judge Paul Healy (ret.), and George Harris, President and CEO International Firearms Consultants, LLC.

I reached out to friends and family, to get their reaction as the chapters started coming together, asking for their opinion to find out if I was getting my story across. My sister-in-law Julie Litchfield Brown, who read my first few chapters and encouraged me to continue, sent me a great book by Stephen King called *On Writing: A Memoir of the Craft* and *The Observation Deck - A Tool Kit for Writers* by Naomi Epel. I would recommend both to any first- time writer. My niece and Julie's daughter, Anita Brown, designed the cover art.

Jim and Doris Walker, both retired English teachers, helped me push forward with their encouragement. We met a few months after I was shot and have been friends for all of these years.

Robert Brand Hanson, another old friend, helped me through the maze of software programs to put my thoughts and memories on paper. Robert is the author of several books on the history of Dedham, MA including *Dedham 1635-1890* and *The Diary of Doctor Nathaniel Ames.* Rob helped shape chapters into a manuscript. He also helped me out with a 'quick and dirty edit' as he called it, when my grasp of structure and punctuation was lacking.

Another person I want to thank, who assisted me with 'writing and promotional issues,' is a family friend Pamela Mansfield-Loomis. Pam is a marketing communications specialist and would read my chapters over and give me an honest appraisal. I kept my writings 'close to the vest,' but would ask friends and contacts from different backgrounds to let me know how it read, including from a woman's perspective. I am not sure it was fair to put family and friends in this position, to say yea or nay to my work, but I felt they would be honest, and they were.

Paul Atlas, an old friend, shared his thoughts and feelings of when he first heard about my shooting, back in 1975.

Father Jerry Hogan, who helped me with the chapter on the Pope, had been there at the event and Mass.

Ellen Carella Valenton, a family friend, had read several of the early versions of chapters and has been very supportive of my project.

Richard Yee, owner of the China Blossom restaurant in North Andover, is a supporter and benefactor.

Maryann Briggs is the mother of Michael Briggs, the Manchester NH Police Officer who was shot and killed back on the evening of October 16, 2006. We have been close friends with the Briggs family since the early 1980s. My wife and Maryann Briggs are two of the strongest women I will ever know in my lifetime. Maryann was kind enough to read my chapters I sent her and could understand more than anyone what my wife Sandy went through when I was shot. Her son Michael was a true hero who made the ultimate sacrifice to protect and serve the public.

In 2011, I joined Grub Street, Inc., an organization in Boston which advertised, *Makes writers better writers. Builds literary careers. Creates audience for good work.* I found the group to be helpful and informative. The best thing that came from it was I had a chance to sit down with Attorney Mitchell Bragg of Ascentage Law. Mitch specializes in helping writers through the legal aspects of writing a book. After a free introductory meeting set up by Grub Street, I hired Mitch as the attorney for my project and book. He helped me through the intricacies of intellectual property law and other legal issues with publishing a 'true crime drama.' Things started to fall into place, much like the mail case, one piece at a time.

Three years ago, I met Christopher Obert, owner of Pear Tree Publishing, when I attended the *New England Authors Expo.* (The NEAE is the largest grassroots literary event in New England and a great place to find out more about writing, publishing and to purchase books.) Chris has given me great advice and support. In fact we became so interested in each other's story that I decided to allow Pear Tree Publishing to market and distribute my book.

I would be remiss if I did not thank all the doctors, nurses and medical staff who saved my life and nursed me back to health. I actually heard from the daughter of one of the ER nurses at Winchester Hospital, who had cared for me the night I was shot.

It took just a few days short of five years to indict the hijackers. What started out as a two year project to write this book, took just short of five years. It seems as though five may be my lucky number!

It has been a wonderful journey and catharsis for me. It makes me realize how fortunate I am to have lived to tell about my story and to be blessed with such an amazing family and group of friends.

## *Biographies*

**Dana C. Owen**

Dana C. Owen served as a Police Officer for 27 years in the Commonwealth of Massachusetts, retiring as a Sergeant and the Armorer for the Massachusetts State Police. He served with the Massachusetts Metropolitan District Commission Police Department (MDC) from 1970 to 1992. When several state law enforcement agencies merged, he became a member of the Massachusetts State Police, until his retirement in 1997. He is the recipient of several police citations including the Metropolitan Police Medal of Valor, the highest honor awarded.

Dana holds a Bachelor Degree in Law Enforcement from Northeastern University. A lifelong resident of Massachusetts, he is also an avid genealogist.

**Ron Gollobin**

Ron Gollobin was a journalist for four newspapers in North Carolina, Virginia and New Jersey, primarily as an investigative reporter. He came to WCVB-TV (Boston) in 1975, where he worked for thirty years as an investigative and general assignment reporter. He filed reports for the BBC, the Weather Channel, ABC, Arts and Entertainment Channel, Chronicle, Oprah Winfrey Show, Phil Donahue and America's Most Wanted, among others.

He won numerous awards as an investigative print journalist, including the NJ Public Service Award and Sigma Delta Chi Public Service. Ron was a Nieman Fellow at Harvard and was twice nominated for a Pulitzer Prize for investigative reporting.

Ron has won five Emmy Awards, a Tom Phillips Award, Massachusetts Broadcasters Association, and other writing and reporting awards. He has taught courses at Harvard, Boston University and Northeastern University.

**Athena Z. Yerganian**

Athena Z. Yerganian has worked with the best minds in American Policing for almost thirty years. Athena seems to understand the cop world better than most, having worked with more than thirty Police Departments. She has held leadership positions including Chief Information Officer (CIO) of the Boston Police and the Los Angeles Police Departments. She is the founder and owner of a technology and organizational strategy consulting firm that helps Public Safety improve its response to crime and terrorism.

Athena is a graduate of the Boston Latin School and holds a Bachelor of Arts from Wellesley College and a Master of Business Administration from the Simmons College Graduate School of Management.